HUMAN RIGHTS AND THE
WORLD'S MAJOR RELIGIONS

Human Rights and the World's Major Religions
William H. Brackney, Series Editor

HUMAN RIGHTS AND THE WORLD'S MAJOR RELIGIONS

VOLUME 1: THE JEWISH TRADITION

Peter J. Haas

William H. Brackney, Series Editor

PRAEGER PERSPECTIVES

Westport, Connecticut
London

Library of Congress Cataloging-in-Publication Data

Human rights and the world's major religions.
    p.   cm.
    Includes bibliographical references and indexes.
    Contents: v. 1. The Jewish tradition / Peter J. Haas—
    v. 2. The Christian tradition / William H. Brackney—
    v. 3. The Islamic tradition / Muddathir Abd al-Rahim—
    v. 4. The Hindu tradition / Harold Coward—v. 5. The Buddhist tradition
    / Robert E. Florida.
    ISBN 0–275–98425–7 (set: alk. paper)—ISBN 0–275–98047–2 (v. 1: alk. paper)—
    ISBN 0–313–30134–4 (v. 2: alk. paper)—ISBN 0–275–98045–6 (v. 3: alk. paper)—
    ISBN 0–275–98381–1 (v. 4: alk. paper)—ISBN 0–313–31318–0 (v. 5: alk. paper)
    1. Human rights—Religious aspects.   I. Haas, Peter J. (Peter Jerome)
  BL65.H78H8595   2005
  201'.723—dc22   2003068987

British Library Cataloguing in Publication Data is available.

Library of Congress Catalog Card Number: 2003068987
ISBN: 0–275–98425–7 (set)
      0–275–98047–2 (The Jewish Tradition)
      0–313–30134–4 (The Christian Tradition)
      0–313–31318–0 (The Buddhist Tradition)
      0–275–98381–1 (The Hindu Tradition)
      0–275–98045–6 (The Islamic Tradition)

First published in 2005

Praeger Publishers, 88 Post Road West, Westport, CT 06881
An imprint of Greenwood Publishing Group, Inc.
www.praeger.com

Printed in the United States of America

The paper used in this book complies with the
Permanent Paper Standard issued by the National
Information Standards Organization (Z39.48–1984).

10 9 8 7 6 5 4 3 2 1

CONTENTS |

INTRODUCTION TO HUMAN RIGHTS AND THE WORLD'S MAJOR RELIGIONS

THIS IS THE FIRST BOOK IN A SERIES published by Praeger Publishers titled, "Human Rights and the World's Major Religions." The purpose of the series is to define the meaning of human rights in a specific religious tradition and to survey its breadth and development across time and cultures. The authors have crafted analytical chapters and selected appropriate source materials that illustrate their analyses. Additionally, these reference works include biographical sketches, extensive annotated bibliographies, a chronology, and an index. The religious traditions in this series are Christianity, Judaism, Islam, Buddhism, and Hinduism.

This volume is devoted to Judaism. Following an overview that defines the problem of human rights in the Jewish religion, and a chronology that spans the settlement of Israel (ca. 1200 B.C.E.) through the end of the second millennium C.E., the author develops his themes through historical analyses of the tradition. The biblical treatment of human rights issues plus the development of Judaism in the context of the Greek and Roman empires constitute an important first chapter. There is in chapters 1 and 2 a fresh look at main passages in the Hebrew Bible and introduction of new terminology in addressing the biblical concepts relating to human rights. Yet, he reminds us that the scriptures contain no systematic exposition of human rights. Next, the unfolding medieval understanding in talmudic and halachic literature is surveyed in chapters 3, 4, and 5, with important commentary on the impact of judicial process and the desire to preserve human dignity. Chapter 6 covers the Enlightenment's impact upon Jewish thinking and the development of Jews in various European nationalities. Here Judaism itself underwent important philosophical metamorphoses. The Jewish articulation of human rights in North America is next paralleled with the emergence of the state of Israel and its regional and national particularities in the last two chapters. Among the major contributions of this book are the distinctions the author makes between the biblical and later rabbinic texts and the continually evolving religious communities comprising Judaism from the classical period to modern Europe. Human rights in the Jewish faith is a complex set of contexts and literatures.

The reference material in Part II is a rich treasury of details. There are more than fifty biographical sketches, selections from ancient and contemporary Jewish thinkers that include biblical, Mishnaic, and Talmudic sources (translated by the author in some cases), and excerpts from modern American Jewish voices from both conservative and liberal perspectives. There is also a user-friendly annotated bibliography.

Professor Peter Haas is a seasoned scholar in Jewish thought and brings to this volume an impressive background. With degrees from the University of Michigan (Ancient Near Eastern Studies), Hebrew Union College (rabbinic preparation), and Brown University (History of Religions and Judaism), he received his Ph.D. under the eminent Judaic specialist, Jacob Neusner. An ordained rabbi, Dr. Haas has taught at Vanderbilt University and the Spertus Institute in Chicago. Since 2000 he is Abba Hillel Professor of Jewish Studies and Director of the Samuel Rosenthal Center for Judaic Studies at Case Western Reserve University in Cleveland, Ohio, where he also chairs the Department of Religion. He has authored or edited six books in Judaic studies, one of which, *Morality after Auschwitz* (1988), was listed as an outstanding book in *Choice*. He has won numerous academic awards and held leadership positions in professional societies. A historian and exegete of texts, Professor Haas is well qualified to speak on the topic of human rights in the Jewish tradition. I am delighted with his contribution to this series.

I commend this important contribution to students, scholars, and general readers alike by an authority in the field.

William H. Brackney
Series Editor

INTRODUCTION |

RATIONALE, SIGNIFICANCE, AND ORGANIZATION

JUDAISM HAS HAD A LONG AND complicated social and intellectual history. Over the course of nearly three millennia, the issue of human rights has been addressed in numerous ways and in a variety of genres, often heavily influenced by outside forces. For this reason it should be clearly kept in mind that there is no such thing as a single Jewish view, but rather there are a variety of views embedded in a complex and ever-changing series of discussions and debates. Jewish discourse on human rights, in short, has been neither monolithic nor stable but rather, has reflected a living intellectual tradition struggling with shifting social, economic, and political realities. To help sort out this discourse, the following discussion can be divided into three large periods: (1) that of the Bible, from roughly 1000 B.C.E. to the end of the first millennium B.C.E., (2) that of classical rabbinic Judaism, from roughly the beginning of the first millennium of the Common Era forward, and (3) that of the modern and postmodern periods beginning for most Jews in the middle of the eighteenth century and continuing to the present. This latest period covers two new and unprecedented Jewish communities: that of North America in which Jews enjoy an unprecedented amount of freedom as well as engagement with the outside world and that of the state of Israel. As will be clear by the end of the discussion, the struggle to define a Judaic view of human rights is far from complete and remains a matter of debate and intellectual exploration.

In this scheme, the biblical literature is both the most difficult to interpret and in some sense the least relevant. The difficulty of dealing with the Bible lies in the fact that it does not comprise a single and systematic exposition of human rights, or anything else for that matter. Rather, the Bible is a collection of diverse writings composed by different authors addressing a variety of issues over a period of several hundred years. Among the voices are priests, prophets, and kings living in periods ranging from the premonarchic tribal confederation of early Israel, to the empires of the mighty kings David and Solomon, to the period of the precarious existence of the two smaller kingdoms of Israel (in the north) and Judah (in the south) and finally into the exilic and postexilic period of Persian hegemony. Adducing a coherent view on any particular issue from this material is nearly impossible, and especially so for a vague concept like human rights. In addition, there is always the question as to the extent to which the Bible is descriptive, telling us what *actually* took place in the villages of ancient Israel, and to what extent the Bible is prescriptive, telling us what certain interested parties, such as the priesthood at any one time, thought *ought* to be the case.

There is, however, a serious question about how relevant the Bible and its religion is to begin with for an understanding of rabbinic Judaism. To be sure there are continuities, and the framers of rabbinic and later Judaisms have always drawn heavily on verses from the Bible to warrant their decisions. But the religion of the Temple and its sacrificial cult overseen by an hereditary priesthood as described in the Bible is far removed from the Romanized religion of the early rabbis, which stressed home rituals, prayers, and the leadership of an elite intellectual caste, the rabbis. In other words, by the beginning of the first millennium C.E., the Bible served as the sacred history of the Greco-Roman Jewish ethnos, but what in fact emerged as the day-to-day religion of that ethnos was hardly a faithful reconstruction of the religion of biblical Israel. Rather, it was a new Roman religion called *Ioudaismos*. Ioudaismos (from which we get the word Judaism) was a creation of the Roman world and reflected Roman notions of religion, ethics, law, and thought. It is absolutely necessary, then, to draw a distinction between the biblical literature and the religious community it describes on the one hand and the religion later Hellenized and Romanized Ioudaioi practiced on the other hand.

As a result, the material treated in this book makes a natural break between what was the case in the biblical literature (chapters 1 and 2), and what became the case for rabbinic Judaism as this tradition developed in

Roman times and forward (chapters 3 through 7). In the latter case, that of the rabbinic tradition, there were concerted attempts to create a more or less unified body of doctrine and law governing all aspects of Judaic life, including relations with others and the Other. Hence, speculations and discussions of human rights appear implicitly and deliberately in rabbinic writings. From these writings one can draw some fairly concrete and detailed conclusions about rabbinic attitudes toward human rights, even though the term "human rights" itself does not appear and was apparently unknown to the authors of the literature.

I have divided my discussion of rabbinic Judaism into three sections: the classical period (chapters 4 and 5), the modern period (chapters 6 and 7), and the contemporary period (chapters 8 and 9). The classical period covers the time of the creation and the definition of rabbinic. It begins with the publication of the Mishnah in the first half of the third century C.E. and reaches a kind of culmination with the compilation of the Mishnah's greatest commentary, the Gemara (or Talmud), in the mid-seventh century. The expanison, consolidation, and elaboration of rabbinic Judaism continued along the lines laid out by the Talmud for the next thousand years. It is during this period from the seventh century to the eighteenth century that both traditional Jewish law and traditional Jewish philosophy (metaphysical as well as moral) reached their highest points. While it is certainly the case that the Jewish community was largely, though not entirely, separated from the surrounding community, and while Jewish legal jurisdiction only extended to the social boundaries of the Jewish community itself, it is nonetheless the case that issues of human rights drawn from the Greco-Roman world did enter into Talmudic and later discussions and were considered and developed in a Judaic context. Although the social, legal, and historical position of the Jewish community changed rapidly in the later part of the eighteenth century, the reader should be aware that the essential legal lines of the classical period have continued down to contemporary times in Orthodox and ultra-Orthodox Jewish communities.

The modern period (chapters 6 and 7) addresses the changes in the Jewish views of human rights introduced by the Enlightenment and the emancipation in the eighteenth century. The emancipation, in this context, refers to the breakdown of the old medieval restrictions and constraints placed on Jewish social and intellectual life by the medieval order. Beginning in approximately the middle of the eighteenth century, the countries of Western and Central Europe began to modify and gradually eliminate medieval rules that restricted Jewish residence requirements (i.e., the ghettoes), work restrictions, access to secular education, and the like. As a result, the Jews of Central and Western (and more slowly Eastern) Europe began to find entry into the mainstream of social, political, and intellectual life. There was a cost, however, namely the need to give up cherished ways of Jewish life in favor of adopting the dress, manner, language, diet, and social customs of the surrounding peoples. The result was a fundamental and thoroughgoing reconstitution of Jewish life in Europe. A new breed of Jewish leaders had emerged by the middle of the nineteenth century—university trained, rabbinic as well as lay, that rearticulated the received rabbinic tradition in terms of Enlightenment and Romantic ideals. In this enterprise, Immanuel Kant and Georg W. F. Hegel, and even Karl Marx, became seminal figures. This new Judaism, which took hold in post-revolutionary France and then bit by bit in the German-speaking areas of Central Europe and then moved west into England and especially North America, came, by the beginning of the twentieth century, to define the Judaism of the vast number of Western Jews. Such current Jewish denominations as Liberal Judaism in Germany and England, and Reform, Conservative, and Reconstructionist Judaisms in North America are the direct result of these changes. Their views of human rights are little more than eighteenth, nineteenth-, and twentieth-century Enlightenment (and in some cases romantic) ideas put into Judaic terms.

Chapters 8 and 9 look at the contemporary debate within and between the two distinct, largely secular, Jewish communities that dominate Jewish life in the twenty-first century. On one side stands the North American Jewish community, now fully integrated and successful. This community largely shares the general American liberal commitment to human rights. On the other side stands the Israeli community, which continues to face both an internal existential need to define itself as a Jewish state and a significant external threat to its very existence. In contrast to the American community, the Israeli community has put communal needs of definition and survival ahead of individual human rights. This variance has created tensions not only within each community, but between them as well. North American Jews, while committed to human rights out of religious and social factors, nonetheless sympathize with Israel's security dilemma. Israelis, for their part, are struggling to create a liberal, Western democracy and are increasingly uncomfortable with the limitations put on individual rights in the name of national security. It is these diverse forces that are animating the contemporary Jewish discussion on the needs and limitations of human rights within the Jewish community.

Finally, to aid the reader I have included some supplementary materials at the end of the book. Part II contains a collection of original sources that illustrate the extent and nature of Jewish literature on the subject of human rights. These materials, some of which are referred to in Part I, should give the reader a sense of the character, discourse, and flavor of the original sources. A second chapter in this section contains biographical sketches of some of the more important authorities cited in the text. At the first mention of each such authority in Part I, I have placed an asterisk (*) after the name to indicate that a biographical sketch is available in Part II. Finally, after the notes, I offer readers who are interested in further study an annotated bibliography of selected works dealing with Jewish ethics, especially as pertain to the area of human rights.

APPROACH AND METHOD

JUDAISM HAS ALWAYS been a religion more focused on creating norms of behavior than on creating philosophical creeds and dogmas. Thus, discussions on human rights, or any other such topic in the traditional Jewish literature, tend to deal not with the topic in an abstract and theoretical way, but with concrete applications in specific situations. This is not to say that more philosophical treatises do not exist, but those that do are often regarded as idosyncratic to the author and have little relevance to how the Jewish community in any one place functioned. Thus, to adduce a Jewish view on any topic means looking more at Jewish common law and accepted practice as these developed over the centuries than at philosophical treatises or dogmatic statements. It is detailed and painstaking work. The discussion in this book is meant to show how this process worked and to sketch out the basic lines of the Jewish approach to the issues at hand. Obviously many areas, as well as some of the dynamic of the debate itself, will be lost in the interest of creating an understandable and nontechnical book for the nonspecialist.

In some sense the work is made easier because of the largely self-contained character of the Jewish community up to modern times. The early rabbis who created the rabbinic Judaism that has become normative down to today drew heavily on the Roman legal tradition, in parallel to the early Christian Church, which drew heavily on Greco-Roman philosophy. To distinguish themselves from Roman pagans, and Christians, the rabbis developed an elaborate network of social norms that included dietary laws, codes of dress and behavior, civil law, and a calendar. As the Roman Empire became Christianized, the Jews found themselves more and more excluded from society and thrown back on their own resources. This was especially true after the fall of Rome and the replacement of the Roman government by the Church. Jews were obviously not subject to Church law and so were allowed (or forced?) to live according to their own legal tradition. This same arrangement took shape as well in the Middle East and North Africa in the wake of the conquest of Islam. As in Europe, the Jews found themselves excluded by the prevailing legal system (in this case the Islamic Sharià) and so fell back on their own self-governance.

Gradually this led to the development in both Christian Europe and in the Muslim Middle East and North Africa of Jewish semiautonomous corporations or ghettos in which Jews more or less were allowed to run their own affairs, religious as well as civil and even criminal, albeit with the general oversight and occasional intervention of the ruling authorities. This semiautonomous situation lasted, as noted, until the modern period and the integration of the vast bulk of Jews into the newly emerging secular civil societies of Western Europe, then Eastern Europe, and now slowly in the Arab lands. In all events, the medieval system meant that the full range of human rights issues became subject to Jewish legal speculation and regulation. It is because of the quasi independence of Jewish communities throughout the classical and medieval periods that we have such a large quantity of material dealing with topics that we today would regard as human rights issues. The chapters dealing with traditional Judaism, then, draw heavily on the legal literature, whether this is Talmud or later rabbinic legal rulings (responsa).

In this regard, the modern period presents a completely different set of interpretive problems. As Jews became assimilated into the secular host cultures, they participated in the social, economic, and political debates of their homelands. In some cases, their views were made in specifically Jewish terms and drew explicitly on Jewish sources. In other cases, the writers were Jewish and their attitudes mirrored those of the Jewish communities from which they came, but their arguments were not explicitly or apparently Jewish. The question then arises as to whether the work in question represents Judaism or whether it is the position of a German, Austrian, Frenchman, and so forth, who happens to be Jewish by ethnicity. The chapters dedicated to the modern period try to focus on the former (i.e., explicitly

Jewish writers writing as Jews) as opposed to the latter (writers who happen to be Jewish but are writing as generic citizens). The criterion for making the decision has generally been the extent to which explicitly Jewish sources are used to warrant the argument.

The problem has become even more complex in the contemporary period. The American situation is especially difficult because it is often impossible to sort out completely whether a work written by a Jewish academic in English is to be regarded as Jewish, as academic, or as liberal. The process of selection is confounded even more by the fact that as the American Jewish community has become more assimilated, it no longer has a stable intellectual center. For example, Jews are still more likely to be Democrats than Republicans, but then many of the neoconservatives are Jewish, and even explicitly so. There are wide and growing rifts within the Jewish community between the orthodox and liberal wings over a variety of issues. So not only is it increasingly difficult to determine what is "Jewish" and what is not, it is also more difficult to discern anything like the Jewish view at all. Mostly, there is little more than a variety of Jewish and semi-Jewish voices in the cacophony of the intellectual marketplace.

The case of Israel presents its own set of nearly intractable interpretive problems. Israel was founded as a state that was to be, according to its founding declaration, both Jewish and democratic. This dual mission has presented Israeli legalists, from academicians to supreme court justices, with a dilemma in that they are often serving two, at times mutually exclusive, ideals. This is because to some considerable extent, to be a true democracy in the Western liberal sense means to refuse to give Judaic culture a place of preference. To what extent, for example, should the state restrict commerce on the Sabbath? Maintaining the Sabbath preserves the Jewish character of the state but violates the rights of its non-Jewish (and secular Jewish) citizens. Another topic is executions for certain crimes. Judicial executions are allowed in Jewish law but are disallowed according to widely held human rights principles. What path should a democratic *and* Jewish state take? This raises a practical question for the practice of law in Israel. Should British common law (from the time the area was under British control after World War I) serve as precedents in Israeli court decisions, or should precedents be drawn from Jewish common law? And if Jewish law is to be a weighty voice in Israeli common law, whose Jewish law should that be: the ultra-Orthodox, the moderate Orthodox, the liberal movements? These and similar conundra are matters of heated debate. Chapter 9 on human rights in Israel tries to find some general grounds of consensus without taking a stand on these internal debates.

To sum up, rabbinic Judaism has developed over the last two millennia a complex and far-reaching system of common law, drawing on but not duplicating biblical rulings and norms. The modern period has broken up Jewish self-autonomy and raised questions about how Jews should act in modern secular cultures. Both in Israel and in North America, the Jewish community is still very much in the process of redefining itself and its Judaisms. While the bulk of Jews have adopted generally liberal Western democratic attitudes, there is a strong sense that the Jewish tradition ought not to be abandoned. The shape any synthesis can or will take is still very much in question. It is for this reason that the following chapters will be able only to sketch out the broad outlines of the Jewish approach. In fact, in the last two chapters in Part I, the discussion will deal more with the questions of how Jewish practice and law should be shaped than with advocating specific solutions.

A BRIEF INTRODUCTION TO JUDAISM

JUDAISM TRACES ITS origins back to the very creation of humankind. According to the biblical story, a series of covenants were established with humankind in which people agreed to obey God and his commandments in return for blessing, protection, and prosperity. The obverse side of the covenant was that people who disobeyed God could expect to encounter punishment, usually in the form of disease, war, and/or death. The first covenant was made with the very first two people, Adam and Eve. They lived in the Garden of Eden, a sort of paradise, and were told all was theirs except the fruit of the tree of knowledge. When they ate that fruit in contravention to God's command, they were punished by, among other things, being expelled from the Garden. Men would have to earn their living by the sweat of their brow and women would have to endure the pain of childbirth. In rabbinic thought this has often been taken as a metaphor for all human existence. Humans know what is right and good, but they constantly fall short and thereby bring the ensuing negative consequences upon themselves.

The pact with Adam and Eve was the first covenant made between the Deity and humanity. As time and history unfolded, God became disillusioned with humankind and determined to destroy it. A great flood was brought that killed all life on earth. The only survivors were Noah and his family, who had been instructed to build an ark and bring one pair of each species of animal aboard. After the flood, God regretted having killed all life on earth and made a covenant with Noah, promising never to bring such a flood again. The covenant was represented by the rainbow. In later rabbinic tradition, it was at this time that the basic moral code for all humans was revealed by God. Called the Noachide laws, this code included a number of stipulations, including a ban on the shedding of innocent blood, outlawing the practice of cutting off the limbs of living animals, and requiring the setting up of a court system.

A third covenant was made with Abraham, who challenged the polytheism that had grown up around him and preached that one God had created everything. The covenant with Abraham promised that God would protect and expand his descendants in return for their obedience to the divine law. The covenant with its promises was passed down to Abraham's son by his wife Sarah, namely Isaac, and then to Isaac's son Jacob. Jacob, whose name was changed to Israel, fathered twelve sons who became the eponymous founders of the twelve tribes of the Children of Israel. The people of Israel were thus bound by two covenants: the overall moral code of Noah and the more specific stipulations of the Abrahamic code, calling on them to become a holy people.

Yet another covenant was made with the people of Israel on their emancipation from slavery under the pharaohs of ancient Egypt. Under the leadership of Moses, the ex-slaves left Egypt and made their way back to the Promised Land, that is, to their ancestral homeland in western Canaan (roughly the area of the modern state of Israel). On the way, the people stopped at Mount Sinai and Moses received a covenant that included the Ten Commandments and the body of material that came to be known as the Five Books of Moses, or the Torah (instruction in Hebrew). This revelation spelled out the specific rules, regulations, and norms that would govern the people when they settled in the Promised Land, including worship, the bringing of various sacrifices and agricultural offerings, and various civil and criminal laws. It is this material that formed the basis of the Bible and later rabbinic legislation.

The People of Israel proceeded under the leadership of Moses and his successor Joshua to arrive at the Promised Land and eventually establish themselves therein, driving out or conquering the local Canaanite population. Gradually the twelve tribes coalesced into a single nation under the kings, Saul and especially David and Solomon. It was at this period that the Jebusite city of Jerusalem was conquered and made into the capital. In addition, David and Solomon oversaw the creation of one central, national Temple that was placed under the aegis of a hereditary priesthood descended from Moses' brother Aaron. All sacrifices to the Israelite God were brought to that one central shrine, all other holy altars being decommissioned. After Solomon's death, the empire broke apart into two kingdoms. The northern one, which contained the bulk of the population, was called Israel and established its capital at Samaria. The southern kingdom, named Judah after its largest and most important tribe, continued to regard Jerusalem as its capital, to regard the Temple there as the only legitimate place to which to bring sacrifices to the Israelite God, and to remain loyal to the dynasty of David and the priesthood of Aaron. After some two hundred years, in 722 B.C.E., the northern kingdom of Israel was conquered by the Assyrians and essentially disappeared from history. Only the southern kingdom survived, and its laws, customs, and practices were handed down to become the basis for the Bible and then for later "Judah-ism."

The southern kingdom, however, was also eventually conquered, this time by the Babylonians in about 586 B.C.E. After about sixty-five years of punishment (as the Bible interprets matters), the Persians, who had conquered the Babylonian Empire, allowed the Judeans to return to their homeland, rebuild Jerusalem, and reinstitute the sacrificial worship at their Temple. This reconstruction is recorded in the last books of the Bible. This renewed Judah continued a precarious existence down to Roman times and eventually became the Roman province of Judea. After decades of unrest under Roman domination, the province rebelled in the late 60s C.E. The rebellion was eventually put down around 73 C.E., but in the process the Temple was burned to the ground, Jerusalem was destroyed, and the population scattered or killed.

Out of this devastation grew two important religious movements. One was Christianity, which claimed that the long-awaited Messiah ("anointed one of God") was coming and would imminently destroy the evils of this world (that is Rome) and usher in the Kingdom of God. The other religion was that of the early rabbis, who attempted to salvage what they could of Judean traditions and writings and reconstruct a religious way of life that could survive until God allowed the Temple once again to be rebuilt. By applying Roman jurisprudential thinking to the rules and norms in the biblical literature, they produced a legal tradition (the halachah, meaning "the way") that would allow individual Jews and their families to replicate in their homes the holiness that once adhered, and would one day adhere again, to the Jerusalem Temple. So all Judeans/Jews were asked to act as though they were priests. All their homes became little Temples and holiday meals, such as the Friday night meal welcoming in the Sabbath and the Passover seder, replicated the offerings once brought to the Temple. In this way, the rabbis argued, the People of Israel, could continue to fulfill the stipulations of the covenant, albeit in a reduced fashion, until God's forgiveness was forthcoming and the exiled people would return to a rebuilt Jerusalem and a renewed Temple. This became the basis of rabbinic Judaism for the next two thousand years. The maintenance of this peculiar and holy lifestyle was made possible, as noted earlier, by the fact that Jews were subject neither to Christian nor to Islamic law and so were allowed in the Middle Ages a high degree of communal autonomy in both Europe and the Muslim world.

This situation changed only in the modern period. Jews in Europe, and gradually elsewhere, were confronted with the possibility of leaving their ghettoes and assimilating into the alluring world of modernity. The price, of course, was to give up their old ways and assimilate into the new. Three basic strategies emerged. One was to forego any change, claiming that modernity was only a form of idolatry. The responsibility of Jews, in this view, was to stay in their ghettoes and continue their full obedience to God's laws. This view represented only a minority of Jews, ultimately some 10 to 15 percent, and became the basis of today's Jewish Orthodoxy. The bulk of Jews, however, found the lure of the outside world and the chance to leave the restrictions of the ghettoes too much to resist. Some took the opposite extreme and left Judaism entirely, often becoming Christians. The third option was to find some middle ground, that is, to move out of the ghetto and assimilate into the surrounding culture in public, but maintain a private religious life that was Judaic in content. How this was to be done was, and remains, a matter of considerable controversy and debate. It is out of this middle way that such movements as Reform Judaism in America, Liberal Judaism in Europe, Progressive Judaism in Israel, Conservative Judaism, and even Zionism emerged. It hardly needs to be said that not only have these groups become more complex internally over the last few centuries, but relationships among them have become contentious. Issues of Jewish continuity and unity have become priority items in the Jewish community's internal discourse.

It is out of the rabbinic law, and the diverse readings of that legal tradition in modern movements that the texts and documents reviewed in this book grow. While opinions vary greatly, what unites them all as part of

Judaic reflection on human rights is the commonly held conviction that they represent the will of God as revealed in the various covenants that formed the Jewish people. While liberal Jews are more ready to look to the outside world for inspiration and traditionalist Jews are more distrustful of the outside world (especially in the wake of the Holocaust), there is thus now a striking preference among Jewish intellectuals and leaders of all persuasions to keep modern Judaic discourse within traditional limits. All agree that their work is being done in the name of God and God's desire to see the world sanctified and redeemed. The drama of the debate as to exactly what this means, particularly with regard to human rights, is what is documented in the chapters that follow.

CHRONOLOGY

1200–1000 B.C.E.	Israelites populate the highland regions of the Land of Israel
ca. 1000	Formation of the kingdom under kings Saul, David, and Solomon
ca. 900	Division of the kingdom into two smaller domains: Judah (north) and Israel (south)
793–700	Destruction of the northern kingdom of Israel by the Assyrians
586	Conquest of Judah by the Babylonians; razing of the Temple and Jerusalem
333	Alexander the Great conquers the Ancient Near East; beginning of Hellenization
167	Maccabean revolt for religious and political freedom
Early First Century	Time of the protorabbis Hillel and Shammai
70 C.E.	Destruction of the Second Temple and Jerusalem by the Romans
ca. 230	Compilation of the Mishnah
ca. 600	Compilation of the Gemära (Talmud)
ca. 1000	Dissolution of the Babylonian Talmudic academies

ca. 1100   Destruction of European Jewish communities by the Crusaders

1178   Moses Maimonides edits the first code of Jewish law, the *Mishneh Torah*

1492   Expulsion of the Jews from Spain

1565   Publication of Joseph Caro's comprehensive code of Jewish law, the *Shulkhan Arukh*

1791   Granting of civil rights to the Jews of France, the first such act in Europe

1881   Repressive May Laws passed in Russia; embryonic Zionist movement begins

1894   First Zionist Congress convened in Basel by Theodor Herzl

1933–1944   The Holocaust

1949   Declaration of independence of the state of Israel

1967   Conquest by Israel of the West Bank and Gaza Strip

Part I
Historical Development and Analysis

1

THE BIBLICAL LEGACY: BIBLICAL ISRAEL CONFRONTS THE OTHER

ANY DELIBERATIONS ABOUT HUMAN rights in biblical Israel have to take into account several different methodological considerations. To begin with, it is most important to keep in mind that for all intents and purposes, the only evidence of attitudes toward human rights in biblical Israel is the written texts that make up the Hebrew Bible. These texts, in turn, were written by different people representing different perspectives over a period of several hundred years, from around the time of the monarchy in the ninth century B.C.E. until well into the postexilic period of the sixth and fifth centuries B.C.E. These later materials include, among others, the books of Ezra and Nehemiah (likely dating from the fourth century B.C.E.), and the book of Daniel, which may be as late as the second century B.C.E.[1] Thus the Bible presents a host of interpretive problems that have to be kept in mind when adducing the biblical view of human rights. First, each book reflects its own time and social context within the unfolding history of biblical Israel. Second, the biblical literature is not to be understood merely as the product of biblical Israel, but also as the product of the larger political and social environment of the Ancient Near East, of which the Israelites were but a small part. As archaeology is increasingly demonstrating, the ancient Israelites were anything but a completely separate and distinct people hermetically sealed off from the populations and cultures around them. Quite to the contrary, they were very much a part of the Canaanite scene, and thus deeply influenced by Mesopotamian and Egyptian culture. So to understand the literature of biblical Israel and its views of human rights, one has to read the literature not only in terms of the historical and social development of the Israelite community, but also in terms of the encompassing Ancient Near Eastern milieu, which itself, of course, was neither monolithic nor stable over time. Given this complex historical and social web, it is somewhat misleading to talk at all about "a" or "the" biblical view of human rights.

On the other hand, despite its embeddedness in the Ancient Near East, biblical Israel did see itself as distinct and even unprecedented among its neighboring cultures. It claimed to have a particular religious and covenantal relationship with the divine. That is, the Israelite community had a shared notion of being different from its neighbors by having been brought into existence by their God for a specific purpose and to fulfill a specific mission. So while biblical Israel is indeed part of the larger Ancient Near Eastern whole, it also has its own distinct features and unique characteristics. For the present book that means that the laws of the Bible dealing with issues touching on human rights have to be seen to some extent as Israel's particular take on assumptions and institutions that were part of the world that the ancient Israelites took for granted. The extent to which the rules, norms, and values of the biblical text are really substantively unique or are little more than regional variations of a larger whole is a question that is still largely unanswered, and maybe unanswerable by archaeological evidence.

Finally, it has to be said that the biblical text is a selection of texts written by some combination of intellectual, political, or religious elites over a period of generations. This means that there is a crucial distinction to be drawn between what these texts say and what actual people were thinking and doing in their day-to-day lives in the towns and villages of biblical Israel. The narrative voice(s) of the Bible, after all, do not represent neutral bystanders and witnesses, but rather engaged narrators with particular social locations and religious agendas. Thus, to some considerable extent, the texts that make up the Hebrew Bible have to be read as reflecting what the authors thought the society *should* be like, not as descriptions as to what it was *actually* like. A good example is made up of the prophetic texts, some of which articulate the wishes of some elite interest group within the society (the priests in Jerusalem, for example) who are highly critical of the "idolatrous" values of the common folk in their day-to-day lives and at other times champion the common folk against the "corrupt" religious and political elite in Jerusalem. Both perspectives are true in their own way, but neither can be taken as absolutely objective descriptions of day-to-day Israelite life among the bulk of the population. This methodological complexity has been increased over the last few decades by a new line of critique that stresses the gender perspectives of the authors. Feminist scholars in particular have reminded us that the narrators are primarily male and have a particular audience in mind, generally a male one.[2]

All of this is to say that one cannot simply assume that what the biblical text says was necessarily the case in the actually lived lives of Israelites. Nonetheless, the biblical text is important because in the end its various books do articulate the views of some powerful and influential strata of Israelite society. Thus, in the following, the reader should regard my descriptions not as an accurate portrayal of real Israelite society (although they might be), but as the vision of some leadership group or groups of how matters ought to be. This itself is an important source of data about how members of that community three thousand years ago, especially its intellectual and literary elite, thought about matters touching on what moderns today would call human rights.

With these thoughts in mind, this chapter will analyze the biblical description of how the weak and powerless were to be treated. The strategy in what follows will be first to consider the larger religious structure that provided the theoretical framework for Israelite ethics and then to turn to the social context in which matters were worked out in the detailed laws and norms spelled out in the texts. In all cases, it is important to remember that the biblical texts are not necessarily an accurate account of what actually was practiced in real life, but rather a model, or even a series of models, of how the elite thought things ought to be.

We turn first to the larger religious picture. According to the structure of the Israelites' relation to their God, they had no inherent rights per se. Their lives were in the hands of God, and God could reward, punish (through war, disease, drought, and so forth), or kill them at will. In fact there are several instances in the early books of the Bible in which God released a plague upon the people, killing thousands, for an infraction committed by a few. In short, there was no inherent right to life, health, or prosperity per se; all depended on the will of God. But oddly enough, even God's will was understood to be not entirely arbitrary. To begin with, of course, God was bound by the stipulations of the covenant. The rules by which the game was played were more or less clearly spelled out and even God had to obey the rules. If the people fulfilled their end of the contract, then God was morally bound, as it were, to fulfill the divine end. Beyond this, there was also a certain sense that God had an obligation to abide by the bare dictates of justice, over and above the details of the covenant, a theory that carries forward into the rabbinic period, as will become clear further along. The flagship passage in this regard is God's decision to destroy entirely the cities of Sodom and Gemorah, as related in Gen. 18:25. In this situation, Abraham argued with God on moral grounds that God had to be just and refrain from wholly destroying the cities should there be innocent and righteous bystanders living there. In Abraham's famous words, "Shall not the Judge of all the earth deal justly?"[3] God, of course, was forced to agree, but in the end the requisite number was not found and the cities were destroyed anyway. But the point of the encounter nonetheless stands: Although God has the right and power to destroy whole cities along with their populations, God is also subject to moral limitations.

This lack of an innate right to life in the face of the omnipotence (albeit limited by justice and morality) of God is played out in several other biblical situations. In some cases, as will be discussed in more detail below, the Israelites are commanded to exterminate certain peoples. There is no question in the Bible that the Israelites are committing no wrong by fulfilling these explicit words of God. The right to life is given by God and can be taken away by God. The same logic applies to the various capital crimes enumerated in the Bible. One convicted appropriately of a capital crime could be executed by the community acting through the court, in accordance with God's word and will. Again the lesson is clear. There were no human rights per se, only certain protections, obligations, and expectations imposed by the community as agent of the divine and as spelled out in the covenant. Those who broke the covenant also thereby forfeited the right to life. Depending on the situation, the punishment could come from the community or from God.

Even though the overall theory does not recognize a right to life, on a practical level, of course, matters were different. The Israelites after all had to live a daily workaday existence in their families, clans, and villages. Many of the biblical stories do indicate that in practice certain types of individual human rights were in fact assumed and respected. Even according to the biblical stories as written, it is clear that people were subject to a certain level of expectation from others and could and did, in turn, make certain moral demands on their neighbors or the wider community. In short, a notion of an innate right to life and respect did function at least in practice. It is to these more practical applications of human rights to which I now turn.

The society of biblical Israel was, as mentioned previously, a more or less typical Near Eastern rural society of the day. This means it would have consisted of a network of fairly small rural farming villages with an occasional settlement large enough to serve as a regional (market) town. As is true of virtually all undeveloped rural farming populations to this very day, such villages would have contained at the most a few hundred people, and in the majority of cases less. For biblical Israel, the very topography of western Palestine would have insured that such villages would remain small and somewhat isolated pockets or clusters in the mountainous terrain. Archaeological evidence from the twelfth and eleventh centuries shows us that Israelite farming settlements occurred first in the relatively difficult terrain of the highlands of central Canaan, and only gradually moved down into the rich farmland of the coastal plane, absorbing Canaanite villages, towns, and cities along the way. The biblical books of Joshua and especially Judges convey a sense of the slow and haphazard way in which the Israelites came to dominate the land. The few major cities that eventually became part of biblical Israel were all ancient Canaanite centers, and likely largely retained their non-Israelite populations and practices long after their absorption into Israel. More sophisticated social and trade networks would have developed only with the emergence of a centralized kingship around the year 1000 B.C.E., but how far that would have reached into the hinterland is still far from clear. In fact the northern tribes broke away from the Davidic dynasty of Jerusalem around 900 B.C.E. and seems to have been a much more pluralistic and open society than was true of the relatively more remote south. The Bible is mostly a southern document, and so tends to represent that perspective.

Demographically, the residents of each village would likely have been related to each other in some way. Most people would never have had the need or means to leave their home village or wander beyond their home cluster of villages. It would not have been uncommon, as is still true in the more traditional communities of the Middle East, for someone to be born, grow up, and die in the same family house. The one usual exception would have been a woman who married a man from a neighboring village and who consequently moved in with his family. But by and large, the population of the villages would have remained rooted to their land and homesteads. It may well have been the case that in larger villages the population broke down into two (or more) large extended families or clans that tended to marry within their own ranks, again much as is true in traditional villages in the Middle East today. Depending on geography, it is conceivable that in some areas, kinship networks might extend over several villages and communities. By the same token, again depending on a variety of historical, geographical, and trade factors, the populations of more distant villages or those in the next valley might be considered friends with whom one could do business, or foreigners, utter strangers, and even enemies. The biblical accounts of this early period clearly indicate that one of the ongoing struggles of the region was the attempt on the part of the central government and priesthood in Jerusalem to create a sense of common peoplehood and "Israelite-ness" in an often vain attempt to overcome the centrifugal forces of history, geography, kinship, and trade relations.

Life in ancient Israelite villages was hard and uncertain, and so social peace and harmony, and even cooperation, were critical to survival. Close kinship ties helped provide a minimum social safety net for those in trouble. It was the obligation of the next of kin, for example, to pay off the debt or redeem land that was about to be alienated from the family/clan because of unpaid debts. On the other hand, of course, large families facing limited land resources could also be a source of friction. One unusual law emerging from this society is that of the so-called levirate marriage. According to this law, in the case of a man dying without a male heir, his widow was expected to have sexual intercourse with the dead husband's brother (the levir) in the hope of producing a male heir for the deceased husband. This would give the woman a family and an inheritance for her old age. But the brother could refuse to fulfill this obligation (in a ceremony called *halitsah*). The woman would thereby be freed to move on, but the deceased brother's family would have died out. Such refusal could presumably be based on the calculation that giving the dead brother an heir would diminish the potential levir's own children's share of the family estate. A case very much like this stands, in fact, at the center of the Book of Ruth. The next of kin of Ruth's dead husband refuses to become the levir on just these grounds, in the process clearing the way for Boaz to marry Ruth.[4] The whole institution of levirate marriage is a good example of the concept of human rights in classical Israel. Individuals in the community, especially women, had little status on their own. Each person had status and identity only (or mainly) as part of a social and kinship network. In other words, normal members of the village population did not have human rights as much as they had rights, duties, and obligations inherent in their social position. On the other hand, the laws of the society seemed to have been shaped so that everyone native to Israel had access to some social position.

One must add to this rather simple picture the actual complexities that form in village life. There would have been many people who somehow fell out of the social network, such as the heirless widow whose levir refused to provide an heir and so did not have a social safety net waiting for her. In addition, as the economy developed and as the social structure became more complex with the rise of the monarchy, a number of changes occurred in village and town life that rendered the old kinship networks obsolete. Maybe most important among these changes was the influx of many foreigners who moved in and through the area. After all, the Land of Israel, then as now, stands at the juncture of Asia, Europe, and Africa, and was a conduit for all manner of travelers and traders. This of course raised new questions about what rights and duties these foreigners had as regards the indigenous population. For these types of people, the normal rules of social obligation in small interrelated villages did not apply and so a more sophisticated concept of what moderns call human rights had to be developed. The biblical laws address themselves to four such types in particular—the orphan, the widow, the stranger (ger), and the foreigner (nochri or zar).

Before turning to these classes of individuals, some comments about the role and position of women are in order. It was taken for granted by the early scholars of nineteenth-century critical biblical scholarship that women were marginalized as a class. This attitude is nicely summed up by Phyllis Bird, professor of Old Testament at Garrett-Evangelical Theological Seminary:

> Underlying these arguments and assumptions concerning the marginal or subordinate status of women in the Israelite culture was a common understanding of early Israel as a kinship-structured society of nomadic origin, whose basic social and religious unit was the patrilineal and patriarchal family. Though it was the agricultural village with its assembly of free landowners that Wellhausen had in mind when he correlated political and religious status, the principle he articulated had broader applicability: "Wer politisch nicht vollberechtigt war, war es auch religioes nicht." Women, who were disenfranchised in the political realm, were disenfranchised in the religious realm as well.[5]

She goes on immediately to point out that even though this assumption continued to reign in the field, there were already in the late nineteenth century scholarly rebuttals to this assumption, arguing that women indeed had a much fuller role to play both socially and economically. This is not to deny the largely androcentric character of the Bible or, likely, the society that underlay it. But modern ethnographic studies show us that even when the social world is ostensibly male dominated, women have a place and a role. For Bird and others, this place diminished, to be sure, as the cult became more centralized under the monarchy and the Zadokite priesthood.[6] But it should not be simply assumed, as Wellhausen and others do, that women had on their own no role or place in Israelite society.[7] Carol Meyers, professor of religion at Duke University, has argued, for example, that women played a role equal to that of men in premonarchic Israel.[8]

In terms of biblical law, surely one of the most troubling passages has to do with the *sotah*, that is, the woman whose husband suspects her of adultery. In this case, according to the laws of Num. 5:11–31, the suspicious husband may make a formal accusation to the priest. The woman must then go through a public and humiliating trial by ordeal, in which she is stripped half-naked, her hair is disheveled, and she is forced to drink a potion while calling a curse down upon herself if she is indeed guilty. This is the only case in the Bible in which such a trial by ordeal occurs. Arguments have raged back and forth whether the drastic nature in which the husband's suspicions are handled are a reflection of a need to keep family, and especially lineage, intact, or a striking case of misogyny.[9] It should be pointed out that there is no direct evidence one way or the other whether or not this ritual trial was ever indeed carried out as prescribed. But its inclusion in the biblical text surely reflects the view of some segment of Israelite society.

The following discussion focuses on the four outsiders that are explicitly recognized by biblical law. The first to be mentioned is the orphan. This individual was, of course, the most socially connected because while the biological parent or parents were dead, the child was still part of the larger extended family of his parents, the various uncles, and in-laws who all had an obligation to raise the child. The practical problem, of course, was that not all uncles, cousins, or whoever, would necessarily be willing or able to take in and raise another child or group of children. This could be the case for a variety of practical or selfish reasons. The Bible is constantly reminding the Israelites that taking in an orphan is a primary obligation. The Bible is also careful to warn the guardians of orphans not to take undue advantage of their young wards' ignorance and lack of legal power. For the biblical text, at least, the orphans had certain claims on the community.

The widow faced a related but somewhat different problem. On marriage, she entered her husband's household and thereby also his kinship network. At his death, that connection was broken, at least legally. There are a number of possibilities for her future that could then ensue. If she were childless, then the rules of levirate marriage dictated that the next of kin, usually her dead husband's brother, was to have a child by her. That child would be deemed the heir of the deceased brother, as already noted. As such, she would still have her place in the (now dead) husband's family network. Should the next of kin refuse this obligation, the woman would be released from the family and could either return to her own parental household or, surely the preferred solution, find another husband. If she had small children, of course, she would retain her position in the family, as she was now raising legitimate heirs and as these children grew to adulthood, she would become their ward, as would any elderly parent. A final possibility is that she would remain neither in her marriage family nor return to her birth family, but become, as it were, a free agent. Such an unattached woman might or might not be able to earn an honest living. The Bible stresses again and again that such a woman has a legitimate call on the community for help, sustenance, and protection, and that, conversely, the care of such women is an obligation on the community. In fact, God is described as paying particular heed to the cry of the widow and the orphan. Exod. 22:21-23, for example, proclaims in no uncertain terms, "You shall not ill-treat any widow or orphan. If you do mistreat them, I will hear their outcry as soon as they cry out to Me, and My anger shall blaze forth." The prophetic book Jer. 7:6 (and also in 22:3) announces that Israel will be allowed to live in the land only if they mend their ways, and mentions specifically the care of the widow and orphan.

The third category, that of the sojourner (ger), refers to what might be called foreign nationals or resident aliens, that is, individuals who are resident in the land for a limited period of time for trade, commercial, or occasionally military, purposes, but who have no family ties to the region. Such a person had no inherent or natural status or social connection to the land, and so, as has been noted, enjoys no inherent or natural rights. What rights he or she had were granted by the community. Nonetheless, the sojourner was assumed to have the right to a certain minimum expectation as regards sustenance and protection outside the normal familial social networks. Such a one was assumed to have the same rights and obligations as a native-born Israelite, such as freedom from work on the Sabbath (Exod. 20:10) on the one hand, and avoidance of leaven during the Passover holiday (Exod. 12:19), and so forth, on the other. Concomitantly, the stranger was to have equal rights under the law: "Hear out your fellow men, and decide justly between any man and a fellow Israelite or a stranger" (Deut. 1:16).

The fourth category, the stranger, was similar to that of a foreigner (although the stranger could apparently be an Israelite from another area), who, for whatever reason, has taken up permanent residence in the community. The term is often explicitly contrasted to *ezrach* (as in Exod. 12:19 or Lev. 24:22), meaning one who is native or indigenous. While the normal social obligations incumbent on the family, clan, and tribe would obviously not apply to these individuals, the Bible is clear in stating that such people are to be treated fairly and accorded basic human rights. In fact, Lev. 24:22 says explicitly, "You shall have one standard for stranger and citizen alike." This demand is stated with even more force in Num. 15:15–16—"There shall be one law for you and for the resident stranger; it shall be a law for all time throughout the ages. You and the stranger shall be alike before the Lord; 16. The same ritual and the same rule shall apply to you and to the stranger who resides among you."

Exodus goes on not only to outlaw false testimony and perjury, but actually to decree that the perjurers should suffer the consequences that they intended to fall on their victim. So there was a presumption that everyone was due a fair trial.[10] It is also clear from this that the distinction between the foreigner and the stranger is often blurred in the biblical text, the obligations and duties applying to the one being assumed to apply to the other. There were, then, attempts to legislate human rights even for those foreigners who were entirely outside the community. It is worth pointing out that the passages from Jeremiah previously referenced include the stranger along with the orphan and widow, upon whose correct treatment the future welfare of the community relies.

One of the earliest passages dealing with these four quintessential outsiders is found in Exod. 22:20–23, cited above:

> 20. You shall not wrong a stranger [ger] or oppress him, for you were strangers in the land of Egypt. 21. You shall not ill-treat any widow or orphan. 22. If you do mistreat them, I will heed their outcry as soon as they cry out to Me 23. and My anger shall blaze forth and I will put you to

the sword, and your own wives shall become widows and your children orphans.

The rationale attached to these pronouncements is worth a moment of consideration. The stranger is not to be oppressed because "you were strangers" (see Exod. 23:9). On the other hand, orphans and widows are to be protected because otherwise your own family will suffer that fate. On the surface neither of these rationales sound particularly like an example of human rights. This is especially true of the second case since the agent's own self-interest is invoked (if you ignore the orphan, then your own children will become orphans). Yet the passage is in fact based on two much more fundamental principles. First, the agent's own feelings are summoned up in both cases. In short, you are not to think of the stranger (or orphan or widow) as experiencing life's difficulties differently than you would. Their needs and rights are the same as yours since they share with you a common humanity. Second, the passage makes it quite clear that the mistreatment of these helpless, or rather disconnected, members of society offends God. In other words, there is a built-in assumption (taken to be a divine truth) that all people share feelings and needs, and you are aware of this because of your own humanity. This commonality transcends family, clan, tribe, and even nation.

Another section of text that is useful in this regard is the so-called Holiness Code (Lev. 17–26). This section contains myriad laws that are designed to make the Israelites into a holy people. As such it addresses the Israelite treatment not only of the four quintessential outsiders, but also marginal members of the community itself. I want to focus attention in particular on the few verses appearing in Lev. 19:9–19:

9. When you reap the harvest of your land, you shall not reap all the way to the edges of your field, or gather the gleanings of your harvest. 10. You shall not pick your vineyard bare, or gather the fallen fruit of your vineyard; you shall leave them for the poor and the stranger (ger): I the LORD am your God. 11. You shall not steal; you shall not deal deceitfully or falsely with one another. 12. You shall not swear falsely by My name, profaning the name of your God: I am the LORD. 13. You shall not defraud your fellow. You shall not commit robbery. The wages of a laborer shall not remain with you until morning. 14. You shall not insult the deaf, or place a stumbling block before the blind. You shall fear your God: I am the LORD. 15. You shall not render an unfair decision: do not favor the poor or show

deference to the rich; judge your kinsman fairly. 16. Do not deal basely with your countrymen. Do not profit by the blood of your fellow: I am the LORD. 17. You shall not hate your kinsfolk in your heart. Reprove your kinsman but incur no guilt because of him. 18. You shall not take vengeance or bear a grudge against your countrymen. Love your fellow as yourself: I am the LORD. 19. You shall observe My laws.

Several features of this block of laws should be pointed out. First, is that, as expected, most have to do with one's countrymen or kinsfolk. Leviticus wants, as it were, a certain level of mutual regard and respect among the members of the social network. The village or clan simply could not function without this basic level of human interrelationship. But the laws address some specific types of individuals as well. Three stand out in particular: The harvest is to be done in such a way that grain is left over for the poor and the stranger; the deaf and blind are not to have advantage taken of their disabilities; and the poor are to be treated as equals, neither favored nor disfavored. It is curious that these three types are specifically mentioned, since they would seem to be covered by the more general norms, as in verse 11 cited above. Illustrated here are specific instances of basic human rights. Each person, regardless of status, has a right to communal sustenance, honor and fairness, and preservation of a certain level of dignity.

The laws of the Holiness Code are regarded historically as a block of material that was absorbed, more or less whole, into the larger priestly layer of scripture of which Leviticus is the core. According to this hypothesis, this layer of material in the Pentateuch would represent a later period in the history of biblical Israel, a time closer to the end of the monarchy and the Babylonian exile. Without getting into the intricacies of these arguments, it is clear that the notion of human rights is much more focused here. It is not just a matter of taking care of displaced or out-of-place members of the community, but involves basic human dignity even for those who are part of the social network (e.g., the poor or the blind). In some sense, this material adds to the earlier sense of basic human rights the notion that part of those rights is also human dignity. Along these lines, David Novak,* of the University of Toronto notes that the *you* addressed by these commands is in the singular and the neighbor who is not to be exploited is also addressed as a single person, not a collective entity.[11] In this same article Novak goes on to point out one of the outstanding examples of individual rights in the Bible. The story occurs in 1 Kings 21:1–2, "sometime afterward the following incident occurred: Naboth the Jezereelite owned a vineyard in Jezreel, adjoining the palace of King Ahab of Samaria. 2. Ahab said to Naboth, 'Give me your vineyard, so that I may have it as a vegetable garden since it is right next to my palace. I will give you a better vineyard in exchange; or if you prefer I will pay you the price in money.' 3. But Naboth replied, 'The LORD forbid that I should give to you what I have inherited from my fathers!' " True, the story is not so much about individual rights per se as it is about the inalienability of family land given to the tribes during the conquest of the land. Nonetheless, it shows that as regards at least family rights, even the king had to observe limits. In the end, the king (or rather, his wife Jezebel) engineers Naboth's death and the king ends up with the field anyway, but the moral point stands: The king himself could not directly confiscate the land of an Israelite subject.

Another story that illustrates this same principle as regards the limitations on the king vis-à-vis the rights of commoners concerns no less a figure than King David. According to the story in 2 Sam. 11–12, David falls in love with Bathsheba and ends up sleeping with her and getting her pregnant. The problem is that she is already married to Uriah the Hittite. David now needs to get Uriah out of the picture. He concocts a plan to have Uriah killed so that Bathsheba will become a widow: then she is free to become David's wife. David accomplishes this by ordering that Uriah be placed in the front lines of a battle so that he is likely to be slain by enemy soldiers. This is what happened and David was able to marry Bathsheba. Although the king surely had a right to order soldiers in battle, the motivation here was wrong, a deliberate violation of Uriah's rights. The Bible goes on clearly to regard David as blameworthy and regards this event as one of the more damning events of his reign. Uriah, even though a Hittite—a foreigner residing in the kingdom—had a right to life and King David was wrong in disregarding this right, especially for his own benefit. It is significant that this story of Uriah's ill treatment is preserved despite that fact that in the end it is Bathsheba's son, Solomon, who became one of the greatest kings of Israel and the builder of the Temple in Jerusalem.

On the other hand, various forms of slavery were allowed in the community, although in some cases this was more like indentured servitude than what moderns would consider slavery *simpliciter*. It is hard to know exactly what this was and how it was practiced since different parts of the Bible describe servitude of this sort in different ways. This is likely because the practice itself varied over time and from place to place. Rather than try to sort out all the details, I will focus on one primary block of material, the laws of Exod. 21, with a few references elsewhere to help fill in the picture. This will provide a fairly reliable and coherent picture of what slavery meant in biblical Israel, even though many variations appear. Again, as with all biblical laws, it is impossible to know if this material accurately describes how slavery actually operated in the biblical community and if so, for what period of time.

In all events, the biblical material makes it clear that slaves had certain rights (and in some cases, duties) within the community, depending on their particular status, of which there were several. The condition most closely resembling the modern concept of slavery was that of the prisoner of war. These individuals served their masters in perpetuity, to the point that they could be passed down to the master's heirs (cf. Lev. 25:46). They were, in essence, the property of their owner. A similar category seems to have been slaves purchased from alien peoples, either non-Israelites living in the land or non-Israelite neighbors. Such people, presumably youngsters, would have been sold by their families to raise money. In all cases, the purchased or captive slaves would become therefore part of the owner's household. As such they were obligated to all the rules (positive and negative) governing other members of the household. Thus they had to be circumcised (Gen. 17:12–13) but they could not be made to work on the Sabbath (Exod. 20:10) or holidays, and they participated as equals in the Passover festivities and offerings.

A second, related, category involves daughters. According to this practice, a father had the right to sell his daughter into servitude with the understanding that she would become married to the new owner or his son. The rules governing this relationship are outlined in Exod. 21:7–11. These women had a status similar to slaves, and could, for example, be bequeathed to heirs. It also appears that the children of such female slaves themselves remained in the status of slaves. It is, in fact, not entirely clear how this differed from a real marriage in which the prospective husband paid a bride-price. In such a case, if matters proceeded as expected, then the woman was, in fact, to be treated as a wife in all respects. Should the master decide not to marry her after all, then he could not sell her to another, but must allow her "to be redeemed." What this means is not clear, but it presumably involves her being sold back to the family for the original purchase price. If the son marries her but fails to meet his various marital obligations, she is free to go.

A final category of slaves are really indentured servants. These are paupers or debtors who sell themselves, or rather their labor, in order to pay off debts. According to Exod. 21:2–6, such indentured servitude could last only six years. On the seventh year the person went free. If he entered such indentured servitude with a wife and child, they left with him. If he were given a slave woman as a wife by the master, the wife and any ensuing children remained behind in their slave status. The Hebrew slave could himself choose to remain a slave to the master for life. In this case a special ceremony was performed that involved piercing the ear with an awl (Exod. 21:5–6). Exod. 22:2 adds that criminals unable to make restitution to their victims may also be sold into such indentured servitude, presumably until they had worked off their debt. It is not clear how far a master's rights over the use and/or misuse of his slave went. One telling law is that of Exod. 21:26–27, which notes that if a master knocks out a slave's eye or tooth, the injured slave was to be set free.

What is to be concluded from these regulations about human rights in biblical Israel, at least concerning those who live within the community? On the one hand, there seemed to be deep concern for maintaining workable interpersonal relations. All residents in the community had an assigned place with its attendant duties and rights. But on the other hand, it is hard to know whether these were based on some higher concept of human rights or were more simply practical or pragmatic regulations to keep social life functioning in a harsh environment. There is only one real invocation to a higher principle that could be construed as a conceptualization of human rights, and that is the call to be mindful of the stranger because "you know the mind of the stranger." This is made even more explicit in Deut. 10:17–19:

17. For the LORD your God is God of gods and Lord of lords, the great, the mighty and the terrible God, who is not partial and takes no bribe. 18. He executes justice for the orphan and the widow, and loves the stranger, giving him food and clothing. 19. Love the stranger therefore; for you were strangers in the land of Egypt.

In other words, insofar as Israel is called to be a holy people, they are to imitate God, and this includes caring for the orphan, widow, and stranger.

Like all social groups, however, the biblical Israelites did not always live up to the high ideals set for them. That this was the case is clear from the fact that later prophets constantly complain about the failure of the people to take care of the needy among them. An especially articulate and early example is the prophet Amos, who lived in the middle of the 700s B.C.E., at a time when Israel and Judah seemed secure and prosperous. But his words could be very harsh. Consider the beginning of Amos 4: "Hear this word, you cows of Bashan on the hill of Samaria—who defraud the poor, who rob the needy." Other prophets are equally outspoken and harsh. Without knowing all the details, it seems clear that these ideals of how to treat the insiders remains, in theory if not always in practice, part of the covenantal legacy of the biblical Israelites. It is the remembrance of this legacy, along with the specific laws attached to it, that become the heritage of rabbinic Judaism several centuries later.

2

THE BIBLICAL LEGACY: BIBLICAL ISRAEL CONFRONTS ITS NEIGHBORS

I N ITS EARLY AND MONARCHICAL periods, the biblical texts only
rarely turn their attention to the issue of human rights outside
their own community. Complete outsiders, when dealt with at all, were regarded either neutrally, that is, as traders or others with whom one might
have a casual economic or social interaction (such as the *ger* or *nochri* discussed in chapter 1), or as enemies, people to be defended against or even
exterminated. This latter category is especially prominent in the texts dealing with the history of the formation of the community, when local
Canaanite groups like the Perizzites, Girgashites, or Amorites were to be
conquered and removed from the land so as not to seduce the Israelites
from the worship of their own gods. The aggressive and belligerent mood
that characterized the beginnings of the community becomes moderated
later as the Israelites settled in and began to establish trade and other relations with their neighbors. Thus, the second view—outsiders as enemies—
gradually gave way to the first view mentioned above—outsiders as trade
and cultural partners.

This moderating tendency took a much different turn in the sixth century B.C.E. as shall be made clear presently. At this point the kingdom of
Judah itself became the subject of foreign military occupation. In fact, in
around 586 B.C.E., Jerusalem was destroyed and much of the intellectual
elite was taken away into exile. The leaders of the community now had to
deal with outsiders not as objects of conquest, or partners in trade and
other cultural exchanges, but as their own conquerors, masters, and even

protectors. More significantly for the development of human rights, they had to confront the challenge of living in a stranger's culture and dealing with the stranger from a nonsuperior position, while maintaining loyalty to their own defeated God. The logic of this situation was to stress human rights of minority populations and to argue for what may be called religious freedom. This line of development accelerated during and after the fourth century, as the even more massive cultural changes brought in by Hellenization swept the region in the wake of the military campaigns of Alexander the Great. By this period the Judeans (i.e., the ethnic group tracing itself back to Judea, wherever it was that they now lived), not only had to deal with foreigners as equals, but had to do so in the philosophical and social context of the Greek tradition, which was highly pluralistic and tolerant of religious and ethnic diversity and syncretism. Chapter 3 will examine how Judeans attempted to do this. Suffice it to say that from the sixth century, Judean intellectuals were challenged to think seriously about how they were to relate to other, non-Judean, human beings outside of the traditional biblical and monarchical context. The following discussion will look at these three periods (conquest, monarchical, and postexilic) in turn.

THE PERIOD OF CONQUEST

IT SHOULD BE noted from the outset that the notion of a massive and fairly rapid conquest of the lands of Canaan by the migrating Israelites is the story as told by the Bible, but is deemed to have been a much more complex process by most modern scholars. Although it is true that the older Canaanite civilization underwent a transformation in the late Bronze Age and a new civilization, subsequently termed *Israelite* by archaeologists, did emerge, it is by no means clear that historically the entire previous population was in fact exterminated or expelled. Rather, it appears that there were a series of social disruptions, some being local insurrections, which gradually led to the emergence of a new cultural complex called Israelite. The resulting population was a mixture that included a large number of local Canaanites who simply became Israelites. It is not within the purview of this book, however, to examine this process or to make historical judgments one way or the other as to how this might have occurred or what it might mean. Rather, the purpose of this chapter is to examine the biblical texts in order to adduce the ideas on human rights that took shape during this period. For this reason the analysis here will follow the chronology of the biblical story. Although in the Bible's own telling of the story there are clear distinctions as to how outsiders were treated (or were to be treated) during the conquest, this chapter will assume that such a period existed and will look at what the text has to say about the outsider in this context.

There are several stories from the preconquest period that illustrate the bellicose nature of Israelite thinking as it struggled for its emergence. This period, lasting approximately from 1200 B.C.E. to 1000 B.C.E., can fairly be described as a period of incessant warfare, rebellion, and social dislocation. From the point of view of the Israelites, at least as this is articulated in the Bible, this was very much in the service of God's plan to return "His" people to the Promised Land and so the fate of the indigenous and adversarial population was given little if any attention. The Israelites were commanded, as it were, to conquer and essentially remove from the land all of the current populations. Even before the conquest, there was a certain sense of tribal loyalty and blood vengeance that was taken as the norm for intergroup interactions. One of the more egregious stories coming from this period is that of the vengeance visited upon the family of Hamor by the sons of Jacob in the wake of the rape of their sister, Dinah. According to Gen. 34, Shechem, the son of Hamor, a local chieftain, took Dinah by force. The father, Hamor, subsequently met with Jacob to arrange a marriage between Dinah and Shechem. Dinah's brothers agreed to the arrangement provided all of Hamor's men be circumcised like the Israelites. Hamor agreed, and the operations were duly performed. The story goes on to report:

> 25. On the third day, when they were in pain, Simeon and Levi, two of Jacob's sons, brothers of Dinah, took each his sword, came upon the city unmolested and slew all the males. 26. They put Hamor and his son Shechem to the sword, took Dinah out of Shechem's house, and went away. 27. The other sons of Jacob came upon the slain and plundered the town, because their sister had been defiled. 28. They seized their flocks and herds and asses, all that was inside the town and outside; 29. all their wealth, all their children, and their wives, all that was in the houses, they took as captives and booty.

Family and clan honor was a primary value, and nothing like what would be considered today to be human rights considerations were to stand in the way of redeeming family honor.

A similar scenario plays itself out years later during the conquest of the land. The story, told in Num. 31, begins:

> 1. The Lord spoke to Moses saying, 2. "Avenge the Israelite people on the Midianites; then you shall be gathered to your kin." 3. Moses spoke to the people, saying, "Let men be picked out from among you for a campaign, and let them fall upon Midian to wreak the LORD's vengeance on Midian." 7. They took the field against Midian, as the LORD had commanded Moses, and slew every male. 9. The Israelites took the women and children of the Midianites captive, and seized as booty all their beasts, all their herds, and all their wealth. 10. And they destroyed by fire all the towns in which they were settled.

And as if this were not enough, Moses scolded the returning warriors for sparing the women and children! He went on to command them to "slay every male among the children, and slay also every woman who has known a man carnally" (Num. 31:17). Again, there were clearly no human rights inhibitions at work. Various groups were to be driven from the land, and some, like the Amalekites, were to be erased completely from human memory (Deut. 25:17–19).

The books of Joshua and Judges are in fact full of stories of brutal battles, sieges of cities, and other acts of war and terror. A particularly brutal series of episodes is related in Judges 19–20. The events here began when an old man in Gibeah in the area of Benjamin took in some strangers for the night. The townspeople, who the text itself describes as "a depraved lot" (Judg. 19:22), demanded that the strangers be handed over to them so that they could "be intimate" with them. The host refused and eventually one of the guest's concubines instead was thrust out of the house into the hands of the mob. She was ravished all night and left dead on the doorstep of the house in the morning. Outraged, her husband took her body home, cut it up into pieces, and sent the parts out across the land, saying that nothing like this had ever happened in Israel before. In the end, the other tribes agreed to avenge the outrage and attacked the tribe of Benjamin, which was roundly defeated. The other tribes also put a sanction on Benjamin, refusing to give their daughters to Benjaminites in marriage. It soon became apparent, however, that because of the death of the Benjaminite women, the tribe was facing extinction. So the Israelites not only gave to the Benjaminites women captured from the Canaanite town of Jabesh-gilead, but also allowed the Benjaminites to capture for their wives the (Israelite?) women who were to go out to Shiloh to celebrate a feast of the Lord. Again, it is easy to see that human rights outside of one's own community was hardly a consideration at this time.

A rather curious story appears in Joshua that indicates that despite this seeming anarchy, a certain military honor had its place. In this story, a group of Canaanites in four cities in Gibeon saw the complete destruction of Jericho and Ai and came up with a plan to protect themselves from a similar fate. They approached Joshua and asked to be accepted as a subject people because they had heard of the Israelite God and so wanted to make a pact with the people of this God. Joshua was eventually persuaded to enter into a treaty with the group. Later he discovered the ruse and realized that he had agreed to spare a part of the Canaanite population, a population he had previously sworn to eradicate. In the end the four cities were militarily attacked and defeated, but because of the treaty, the inhabitants were not killed. In other words, the sacredness of an oath, even with the Canaanites, was taken quite seriously. The Gibeonites were instead enslaved as "hewers of wood and drawers of water," a caste status that they maintained for generations ("as they still are," Josh. 9:27).

THE MONARCHY

THIS BRUTAL PERIOD of tribal warfare changed once the Israelites were settled in the land and began to build their own civilization under the kingships of Saul and especially David and Solomon. This period of nation building began with the appointment of Saul as chief warlord. His victories brought a measure of peace and security to the Israelite tribes and some sense of communal identity. He was followed by David and then David's son Solomon as kings. During the reigns of David and Solomon, the empire of Israel reached its greatest extent: Jerusalem, conquered from its Canaanite owners, became the capital; the central Temple was constructed, and a certain Israelite national identity was formed. With the establishment of a formal government, the community made the transition from conqueror to a settled population. It was at roughly this time that the community began to legislate a safety net for its more vulnerable members. But relationships with outsiders also became more regularized. To be sure, warfare, with all its attendant atrocities, continued. But the Israelites also now began to deal with their neighbors on a more diplomatic and tactful level. While certain peoples continued to be regarded with disdain, such as the Ammonites and the Moabites, there are no more calls for mass exterminations and genocides. Other peoples could be regarded as aliens and even enemies, but this no longer entailed their dehumanization. Trade relations developed, and members of these groups could live among Israelites as strangers who had a certain level of recognition and protection, as has already been noted.

After the kingship of Solomon, the biblical community broke up into two somewhat contentious rival kingdoms: Israel in the north with its capital at Samaria and the bulk of the population, and Judah in the south, centered on Jerusalem and with a relatively sparse population, given the desertlike quality of most of its terrain. In around 722 B.C.E., Assyrian armies conquered Samaria and absorbed all of the northern kingdom of Israel into their empire. This was accomplished in part by transplanting Israelite families to Mesopotamia and bringing in foreign settlers to dilute the Israelite character of the remaining indigenous population. In all events, the independent existence of an Israelite community in the north ceased (except in the form later on of the Samaritan religious sect). Although Jerusalem also was threatened at this time, it was not actually taken, and so the southern kingdom of Judah continued to exist.

A new attitude slowly began to take hold in the biblical books as the Israelite empire broke up and finally suffered defeat. These events quite naturally led to speculation about the nature of the covenant, theodicy, and the rule of God. If God could use the Assyrians or the Babylonians for divine purposes, then the Israelite God was indeed the God of all history and so of all peoples. In fact, it would follow, this God could just as easily punish the Judeans as it could the Israelites, or the various Canaanites, as the first two chapters of the book of the prophet Amos attest:

For the three transgressions of Damascus / For four, I will not revoke it: . . .

For the three transgressions of Gaza / For four, I will not revoke it: . . .

For the three transgressions of Tyre / For four, I will not revoke it: . . .

For the three transgressions of Edom / For four, I will not revoke it: . . .

For the three transgressions of the Ammonites / For four, I will not revoke it: . . .

For the three transgressions of Moab / For four, I will not revoke it: . . .

For the three transgressions of Judah / For four, I will not revoke it: . . .

For the three transgressions of Israel / For four, I will not revoke it: . . .

A few centuries later, the prophet Isaiah could proclaim, "For my House shall be called / A house of prayer for all peoples" (Isa. 56:7). From this perspective, it became possible to conceive of human rights in a more universal, inclusive sense.

THE EXILE

ALTHOUGH JUDAH SURVIVED the Assyrian incursions in the eighth century, the southern kingdom remained extremely vulnerable. When the neo-Babylonian Empire replaced the Assyrians, the drive to conquest continued and Judah came under renewed threat of conquest. In the late 600s B.C.E. and early 500s B.C.E. the inevitable happened and Judah fell to the armies of the Babylonian Empire and lost its independence. In around 586 B.C.E. facing a series of insurgencies, the Babylonian ruler, Nebuchadnezzar formally dissolved the Kingdom of Judah and exiled its royal family, priestly leaders, and other major families to Babylon. Thus began the Babylonian exile, which by all rights should have ended the existence of biblical Israel. But some fifty years later, around 538 B.C.E., the Persians, who had in turn conquered the Babylonians, instituted a policy that allowed the exiled Judean families in Babylonia to return to their homeland, to rebuild Jerusalem, and to restore the Temple under the leadership of the local priesthood.

The actual process of this return and reconstitution was a long, complicated, and multilayered affair that is not relevant here. Suffice it to say that the Temple, or some semblance of it, was in fact rededicated in around 520 B.C.E. The restored province of Judea, or Yahud as the Persians called it, was a far cry from the previous kingdoms. It comprised little more than Jerusalem and the surrounding countryside such that most Judeans now lived outside Yahud, some in what was formally Judean or Israelite territory, and some in a far-flung diaspora that stretched from Mesopotamia to Egypt. What is important here is that along with this return of the ruling elites, and especially the priesthood, came a kind of religious national ideology that saw this rump province as the seed for the reborn empire of David. This ideology was one of a number of views that set off a massive debate within the community about the very nature of the resurrected society and how its members should relate to outsiders. Over the next few hundred years, this internal debate, chronicled at least in part in the last books of the Bible, resulted in a whole new conceptualization as to what it meant to be part of the people of Israel and how that people in turn were to relate to outsiders. Part of the debate involved the universalization of the Israelite God, from the national god of one people, to the ruler of the whole world, and the creator and protector of all peoples, a process already under way during the monarchy. Others saw the exile itself as a punishment for being too open to foreign and ungodly ideas, and so called for an even more exclusivist attitude. This intellectual shift had, of course, a profound effect on discussions of human rights as these were to be understood in the reborn community.

One extreme is without doubt represented by the priestly scribe Ezra, who was sent by the Persian government to help reorganize the Judean community in the late fifth century B.C.E. Ezra arrived with the understanding that the people of Israel were a holy race that had to maintain its genetic purity, especially as regards the priesthood, which had exclusive access to the inner sanctum of the Temple. The shocking and brutal story of his attempt to impose an extraordinarily exclusivist policy on the people is related in chapter 10 of the Book of Ezra. It is worth citing the account at length:

> Then a proclamation was issued in Judah and Jerusalem that all who had returned from the exile should assemble in Jerusalem, 8. and that anyone who did not come in three days would, by decision of the officers and elders, have his property confiscated and himself excluded from the congregation of the returning exiles.
>
> 9. All the men of Judah and Benjamin assembled in Jerusalem in three days; it was the ninth month, the twentieth of the month. All the people sat in the square of the House of God, trembling on account of the event and because of the rains. 10. Then Ezra the priest got up and said to them, "You have trespassed by bringing home foreign women, thus aggravating the guilt of Israel. 11. So now, make confession to the LORD, God of you fathers, and do His will, and separate yourselves from the peoples of the land and from the foreign women."

According to the remainder of the story the people readily agreed to do this. But it is clear from other writings subsequent to this edict that the matter was hardly settled in such a swift and simplistic way. In fact, there are significant late biblical writings that argue precisely against Ezra's exclusivist view and for a broader acceptance of others.

Before proceeding, it will be helpful to sketch out the massive social changes the community was facing. Within a century or so of Ezra's decree, Jerusalem and Judah found themselves caught up in the process of Hellenization, brought about by the conquests of Alexander the Great, who came through the region in the 330s B.C.E. One of his policies was to bring Greek administration into the newly conquered territories of the Middle East. Along with this came Greek language and not far behind Greek education, philosophy, science, religion, and culture. In the event, one of the outstanding characteristics of Alexander's policies was a process in which Greek culture blended and merged with traditional Middle Eastern cultures to create a vibrant new synthesis called Hellenism. Needless to say, this was hardly a monolithic culture that took hold everywhere in the same way and at the same time. Hellenism was really more of a profound cultural transformation that continued to unfold unevenly across the Middle East over several hundred years, taking on different forms and content in reaction to a variety of local factors. But there is no doubt that throughout the Middle East an ongoing process of syncretism was under way that brought together into new cultural complexes a vast variety of peoples, ethnic groups, languages, religions, and cultures.

The transformation of religion yields some insight into the process. The local Canaanite Baals, for example, became manifestations of Zeus and local religious practices became Hellenistic mystery cults celebrated across the Hellenistic world and explained in terms of Persephone's descent to Hades or the resurrection of the Egyptian goddess Isis. These were practiced not only by "natives" but by hangers-on and children of mixed parentage as ethnic groups of every variety both blended with others and struggled to identify their uniqueness as distinct peoples in their various diasporas. Even in its relatively isolated position up in the hill country, away from major trade routes, Jerusalem was not immune to the cultural, intellectual, and religious changes swirling around it. The need to keep Judea and Jerusalem intellectually, religiously, and ethnically pure as Ezra proposed seemed not only less and less possible, but also less and less desirable. In fact, the story of Ezra may itself reflect, ironically, this process of assimilation and syncretism. The letters he quotes, for example, are written not in Hebrew, but in the Babylonian imperial *lingua franca*, Aramaic, which itself shows some Greek influence. Ezra thus found, and had to work within, a community already well on its way to cultural and ethnic reconfiguration and vulnerable to pluralism, a reality that infected him even as he fought against it. Counterparts to Ezra's vision that stress instead the universality of God's rule and the common humanness of all peoples were composed by Judeans during this same time, and some found their way into the Bible, alongside the books of Ezra-Nehemiah. The Bible preserves for us the elements of the Hellenizing versus exclusivist debate.

One of the most remarkable biblical countertales is the Book of Ruth. While the story itself takes place in the time of the Judges, that is, premonarchic Israel, the language and sentiment clearly point to the Hellenistic period as its time of origin. The story concerns Naomi, a Judean woman who travels with her husband across the Jordan river to Moab. There her sons marry local women. Now the reader needs to be aware at this point that the Moabites were one of the most despised people in early Israel. Deut. 23:4–5, states quite baldly, for example:

> 4. No Ammonite or Moabite shall be admitted into the congregation of the LORD; none of their descendants, even in the tenth generation, shall ever be admitted into the congregation of the LORD, 5. because they did not meet you with food and water on your journey after you left Egypt, and because they hired Balaam, son of Beor, from Pethor of Aram-naharaim, to curse you—.

So the move of Naomi to Moab, and the coming of Ruth the Moabite woman to Judah, are not just random referrals to an alien people. Moab and Ruth represent the quintessential hated outsider.

It is precisely this fact that makes the rest of the story so remarkable. Tragedy struck the family and Naomi's husband and eventually both of her sons died, leaving the three women without male support. Naomi decided to return to her homeland and told her two daughters-in-law to find new husbands for themselves in Moab. One of the daughters-in-law, Orpah, does so, but the other, Ruth, refuses, choosing instead to stay with her mother-in-law, announcing in her famous soliloquy, "For wherever you go, I will go; wherever you lodge, I will lodge; your people shall be my people, and your God my God" (Ruth 1:16). So these two women return to Judah, in the region of Bethlehem, where Ruth eventually married a wealthy relative of her late husband and bore a son, Obed. The conclusion of the book recounts that Obed in turn was the father of Jesse, who was the father of the future King David.

It is, of course, no coincidence that the story involves precisely the Moabites, and lest the point be lost, Ruth is referred to as "the Moabitess" throughout. The point clearly is that the old enmities between peoples no longer makes sense in the Hellenistic milieu, and that in fact the greatest period of Israel's history, the golden age of David's rule, was the result of just such a crossing of boundaries. Ruth the Moabitess was accepted into rural Judean society. She adopted its practices, reaped its rewards, was able to marry into a prominent family and in fact became the progenetrix of King David. Clearly the narrator of this tale had no problem with racial purity, in sharp contrast to the attitude of Ezra, even as regards the classically excluded groups such as the Moabites. So one of the major lessons of the story is the breakdown of the ethnic barriers erected in early Israelite legislation, a sentiment perfectly in keeping with the increase in ethnic permeability ushered in by Hellenization.

A second example of this universalizing tendency is found in the short book of Jonah. Jonah is called by God to preach to the people of Nineveh, the capital of the hated Assyrian Empire. This, it is worth remembering, was one of the worst and most brutal enemies of the Israelite people, responsible for the complete destruction of the Northern Kingdom of Israel. Confronted with this demand to bring salvation to the Ninevites, Jonah refused and tried to flee. In the end, he found that he could not escape God and so reluctantly went to Nineveh. The city, as he feared, repented and Jonah went off to sulk in the desert. At that point, God created a bush to give Jonah shade and then just as Jonah settled down, God destroyed the bush. When Jonah grieved about the loss of the bush, God responded, "You cared about this plant, which you did not work for and which you did not grow, which appeared overnight and perished overnight. And should not I care about Nineveh, that great city, in which there are more than a hundred and twenty thousand persons" (Jon. 4:10–11).

This sentiment of openness to others reached its apex in the prophetic period, perhaps in the prophet Micah, who was active in the fifth century, during the early days of the Second Commonwealth. He is probably best known for his oration in chapter 4:

1. In the days to come, the Mount of the Lord's House shall stand firm above the mountains; and it shall tower above the hills. The people shall gaze on it with joy, 2. and the many nations shall go and shall say: "Come, Let us go up to the Mount of the Lord, to the House of the God of Jacob; that He may instruct us in His ways, and that we may walk in his paths."

For instruction shall come forth from Zion, the word of the Lord from Jerusalem. 3. Thus He will judge among the many peoples, and arbitrate for the multitude of nations, however distant; and they shall beat their swords into plowshares and their spears into pruning hooks. Nations shall not take up sword against nation; they shall never again know war; 4. but every man shall sit under his grapevine or fig treee with no one to disturb him. For it was the Lord of Hosts who spoke.

This openness to others was hardly new or unprecedented in biblical Israel. Many of the classical prophets were already moving to a concept of the universality of God as the Lord of all people, with the concomitant notion that thus all people, all God's creatures, enjoyed certain inalienable rights. One of the flagship examples of this early orientation was the prophet Amos of the eighth century. For him and others like Isaiah, the Israelite people have no special claim or privilege vis-à-vis the surrounding population groups. That is, Israel's and Judah's special covenant or relationship with God grants them no special protection when it comes to the exploitation of others. This is a universal demand of human rights that applied to Israel as much as to the foreigners of Tyre. But it is surely in the Hellenistic period that this view came into full blossom.

The intellectual and religious struggles of the Judeans in the Hellenistic world came to represent a crucial turning point in the history of Judaism. With the generations following Alexander's incursion into the region, there was a transmogrification from the old tradition of biblical Israel to the new, Romanized version commonly known by its Greek name, Ioudaismos. This new pattern of belief and practice gave rise to rabbinic Judaism. This transformation is the subject of chapter 3.

3

"Judaism" and Human Rights in the Greco-Roman World

A FEW WORDS ABOUT TERMINOLOGY are necessary before entering the substance of this chapter. For purposes of this discussion, the term Greco-Roman is meant to describe the period from roughly 300 B.C.E. to roughly 230 C.E. In around 300 B.C.E., Alexander the Great conquered the Middle East and began the process of introducing Greek culture into the region, a process generally called Hellenization. The period ends in 230 C.E., with the publication of the Mishnah, the earliest extant text of rabbinic Judaism. The 530 years or so covered in this chapter saw the transformation of the Ancient Near Eastern religion of biblical Israel into the Romanized religion constructed by the earliest rabbis. Because the term *Judaism* is so connected with the rabbinic Judaism that has come down to modern times, the Greek term *Ioudaismos* will be used in this chapter to indicate the transitional forms that took shape between the older biblical religion and the normative rabbinic Judaism of the third century forward. It should be noted that the transition from the older religion described in the Bible to its rabbinic descendant was not a simple or linear process. Rather, a variety of competing forms of Ioudaismos emerged, some of which disappeared, and others of which survived, merged, split, and recombined into a variety of different configurations. Rabbinic Judaism is but one of the many competing streams to take shape during this period. Its emergence as the normative Judaism of the Middle Ages was the end result of a long and tortuous process.

In a way, the confusion inherent in the transition from the biblical religion of ancient Israel to what we call Judaism is reflected in the ambigu-
ities of the Greek term Ioudaioi, which first came into common use
during this period. Its original and simple meaning, of course, was one
who either was or whose family had been from the geographical area
known to the Greco-Romans as Judea (biblical Judah; Persian Yahud).[1]
Over the period under discussion, however, the term gradually took on an
entirely different meaning, namely, one associated with a particular ethnic, religious philosophy, termed *ioudaismos*, which was widely practiced
in a number of loosely related forms across the empire and which was
only in complex and indirect ways connected with the eponymous land
of Judah. To be sure, many Ioudaioi did trace their roots and their religion
back to Judah, but by the turn of the millennium it is abundantly clear
that a significant number, if not the majority, of Ioudaioi had more of a
mythic than an actual physical connection to that land. By Roman times
the people who were called Ioudaioi were more than likely to have been
natives of Babylonia, northern Egypt (especially Alexandria), Rome, or
other areas of the empire and were labeled Ioudaioi only by virtue of the
fact that they claimed descent from or religious association with Judea.
Even in Judea, the indigenous Judeans who could claim family and religious descent from biblical Israelites and who practiced Ioudaismos may
well have been a minority while many Greeks practicing a variety of syn-
cretic religions lived and even ruled in the area of Judah. Jerusalem and
its environs, the very heart of Judea, was only sporadically under indigenous Judean rule. In fact, from about 44 B.C.E., with the beginning of the
reign of Herod, who was himself not Judean but Nabatean, Judea was essentially a province ruled from Rome by non-Judean procurators, with
only a brief exception under King Agrippa from 40 to 44 C.E. There was,
then, a growing disconnection between living in Judea and practicing
Ioudaismos. Scholars regularly have to deal with the anomaly that local inhabitants of Judea were called Ioudaioi in a geographical or political sense
even though they might not be practicing Ioudaismos, while Ioudaioi in
the diaspora, while not geographically or politically connected to Judea,
were nonetheless called Ioudaioi because they participated in the ethnicity,
culture, and religion of what was called Ioudaismos.

To confound matters even more, there is strong evidence that in Roman times many people from a variety of ethnic and geographical backgrounds, both in Judea but also in the diaspora, had adopted some form of
Ioudaismos in their religious life. The ancient religions of the East held a

certain fascination for Romans of all types, and Ioudaismos was by far no exception. There thus formed a large population of *Judaizers* (or *sebomenoi*, as they were called) of various sorts who brought their own ideas and rituals into their practice of Ioudaismos. Estimates are that at one point up to 10 percent of the Roman Empire were Judaizers of some kind or the other. To what extent such people were actually Ioudaioi in any meaningful sense (i.e., they participated in Ioudaismos in a substantial way, not just incorporating certain amulets or prayers into their own otherwise pagan religious practices) was then, and is still now, an open question. The term *Ioudaioi* thus became so diffuse that it lost its inherent meaning. Because of this, the Greco-Roman period presented Ioudaioi of the time with the immensely challenging task of defining boundaries; that is, of determining which people were really Ioudaioi and which were not, and which practices were legitimate expressions of Ioudaismos and which were not, and to what extent the two terms were congruent.[2] This confusion of terms became especially significant after 70 C.E., when revolts in Judea led to the Roman destruction of Jerusalem, the dismantling of the Temple, and the eventual banishment of Ioudaioi from Judea. This was the worst rebellion the Roman Empire ever faced and convinced the Roman leadership that Ioudaioi (meaning those living in Judea) were unassimilable misanthropes. Yet despite this suspicion of Ioudaioi, the attraction of Ioudaismos continued unabated and provoked vicious attacks by upholders of traditional Roman values (like Seneca* and Cicero*). This led to the anomalous situation of Ioudaioi being both a homeless and defeated minority in one sense and a (perceived) threat to the dominance of traditional Roman religion and values in another sense. One result of this confusion of terms was the negative picture of Jews that was later taken up by the Church as a people both defeated and powerful.

The chaos reflected in the terms Ioudaioi and Ioudaismos indicates the broader reality of the Hellenistic and Greco-Roman worlds, namely the intermixing of a wide variety of national and religious groups across the empire. Needless to say, these social realities had an overwhelmingly important impact on how Romans in general, including Ioudaioi, thought about the issues of human rights. The intermixture of peoples, ideas, and cultures that began in the Hellenistic period with Alexander the Great's conquests and continued right through Roman rule, and of which Ioudaioi were an integral part, created a new set of tolerant values and laws in the Greco-Roman world. While, to be sure, there were Roman intellectuals who worried about the preservation of traditional Roman values and customs, the bulk of the population seemed quite ready to draw on the available religious traditions, cults, and practices around them and to combine elements as they saw fit. All religious traditions, especially those of the East, adapted to Roman culture, intermixed with each other, and syncretized (so that Baal in one context was Zeus in another, and so forth), such that a variety of mystery cults, gnostic sects, and other groupings took shape. Roman law itself helped promote a high level of tolerance for this kind of diversity of peoples and religious traditions in that it assumed a concept of natural law or natural rights, which implied the existence of certain human rights. Of course, the exact the meaning and content of natural law was itself the subject of debate and fundamental disagreements among intellectuals. The philosophical debates around such issues are much too complicated to go through here, but a single example, that of the impermissibility of slavery, might be helpful. Slavery of one sort or another was widely practiced in the Roman world. Yet, many philosophers argued that it was against natural law, although they could not agree on why. Aristotle and his followers argued early on that slavery was a violation of nature insofar as it went against the very *telos* or the ultimate end of being human (although Aristotle himself tolerated the institution on practical grounds). The stoics, such as Cicero, argued that slavery was wrong because private property was altogether not a natural right since the resources of nature are, by nature, available to all people. In this constant ebb and flow of religious and legal argumentation on virtually every topic in the Roman world, one effect was the breaking down of absolutes among various groups and the encouragement of universal tolerance (within ill-defined limits).[3] Ioudaismos itself benefited from this tolerant attitude by being declared a licit (or official) religion. Thus, Ioudaioi enjoyed certain legal rights (e.g., observance of the Sabbath) while being reviled by others for just those privileges in that such special status represented the triumph of the particular over the universal and natural.

All of this had, of course, a tremendous effect on the interior character of the Ioudaioi and their various struggles to define themselves and their religion. From the Dead Sea Scrolls, through the apocalyptic literature, and into the New Testament, one gets a glimpse of the fierce internal debates within the community of Ioudaioi as to what was the proper content of the religion and who had a right to say so. What does seem to emerge clearly from the diverse and difficult literature of the time are two opposing trends. On the one hand were people who saw Ioudaismos as the very essence of true religion. The fulfillment of history would see the full conversion of all peoples to the worship of the one true God. This, for some, might involve a supernatural, even messianic, intervention that would redeem the world and issue in a new era in which everyone would look to Jerusalem for religious and moral guidance (along the lines of the vision of Micah, chapter 4, cited in chapter 2). For others, this conversion would happen slowly as more and more people recognized their own religious and philosophical traditions as just pale reflections of the true teachings of Moses. Others saw exactly the opposite, namely, that the preservation of Judaism was possible, in line with Ezra's vision, only in the absolute segregation and protection of the true lineage of the righteous, God-fearing remnant of the faithful. For holders of this view, including the Therapeutai described by Philo* and possibly also the people who settled at Qumran near the Dead Sea, the only way to bring about God's blessing on Israel was to segregate themselves in holy purity in their own tightly controlled communities according to strict interpretations of Biblical priestly law. It hardly needs to be said that each of these groups understood human rights in utterly different terms.

The surviving literature seems to indicate that the vast majority of Ioudaioi (and Judaizers) took something much closer to the first position mentioned above. They were open to the wider world and its various influences and were quite ready to participate openly in Roman life in a variety of ways. That is, the bulk of Ioudaioi rejected the exclusivist attitudes of the Essenes and their ilk. But this did not mean that they thought all religions and philosophies were equal. They, of course, wanted to show that Ioudaismos was not just another religion but that it had a special message to offer. In fact, some Judaic literature from the Hellenistic period portrayed Moses as a great human teacher who even helped instruct Plato and Aristotle, although it is not clear whether the intended audience were Greeks who, knowing this, would feel more comfortable in adopting Judaic teachings, or if the message was addressed to Ioudaioi who could now feel more a part of the surrounding world. In any case, a common message was that even clearly foreign peoples, like the Greeks, had access to the Truth, and in this were indebted to biblical Israel, even if they did not always recognize their indebtedness. The large penumbra of Judaizers the Roman world produced is striking evidence of the success of this kind of missionizing outreach. On the other hand, the notion that all wisdom could be traced back to Moses gave non-Judean religions and philosophies a certain status among at least some segments of Ioudaioi, an attitude that would not have been have found a thousand years earlier. Recall, for example, biblical Israel's attitude toward the Moabites and Ammonites. The common humanity of all peoples and religions, if not the equal worth of all beliefs, became part of the basic assumptions of a good part of the Hellenistic Judean intellectual world, especially in the diaspora. Nothing human was foreign to Ioudaismos and it, in turn, was not foreign to any human endeavor. Only marginal groups, like the Essenes or Jewish gnostic sects, held that they had a secret truth that was available only to a blessed or chosen circle of believers.

There was, of course, a reverse side of this optimistic view of humankind and its collective heritage of wisdom. This negative side manifested itself in the various religious movements that scholars have come collectively to call *gnosticism*. The term covers a variety of attitudes, sects, cults, and doctrines, but it is nonetheless possible to describe in a broad way the attitude that they all shared. In broad terms, gnosticism drew on the foundational Greek philosophical distinction between the ideal realm and the material realm. Gnosticism in general followed the Platonic attitude that the ideal realm was the more real and meaningful while the material realm was but an imperfect and distorted reflection of that perfect realm. But many Gnostics took this orientation a step further, arguing that, contrary to biblical teaching, a good Creator God did not in fact create the material realm; only the purely spiritual realm was the creation and domain of the good Creator God. The material world, in opposition to this, was created by an evil originator often termed the *Demiurge* (literally, craftsman). The idea behind this act of the Demiurge was the subject of much speculation among various Gnostic groups and thinkers, but generally came down to the idea that the Demiurge hoped to capture the souls of people—souls that came from the good Creator God—and so eventually weaken the hold of the good God. In some cases, this was seen as part of a cosmic battle between good and evil. In all events, human souls, which yearn to return to their true Maker instead find themselves entrapped in physical bodies and progressively drawn away from the spiritual into the material web spun out by the Demiurge. In this way the soul is turned from the good toward sin and damnation.

The point of gnosticism is that such souls can be saved from this fate by knowledge of their true condition and contemplation on the divine and true and rejection of the merely physical. Knowledge, of course, being nonmaterial, is the very substance of the soul. The problem is getting this knowledge, *gnosis*, to the souls. To do so, some savior, prophet, teacher, master, or other such figure appears and transmits this special teaching or insight to those who are still able, and ready, to receive and act on it. People in this position then learn to shun the world and its seductions and turn their thoughts instead to the proper goal of the soul, contemplation of the divine. It is these souls that, upon death, are able to transcend, or ascend from, the material realm and enjoy a divine existence. This was of course a powerful orientation in early Christianity, itself a form of Ioudaismos, but it is also apparent in at least some of the earlier scrolls found near the Dead Sea. Some Ioudaioi were themselves gnostic, and saw the Teacher of Righteousness or Moses (or Enoch, or Jesus) as the bearer of this salvific knowledge.

From this point of view, which seems to have been quite widespread among religious groups of various sorts in late antiquity, including various clusters of Ioudaioi, there was really no such thing as human rights per se. The material world of the Demiurge was a realm of evil to be escaped and really not expected to be anything other than unfair and sinful anyway. In fact, suffering and even death could be salvific in that these could serve the higher goal of de-emphasizing the physical body and its pleasure and putting emphasis on the soul and its needs. This is not to say that all gnostics were psychopathic criminals, wife-beaters, or abusive. It is to say that for them human rights, as moderns understand them, did not really exist except insofar as every soul had a right to gnosis and salvation, if it were prepared to receive it. What happened to the physical body was of no consequence, and in fact, its suffering could even lead to a higher good.

On the other hand, gnosticism, by placing considerable emphasis on the rights of the human soul, could also be taken to justify human rights as well. It thus should not be surprising to find that some Ioudaioi focused their attention precisely on the soul and its career. One of the outstanding examples of this way of thinking was Philo of Alexandria. Overall, Philo's reading of scripture was heavily influenced by neo-Platonism. He drew, for example, a sharp distinction between the lower, earthly realm of opinion and the higher realm of truth. One earned a right to the higher truths of the abstract realm only after fulfilling one's role in the lower, earthly life. Thus, the entire earlier history of biblical Israel was read, by Philo, as an allegory of the good life in which the path of the good person is a sort of journey modeled by the biblical patriarchs, who show how one gradually advances from simple interaction with the physical world to higher levels of insight and knowledge. It is this growth of the human soul into contemplation that earns for the soul a kind of salvation consisting of peace and a sharing in the divine nature. For Philo, all human souls have the innate ability, or right, to achieve this goal, albeit not all individuals will in the end be able to realize this potentiality. Philo, of course, never talks about human rights in the modern sense, but he clearly believed, in standard Greco-Roman form, that the human soul does have a special place in the cosmic scheme of things and ought to be nurtured by its owners, and others, to move toward its ordained end.

There are, to be sure, a number of questions as to how much of the Judean community Philo can really be said to represent. Opinions range from a community of one (Philo himself) to the generality of (at least diasporic) Ioudaioi.[4] It is of course at some level impossible to pin down an answer with any definitiveness. Our sources from this period are few and far between, and, ironically, largely preserved by the Church for its own purposes and not by later Judaism. But given the pervasiveness of this general style of thought in the Greco-Roman world, represented by Greek, Roman, and Christian writers and artists and, according to Goodenough, in Jewish art of the epoch, there is little reason to doubt that Philo reflected something larger than his own private philosophy. In fact, specific Jewish contemplative sects are mentioned by both Philo and the historian Flavius Josephus.* In "De Vita Contemplativa," Philo describes a Judaic monastic order, the Therapeutae, located in the desert of Egypt. Josephus, the Roman Jewish historian, makes similar claims for the Essenes. Erwin Goodenough sees this philosophy permeating the entire early synagogue stream of Greco-Roman Judaism. So Platonic types of mysticism seem to have a large, if not overwhelming presence. In short, the entire range of Greco-Roman thought, from natural law to the various readings of gnosticism, had deeply insinuated itself into the internal discourse of Ioudaioi and Ioudaismos.

There was also a more particularistic strain within Ioudaismos. The combination of exclusivist groups on the one hand, and missionizing outreach on the other, convinced many traditional Roman thinkers to see Ioudaisimos as an entirely alien and even dangerous and immoral religion that inherently hated others. To make this claim they could point to groups like the community of the Dead Sea and maybe even the early pre-Pauline Christians. These thinkers began a literary tradition now called "adversus Judaeos," that systematically denigrated Ioudaismos. One of the earlier and extensive accounts is that of Lysimachus, who had Egyptian roots. Addressing himself to the biblical story of the Exodus from Egypt, he is reported by Josephus to have recorded the following:

In the reign of Bocchoris, king of Egypt, the Jewish people, who were afflicted with leprosy, scurvy, and other maladies, took refuge in the temples
and lived a mendicant existence. The victims of disease being very numerous, a dearth ensued throughout Egypt. . . . Bocchoris summoned the priests
and servitors at the altars and ordered them to draw up a list of the unclean
persons and to deliver them into military charge to be conducted into the
wilderness, . . . on the next day a certain Moses advised them to take their
courage in their hands and make a straight track until they reached inhabited country, instructing them to show goodwill to no man, to offer not
the best but the worst advice, and to overthrow any temples and altars of
the gods which they found. The rest assenting, they proceeded to put these
decisions into practice. They traversed the desert, and after great hardships
reached inhabited country: there they treated the population, and plun-
dered and set fire to the temples, until they came to the country now called
Judaea.[5]

Many Roman authors referred to the Ioudaioi's stubborn attachment to
their superstitions as a threat to traditional Roman values. Quintilian* is a
good example of this attitude. He wrote, "The vices of the children bring
hatred on their parents; founders of cities are detested for concentrating a
race which is a curse to others, as for example, the founder of the Jewish superstition."[6] Valerius Maximus reports in the first century C.E. that a certain
Cornelius Hispalus at one point "banished the Jews from Rome, because
they attempted to transmit their sacred rites to the Romans."[7] The philosopher Seneca, writing also in the first century, laments, "Meanwhile the customs of this accursed race have gained such influence that they are now
received throughout all the world. The vanquished have given laws to their
victors."[8] While it is true that many Greco-Roman writers wrote about
Ioudaioi in neutral, or even complimentary terms, the notion of the Jews as
misanthropes and as dangerous to Roman civilization remained a constant
trope among certain members of the Roman intellectual elite. It gained
considerable power in the wake of the continued violence and eventual
bloody rebellion in Judea. The ensuing war, lasting from 68–73 C.E., was
one of the bloodiest of Roman imperial history and convinced many Romans that Judeans were indeed unable to get along with others.

To counter the anti-Ioudaismos of these Roman thinkers, especially after the rebellion of 67 C.E., the historian Josephus wrote extensively on
the Jewish Wars in an attempt to show that it was the work of a small group
of fanatics, malcontents, and zealots. For Josephus, himself a Judean and

one of the early commanders of the resistance against Rome, the Judeans as a whole were not to be blamed. They, in fact, were almost model Romans, deserving respect and even praise for their ancient wisdom and moral way of life. But, in the end, Josephus failed to convince many. In part this was due to the die-hard Judeans themselves, who believed that God would defeat the arrogant Romans and restore the Holy City of Jerusalem, just as he had humbled the Babylonians and allowed a return to the city six hundred years earlier. Those who knew biblical history knew that a period of some sixty-five years passed between the destruction of the First Temple (around 586 B.C.E.) and the building of the Second Temple (completed about 520 B.C.E.). It is thus probably not a coincidence that sixty-five years after the first rebellion, a second one broke out.

In 132 C.E., a leader called Simeon Bar Kochba ("Son of the Star") led a new attempt to liberate Judea from Rome. He even had his own coins minted celebrating years one, two, three, and four of the liberation and depicting a model of the (soon to be rebuilt) Temple. As before, the rebellion was brutally suppressed and Jerusalem was entirely laid waste. There is even evidence that Ioudaioi were forbidden from entering the city, which was now dedicated to the Roman gods and renamed Aelia Capitolina. Hadrian had a coin minted showing the plowing over of the ground of the erstwhile city. But even after Bar Kochba it is clear that some segments of the Judean community held on to their messianic expectations. As late as Emperor Julian the Apostate (ruler from 361–363 C.E.) there was hope that a new, third temple would be built and the golden age of David would return.

The continuing anti-Roman agitation of Judeans only added fuel to the notion that the Judeans (and by extension all Ioudaioi?) simply were unwilling to deal with other people on other than their own terms. This attitude, which seems to have had widespread circulation among the Roman upper classes, is illustrated by Tacitus,* who wrote:

> The Jews . . . reveal a stubborn attachment to one another, an active commiseration, which contrasts with their implacable hatred of the rest of mankind. They sit apart at meals, they sleep apart, and though, as a nation, they are singularly prone to debauchery, they abstain from intercourse with foreign women.[9]

There is little evidence of Judean reaction to these attacks. One outstanding example of a Jewish answer, written even before the Bar Kochba rebellion and its anti-Ioudaioi backlash, is a late work by the same Flavius Josephus encountered earlier. In a pamphlet entitled "Contra Apionem" (Apion was a Roman author who penned a vitriolic attacks on the Judeans), Josephus vigorously defended his countrymen. One item he addressed in particular is remarkably reminiscent of Tacitus's allegations about Ioudaioi. The passage in question is as follows:

> Apion also tells a false story, when he mentions an oath of ours, as if we "swore by God, the Maker of the heaven, and earth, and sea, to bear no good will to any foreigner, and particularly to none of the Greeks."[10]

Josephus's reply, as is characteristic of his defense as a whole, is acerbic. After claiming that quite to the contrary, many Greeks, rather than finding themselves held at arm's length, actually came over to Judaism, Josephus goes on to note, "[N]or did anybody ever hear this oath sworn by us: Apion, it seems, was the only person that heard it, for he indeed was the first composer of it."

Josephus went even further, claiming that the law of the Jews, ascribed not to some earthly legislator but to God, represents a good that all people can recognize:

> [B]ut he ordained our government to be what, by a strained expression, may be termed a Theocracy, by ascribing the authority and the power to God, and by persuading all the people to have a regard to him, as the author of all the good things that were enjoyed either in common by all mankind, or by each one in particular, and of all that they themselves obtained by praying to him in their greatest difficulties. He informed them that it was impossible to escape God's observation, even in any of our outward actions, or in any of our inward thoughts. (2:1:17)[11]

Near the end of this book, Josephus addressed the charge (presumably reflective of general attitudes in the Roman upper classes) that Jewish law does not recognize the dignity or rights of non-Jews. It is worth citing his answer to this charge at length:

> 29. It will be also worth our while to see what equity our legislator would have us exercise in our intercourse with strangers; for it will thence appear that he made the best provision he possibly could, both that we should not dissolve our own constitution, nor show any envious mind towards those

that would cultivate a friendship with us. Accordingly, our legislator admits all those that have a mind to observe our laws to do so; and this after a friendly manner, as esteeming that a true union which not only extends to our own stock, but to those that would live after the same manner with us; yet does he not allow those that come to us by accident only to be admitted into communion with us. 30. However, there are other things which our legislator ordained for us beforehand, which of necessity we ought to do in common to all men; as to afford fire, and water, and food to such as want it; to show them the roads; not to let any one lie unburied. He also would have us treat those that are esteemed our enemies with moderation; for he doth not allow us to set their country on fire, nor permit us to cut down those trees that bear fruit; nay, further, he forbids us to spoil those that have been slain in war. He hath also provided for such as are taken captive, that they may not be injured, and especially that the women may not be abused. Indeed he hath taught us gentleness and humanity so effectually, that he hath not despised the care of brute beasts, by permitting no other than a regular use of them, and forbidding any other; and if any of them come to our houses, like supplicants, we are forbidden to slay them; nor may we kill the dams, together with their young ones; but we are obliged, even in an enemy's country, to spare and not kill those creatures that labor for mankind. Thus hath our lawgiver contrived to teach us an equitable conduct every way, by using us to such laws as instruct us therein; while at the same time he hath ordained that such as break these laws should be punished, without the allowance of any excuse whatsoever.[12]

Josephus's point, of course, is that the anti–human rights attitude ascribed to Jews and Judaism by Roman authors is completely false. It is true that on the one hand Josephus has an agenda, namely to rehabilitate the reputation of Jews in Roman eyes after the rebellion in Judea, and so will of course put his people in the best possible light. On the other hand, demographic evidence from the time suggests that Ioudaioi were living, and prospering across the Roman world. Judaizers, as noted earlier, were spreading throughout the empire, possibly even reaching into the imperial court (Nero's wife is reported to have been a Judaizer by Josephus in *Antiquities* 20:189–196). There is also evidence that Judeans were not uncommon in the Roman army. These facts would hardly seem to reflect a population that was misanthropic and refused to mingle with others. This is not to deny that there were Judeans who were in fact misanthropic or who had little regard for others. But the evidence overall, including the fear of Judaization by Roman elites, indicates that the bulk of Ioudaioi apparently had good, open relationships with their neighbors. In his writings, Josephus displays for us the entire spectrum of Ioudaioi. There are highly Romanized Ioudaioi (like Josephus himself), zealous and intolerant Ioudaioi (such as the Zealots whom he blames for the rebellions), anti-Judaic Roman intellectuals, and masses of Roman Judaizers. The internal debate within this community must have been impassioned and complex.

It is important to remind the reader at the conclusion of this chapter that the Greek terms Ioudaioi and Ioudaismos were used purposefully so as not to leave the impression that a normative Judaism had yet taken shape. The reason for this choice should now be clear. What occurred in the centuries surrounding the turn of the millennium is a widespread Judean diaspora with little or no connection to the center of religious life, that is, the Temple in Jerusalem (which in any case was razed by the Romans in 70 C.E.). So rather than a Judaism with a Judaic tradition, it is necessary to think of a vast, diverse, and dispersed population of Ioudaioi—some descendants of Judeans, some Judaizers (*sebomenoi*), and some sympathizers—all of whom understood the requirements of the Judean tradition in their own ways without any central authority to direct or place parameters around what the contents of that tradition might be.

So to talk about the Jewish attitude toward human rights at this period is an exercise in futility. Rather, it is a matter of the religion and traditions of biblical Israel shattering into a mass of new and often conflicting Judaistic traditions and rituals, which themselves proceed to break apart and reform into new configurations. No Judaism as such is apparent. But out of this jumble, the beginnings of attempts to regroup, reorganize, and redefine a Judaism that could survive in the new world order of late antiquity did slowly emerge. At the end of the day it is becoming more and more clear that there were several attempts to formalize the traditional memories and create a Judaism, just as the plethora of Christians were slowly forming the bases of a "catholic" church. Some of these Judaisms merged to create what is now known as rabbinic Judaism. Other Judaisms persisted for a while before fading away (a non-rabbinic Judaism, later called Karaism, remained a significant presence until well into the Middle Ages), and others remained small and marginal sects, including some forms of gnostic mysticism that resurfaced in the Middle Ages. But in all cases, by the end of the Greco-Roman period, the older biblical views had given way to a human rights discourse that was heavily dependent on

Greek and Roman thought with all of its complexities. The Judaisms that emerged were thoroughly Hellenized, and their discussions on human rights had shifted accordingly.

In looking at the rabbinic Judaism that is now accepted as authentic and normative, two facts are clear. One is that this form of Judaism did not emerge overnight but took centuries to coalesce into the recognizable Greco-Roman religion called Judaism today. The other is that the earliest record of what was to become rabbinic Judaism is the sectarian book known as the Mishnah, edited in roughly final form around 230 c.e. With the publication of this work, it is finally possible to begin to talk about rabbinic Judaism in something approximating its modern meaning. Although the Mishnah seems in its early decades to have represented only a small sect of Jews in Roman Palestine, it, for whatever reason, was slowly taken up as a basis for Jewish life in Babylonia as well and so became the basis over the next few centuries of the Gemara (or Talmud) and thus of rabbinic Judaism in its mature form. It is the development of the rabbinic tradition and its literature that are the topics of the following chapters.

4

HUMAN RIGHTS IN THE TALMUD

A S THE HELLENISTIC PERIOD GAVE way to late antiquity, the creators of rabbinic Judaism faced the problem of how their shattered religious community was to create and maintain a coherent identity after its central shrine, the Jerusalem Temple, had been destroyed and its population dispersed in a diaspora among "the nations." The decision of the rabbis was to focus on the development of the *halachah*, that is, praxis, rather than on theology or the development of dogma. The idea seems to have been that the real fulfillment of the Torah consisted not in holding certain beliefs or developing a certain state of mind—something more common in Greco-Roman, and especially Platonic and gnostic thought— but in fulfilling the divine command to be a "kingdom of priests and a holy nation." To this end, the framers first of the Mishnah (mid-third century C.E.) and then its great commentary, the Gemara (completed around the late sixth century C.E.), focused on establishing Jewish norms of behavior, or halachah ("the way" to act), which would turn every Jewish household into a kind of temple and every Judean into a kind of priest. It is the decision to move in this direction rather than some other that has given rabbinic Judaism its characteristic legalistic flavor and made the Talmud its defining literature. It also meant that the various forms of Judaism that placed emphasis on doctrine, dogma, or philosophies were gradually relegated to the margins.

Before proceeding, two points should be emphasized. One is that the triumph of this project was the result of a gradual historical process. The creation of a halachic Judaism was neither uncontroversial nor instantaneous. Other forms of Judaism existed and continued to exert their influence for centuries—the mystical tradition for example, or the more biblicist Karaites who were still powerful as late as the beginning of the second millennium. While at various times variations of these other Judaisms emerged to challenge the hegemony of rabbinic Judaism, all were eventually either *rabbinized*, that is, absorbed into rabbinic Judaism, or they became sectarian counter-Judaisms. The second point to be emphaized is that this rabbinic/Talmudic approach to Judaism grew up alongside, and in more or less conscious competition with—and even in opposition to— the simultaneous consolidation of a catholic Christianity. While the Church focused more on the Platonic ideals of contemplation and correct thought, rabbinism took the alternative, more Aristotelian track of focusing on concrete actions in the material world in order to realize the perfection (or redemption) of the holy potential inherent in Creation. In other words, both Christianity and Judaism underwent consolidation over the first few centuries of the Common Era in remarkably parallel Greco-Roman terms, and in similar fashion, with a normative (or catholic) movement emerging that rendered competing forms sectarian or heretical.

This having been said, the rest of this chapter will focus on human rights as these developed in Talmudic/rabbinic Judaism. As noted above, the aim of developing Mishnaic, and subsequently Talmudic, law was to define what the Children of Israel in their homes and communities could do to remain holy, the ultimate point being to convince God to end the exile and bring back the Temple. To this end, the framers of this form of Judaism began with the one resource that remained to them after the loss of homeland, holy city, and Temple, namely, the community's shared tradition as found and preserved in their traditional literature, which now was becoming canonized as the Hebrew Bible. But despite their close adherence to the biblical text, these writers were also Greco-Romans and thought in Greco-Roman terms. That is, they not only created a canon (a typical Greco-Roman act of the time), but they also went on to read this canon as a Greco-Roman would. One major task was to translate the norms commanded in the Bible, which were shaped around a small agricultural society, into terms useful for Roman urban householders. Thus, what one encounters in the Mishnah (and its Gemara) are largely legal and normative exercises that work out in detail, using Roman legal categories, how the common people of Israel should lead biblical or "Torah-true" priest-like lives within the Hellenistic and post-Hellenistic urban contexts in which they found themselves. In essence, the rabbinic authorities tried to define what it meant to be a holy people by developing a sort of common case law based on their specialized reading of the canonical scripture they had created.

The authorities of the Talmud set for themselves a second task as well. As noted above, other forms of Judaism were around and posed considerable challenges to the authority of the rabbis. As a consequence, the rabbis of Mishnah and especially Talmud had not only to redefine Judaism into a new and usable idiom, but along the way they also had to establish the basis of their own authority and sell their Judaism to the community. This was more complicated than in the case of Christianity, since no central organization or councils of bishops existed, although organizationally there was more of a governmentally imposed unity in Babylonia (or Sassanian Persia), than in the West. In any case, the early rabbis had to argue their form of Judaism in the (at least Jewish) public marketplace of ideas. In the process, the Talmudic authorities never mention human rights per se, but they clearly did take such values into account. Our goal in the following analysis will be to tease out of the Talmudic legal tradition where the concept of human rights seems to have been a determining factor in how one decision rather than another came to win the day.

Before turning to these examples, it will be helpful to say a few words about how the rabbis attempted to establish their own authority. One story about how the rabbis tried to make their exercise of authority more transparent to the public is illustrated in a famous story recounted in the Talmud Baba Metzia 59b that deals with the so-called oven of Akhnai. In this story, Rabbi Eliezer (ben Hyrcanus)* had been trying his best to convince his colleague, Rabbi Joshua (ben Hananiah),* of a certain point of law regarding the ritual cleansing of a particular kind of oven and had so far been unable to do so. In frustration, he resorted to calling on a series of miracles to prove his point. In each case, however, Joshua refused to accept the testimony of the miracle. Finally, Rabbi Eliezer, in utter frustration, called down a voice from heaven, which duly announced publically that he (Rabbi Eliezer) was, in fact, correct. But his opponent, Rabbi Joshua, obstinately deflected even this divine support by invoking Deut. 30:12: "It is not in heaven."[1] In short, Joshua told heaven to go and mind its own business since the development of Jewish law had been given to the sages, and he even cited the Torah itself to support this contention. In the end, this retort clinched the argument in Joshua's favor, even though it was now clear to everyone that his position was in fact wrong.

The point of the passage is to establish the principle that it is up to the human jurists at the time and place to develop the law logically. Eliezer's failure was not that he was wrong (for the text makes it clear that he was in fact right), but rather that he was not able to convince others on the basis of reason and logic.

For the Talmudic rabbis, prophecy, miracles, and personal revelations were simply ruled out as sources of Jewish law. Rabbinic law was to be the result of a process of open and public debate, not the secret edicts of a religious elite.[2] In so doing, they staked out a position not only in contrast to the Church, but to other, competing, forms of Judaism.

The importance of the triumph of this theoretical approach should be seen in the larger context in which the Jewish community was situated. In the Persian Empire in particular, but also in the West to some extent, the Jewish community was something of a self-governing corporation within the larger empire. In the West this was more a matter of legal status, since after Christianity became the official religion, Jews, as non-Christians, were not subject to Church law. In Sassanian Persia, the Jews were not part of the majority religion, but were, in fact, legally organized by the central government as a distinct semi-self-governing entity under the aegis of the officially appointed *resh galuta* or exilarch ("leader of the exile"). In either case, the practical result of this governmental status was that the Jews, in some ways like other minority ethnic and religious communities, exercised a certain measure of control over their own internal communal affairs, provided that imperial taxes, and other such obligations were rendered to the central authorities as appropriate. In the course of the third–eighth centuries C.E., this was especially significant in the East, where the officially appointed office of the exilarch worked through a trained body of civil servants (the Rabbis) because of the latter's demonstrated literacy and competence in biblical (and Mishnaic) law. The result was that the Persian community became progressively more professionalized and homogenized in a rabbinic sort of way. This same process took place in the West, albeit more slowly because of the less formalized organization of Western Jewry. Because of this difference, it turned out that by the end of the first millennium, even the Jewish communities of Europe and North Africa had come to orient themselves toward Persia and its Talmudic academies as the intellectual center and basis of their own communal governance.[3] Because these Talmudic rabbis had foresworn miracles and had committed themselves to establishing their credentials (at least within their own estate) in open debate, as the story of Eliezer and Joshua illustrates, there was a constant interplay between rabbi and community. This is important because, while never invoking explicitly the principle of human rights, there is nonetheless a clear sense that the rabbis found it urgent to rule with the consent of the ruled and to keep those interests always in mind. Ishmael ben Elisha* expressed this sentiment in the Babylonian Talmud Bava Batra 60b in the following words: "Lay no burden on the public which the majority cannot bear." Thus, unlike the Church (and maybe as a result of conscious contrast to it), Jews were treated more as citizens than as subjects of the religious establishment.

HUMAN RIGHTS IN THE APPLICATION OF THE HALACHAH

BECAUSE THEIR ATTENTION was focused on the practical, day-to-day realities of Jewish common law, the rabbis as administrators, judges, and adjudicators rarely raised the discussion to broader theoretical concepts, such as that of human rights.[4] This means that rabbinic attitudes as regards these matters have to be teased out of the norms, rulings, and legal decisions that they enacted along the way. Consequently, the following discussion of rabbinic positions on human rights in Talmudic and Medieval times will of necessity have to involve us to some extent in the minutiae of rabbinic law (halachah) and legal reasoning. Through this process, it will become clear that a concept of human rights in some form was in fact operating, albeit usually behind the scenes. As a general rule, these norms, rulings, and decisions will be framed as obligations on the individual rather than as rights due to the other. Since duties and rights are opposite sides of the same coin, it will be fairly easy in most cases to move from the duty imposed by the rabbinic lawyers to the rights deemed due to the other side.[5]

As a broad generalization, the halachah as a system has been described as growing out of the conviction that its adherents should engage in "imitatio dei"—that is, they should try in their day-to-day lives to imitate the holiness of the Deity; hence, becoming as Exod. 19:6 states, "a nation of priests and a holy nation." Part of this *imitatio* is of course the just and fair treatment of others, just as God is just and fair. As Shabbat 10a states in no uncertain terms, "as regards any judge who delivers a just judgement even one time, the Scripture regards him as having become a partner with the Holy One Blessed Be He in the act of Creation."[6] The modern Jewish ethicist David Novak captures this principle well in his claim that "denial of God's kingship always leads to injustices against those created in God's image."[7] So the mere fact of being created human, that is, in God's image, establishes a foundation for a minimum regard for each person's rights as a person. In the messiness of day-to-day life, one of the jobs of the rabbinical court judge was to recognize the humanity in both the plaintiff and the defendant. It is with this attitude in mind that Mishnah Sanhedrin 4:5 discusses how witnesses are to be sworn in. In cases of capital punishment, such witnesses are to be reminded that the blood of the victim (and all his descendants) are on their hands if their testimony leads to a false conviction and execution. The Mishnah goes on to say:

> therefore was Adam created alone, to teach you that as regards anyone who wastes a single soul in Israel, the Scripture applies as though he had destroyed an entire world; and as regards anyone who preserves a single soul in Israel, the Scripture applies as though he had preserved an entire world; and (the common descent from Adam serves to promote) peaceful relations among people, so that no one might say to his fellow, "my ancestors are greater than yours."

In the event, of course, law can be a blunt instrument towards achieving this goal. Even though it is open and presumably fairly applied, the strict application of law can often lead to unfairness or injustice. The Talmudic discussants thus stress precisely that the halachah is only a minimum standard and that at times one may (or even must) go beyond what the law requires in order to truly act justly toward others. The most commonly cited Talmudic passage to illustrate this principle is Shabbat 31a, which concerns a stranger who goes to the two famous rivals of early rabbinic Judaism, Hillel* and Shammai,* and asks each to teach him the entire Torah while standing on one foot. Shammai angrily chases the man off. Hillel, however, accepts that challenge and thereby articulates his famous and oft-quoted response, "What is hateful to you, do not do to your fellow. This is all of the Torah in its entirety, the rest being commentary. Go and learn." In line with Hillel's perspective, a good part of Talmudic discussion, in fact, revolves around precisely the issue of how to fulfill the letter of the law on the one hand while not violating the spirit of justice, which is the very foundation on which the law rests, on the other.

The theoretical foundation for this view is worked out in a debate between Rabbi Akiba (ben Joseph)* and one of his outstanding students,

Simeon ben Azzai. According to a passage in Sifra 7:4 (and also the Jerusalem Talmud Nedarim 9:3/14c), Akiba taught that the greatest command in the Torah is Lev. 19:18, "You shall love your neighbor as yourself."[8] Ben Azzai disagreed, citing instead Gen. 5, "1. This is the record of Adam's line—When God created man, He made him in the likeness of God; 2. male and female He created them." The question, of course, is what ben Azzai sees as wrong in Akiba's assertion. The problem, ben Azzai argued, is that one cannot be *commanded* to love another person. In fact, I think, for him the whole notion of love in dealing with another person is irrelevant. Rather, by stressing that Torah teaches that all people are descendants of Adam, it places the right to equal honor and respect on our common humanness, independent of our emotions. It is less important to love the other person than it is to treat the other as a fellow human being also created in the image of God, even if one does not have any particular emotional attachment to that person.[9]

The implication, as already noted, is that sometimes it might be required to disregard the letter of the halachah in the interest of achieving its higher goal of dealing justly with one's fellow human being. This notion of serving justice even if it means bending or even violating the letter of the law has become so entrenched in rabbinic thought that it has been given its own term: *lifnim mishurat hadin*, a phrase that appears often in the legal literature itself, and translates as something like "beyond the limits of the law."[10] As an example, consider the case presented in the Babylonian Talmud Baba Metzia 30b, which reports the following statement of Rabbi Yohanan ben Zakkai* and the ensuing discussion it sparked: "Rabbi Yohanan once said, 'Jerusalem was destroyed only because we judged according to the laws of the Torah.' Later authorities ask in disbelief, 'So should we have judged according to the laws of others [*megizta*— the exact meaning of the word here is not clear]? Rather let us say that [what Yohanan meant was that] they based their rulings *only* on the laws of Torah and did not go beyond the limits of the law [*lifnim MiShurat HaDin*].' "[11] In the minds of later authorities, then, Yohanan is saying that a literalistic application of the law is insufficient in and of itself. The halachah is meant to serve a higher end, namely sanctifying the name of God by honoring all those created in the divine image. If following the law violates this higher purpose, then one must ignore the letter of the law. Failure to do so endangers the whole enterprise of Judaism.

One recent articulator of this view is Haim Cohen, former deputy president of the Israeli Supreme Court. In the following he addresses cases where the law really cannot reach, namely, private interactions between people. In this regard, he writes:

> There are many "good and proper actions," in the words of Maimonides,* many actions which it is very difficult to impose upon man—actions which are more ethical and moral than legal. Take, for example, the commandment of "You shall rise before the hoary head and honor the face of the old" or that of "you shall not place a stumbling block before the blind," or those actions which take place in privacy, of which no other person can be aware; it is in regard to these that the Torah often writes, "you shall fear your God—do what you have been commanded to do and do not do that which are forbidden to do, and do not fear any man or judge, but your God."[12]

In short, the legal discussions and rulings of Talmudic Judaism are universally understood to provide the basic framework within which Jews should construct their lives, but in no way should they be taken as barriers to doing more for other people than strictly required. The demands of justice take precedent over the law, even according to the law itself.

In the actual application of the halachah, it was taken for granted that everyone had a right to a trial, that is, meting out justice was not the prerogative of a single monarch or other authority. Rather than relying on the jury system as is the case in the Anglo-Saxon tradition, Jewish law stipulates that the trial was to be carried out before a panel of at least three judges who were free to investigate the evidence and question witnesses as they saw fit. The judges then voted both on guilt and on the sentence. The accused was present at all times and so was a witness to the proceedings. For this reason, court process was a matter of some consideration. Mishnah Sanhedrin (and Babylonian Talmud Sanhedrin 40b) set out the minimum standards that such trials were to meet. In general, anyone brought to court had the right to expect proper inquires and examinations to have been accomplished. In particular, the passage points out, care had to be taken to ascertain the nature of the act, to fix the time and place of the alleged offense, and to cross-examine the witnesses sufficiently to establish their credibility. It was taken to be a general principle that the more thorough such inquiries and examinations, the better (Mishnah Sanhedrin 5:2).[13] In addition, self-incrimination and confessions were not allowed (Babylonian Talmud Sanhedrin 9b) since "no man calls himself a wrongdoer."[14] Conviction had to be based on the facts, that is, on credible witnesses and corroborating evidence.

To ensure a fair hearing, the Talmud also recognized something like a right to free expression, albeit with certain pragmatic qualifications and exemptions. Scholars certainly had a right to express dissenting views and such minority views are often preserved and even honored in the literature. Mishnah Sanhedrin 11:2 even rules that if a (dissenting) judge returns to his own city and continues instructing according to the way he used to (i.e., in an idiosyncratic way, at odds with local expectations), he is exempt from punishment unless he teaches one to act (explicitly contrary to the law). Similarly, Mishnah Eduyot asks, "[W]hy is the view of a single scholar reported along with that of the majority since the halachah is always that of the majority?" The answer is, "[S]o that a future court might agree with that view and so have a (precedent) to rely on." So at least at the level of the ruling classes, dissent and diverse opinions were allowed and accorded some status and protection. This goes back to the principle that legal decisions are in the hands of current authorities who must make their point in publicly available discourse.

In terms of actual court cases, this had certain pragmatic ramifications. There is a general understanding in the Talmud that no halachic court can overturn the rulings of a predecessor court unless the current court is greater in wisdom than the former. This insured a certain predictability in the law. The Talmud in tractate Avodah Zara invokes this principle and then tells of an incident in which a court reversed itself in a particular case because it found that there was no popular backing for its new interpretation. In so doing, the text cites the saying, found in numerous places, that according to Rabbi Eleazar ben Zadok* one issues an edict on the public only if the bulk of the public is able to accommodate itself to it.[15]

Another broad generalization of Talmudic law is that one is punished (or rewarded) on the basis of one's own merits and deeds, not on those of one's ancestors. As an example of this, there is an extended discussion in Berachot 7a turning on the question as to why there are righteous people who suffer and righteous people who prosper, and conversely, why there are wicked people who prosper and wicked people who suffer, thus, there being seemingly no consistency in suffering and prospering. How could this be in a world ruled by a just Deity? The struggle to find an answer to this conundrum is a matter of much discussion and disagreement in the Talmudic and later literature. One argument is that a righteous person who prospers does so because not only is he righteous but he is the son of a righteous person; while if he suffers, it is because although he is righteous, he is the son of a wicked person. This explanation is immediately rejected by pointing to 2 Chron. 25:4, "[F]athers shall not die on account of the sons, nor sons die on account of the father, but each person on the basis of his own sins will die." This retort is accepted and the argument moves on to whether the apparent discrepancy between those who suffer and those who prosper revolves around whether the person in question is fully righteous or fully wicked. The logic is that the purely righteous will prosper while the partially righteous (i.e., the bulk of humanity) will suffer some in this world in order to be purged of the evil and so be able to receive a good reward in the afterlife. Conversely, a purely wicked person will suffer in this world, but a wicked person with some good might prosper in this world as a reward now for the good so as to receive full punishment in the next life. A variation on this argument focuses on whether, and to what extent, the person in question follows the footsteps of a righteous or wicked parent.

The upshot of the argument is that it is the decisions and actions of the individual in question that in the end determines reward or punishment. After all, whether someone does or does not follow in the footsteps of a righteous or unrighteous ancestor is itself a moral decision. By framing the argument in this way, the merit or demerit of ancestors does end up playing a role in the prosperity or suffering of the present agent, but only insofar as the person in question has him- or herself chosen to emulate the model of the ancestors. Thus, the nature of a person's righteousness or wickedness, and the role of choice and intention, come together in a complicated calculus that makes it often impossible for others to see direct links between a person's present deeds and whether he or she prospers or suffers in this world. Nonetheless, the Talmud assures its readers that, in the end, the amount one suffers or prospers in this life and the next bear a direct relationship to one's good and evil deeds.

This point is illustrated nicely in the Babylonian Talmud tractate Nazir 23a: "Ulla said, 'Tamar fornicated and Zimri fornicated. Tamar fornicated and kings and prophets came forth from her; Zimri fornicated and several tens of thousands of Israelites fell on his account.'" The difference, of course, was the intention of the two. Tamar "played the harlot" in order to get Judah to fulfill the laws of levirate marriage (Gen. 38:6ff). In other words, Tamar violated the law on one level to provoke a greater act of justice. She was correspondingly rewarded with good descendants. Zimri's act of fornication, on the other hand, was to bring in a forbidden foreign woman (a Midianite) into the congregation of the Lord (Num. 25). His violation of the law was not in the name of a higher good but for personal gratification. His act led to death and suffering. So what appears as two very similar acts (fornication) end up having drastically different outcomes because of the different *intentions* of the agents themselves.

A basic set of assumptions threading its way through this and similar Talmudic discussions, then, is first, that individuals are to be judged on their own merits or demerits and, second, that part of these merits and demerits reside in the defendant's intention. This has raised in the minds of some Talmudic authorities the question as to whether intention alone is enough to convict a person. In several instances, the Talmud considers cases in which a person acted out of evil or criminal intent but ended up doing nothing illegal.[16] In all these instances, an evil intent that did not yield an actual illegal deed was regarded as not actionable. It would thus seem fair to sum up this area of Talmudic law as holding a person liable for punishment only if an actual illegal act was committed, but that at the same time, the intention of the agent when committing the crime was deemed a legitimate part of the deliberations. Thus, the evil of an illegal act can, in effect, be mitigated if the intention of the agent was to do good. To put matters in an other way, the defendant always had the benefit of the doubt—a bad act that resulted from the misapplication of a good intention was judged with due consideration of the good intention, although a good act resulting from the perversion of a criminal intent was to be judged on the basis of the act alone.[17] In the end, concrete justice should always be the ruling concern, even if this means that at times one has to go beyond the bare facts, or the simplistic application of the letter of the law. A corollary to all this was the notion that in the end God was the ultimate judge and all would be worked out justly, if not in this life then in the life to come.

THE BASIC HUMAN RIGHT TO LIFE

TURNING TO MORE specific topics, it is clear that one of the most basic human rights is the very right to life itself. So important is this value that it is already invoked at the very beginning of humankind. The first two people that God created, Adam and Eve, had two sons, one of whom (Cain) killed the other (Abel) in a fit of rage. The biblical story goes on to record God's reaction in Gen. 4:9–11:

9. The Lord said to Cain, "Where is your brother Abel?" and he said, "I do not know. Am I my brother's keeper?" 10. Then He [namely, God] said,

"What have you done? Hark, your brother's blood cries out to Me from the ground! 11. Therefore, you shall be more cursed than the ground, which opened its mouth to receive your brother's blood from your hand."

The utter sanctity of human life is recognized in the Talmud as well, to the extent that it is raised to a fundamental axiom with its own term, *pikuach nefesh*. This phrase refers to the principle that in any situation, the preservation of human life is to take precedence over all other laws, with only a few specific exceptions, examined below. The importance of this principle is illustrated in Talmud Yoma 85b, where the sages are engaged in a discussion about whether it is permissible (or even mandatory!) to violate even the Sabbath in order to rescue a person whose life is in only potential danger. That is, is the mere *possibility* of the loss of a human life sufficient cause for a certain and purposeful violation of one of the most important of Jewish holy days. From the ensuing discussion in the Talmud, it is clear that the nub of the problem is the doubtful nature of the danger to life; were a human life *certainly* in danger, there is not even a question that the Sabbath was to be violated. Not surprisingly, the determination at the end of the discussion is that the matter of doubt is irrelevant. Even if a human life is only potentially in danger, the rules of the Sabbath are to be suspended.

Interestingly, several reasons are given for this principle, indicating that the decision was arrived at first, "outside the limits of the law," as it were, with the rational being identified only after the fact. The discussion as to reason proceeds as follows, "R. Yohanan b. Yosef says, 'it is holy unto you' (Exod. 31:14). This means it [i.e., the Sabbath] is given over unto you; you are not given over unto it. Rabbi Simeon Ben Menasia* says, 'And the Children of Israel shall observe the Sabbath (Exod. 31:16).' The Torah is saying that one should desecrate one Sabbath on this account so that he will observe many Sabbaths."

There is, however, a difficulty in the pure application of the principle of *pikuach nefesh*. Although on the surface, the principle of *pikuach nefesh* holds that all humans are created in the image of God and so have an inalienable right to life, matters turn out to be more complicated. Biblical law, and so the Talmud, recognize capital punishment. For example, in addressing itself to the heinous character of murder, Gen. 9:3–6 announces that:

3. Every creature that lives shall be yours to eat; as with the green grasses, I give you all these. 4. You must not, however, eat flesh with its life-blood in

it. 5. But for your own life-blood I will require a reckoning: I will require it of every beast; of man, too, will I require a reckoning for human life, of every man for that of his fellow man! 6. Whoever sheds the blood of man, / By man shall his blood be shed; / For in His image / Did God make man.

This passage carries with it the clear implication that a murderer deserves capital punishment, that is, the shedding of his blood, in recompense. In fact, the problem is even more complex, because the Bible specifies a number of other types of capital punishment and the misdeeds for which they are to be imposed. Executions are to be carried out, for example, by stoning in response to a number of crimes such as offering a child to Moloch (Lev. 20:2), invoking a spirit (Lev. 20:27), pronouncing the name of God (Lev. 24:16), and violating the Sabbath (Num. 15:35). Other means of execution included burning in response to certain cases of sexual immorality and hanging (usually in reference to non-Israelites). In addition to these, the Talmud adds two other methods of execution: slaying (i.e., by the sword) for murders and those who subvert towns and strangling (for anything else). So there seem to be clear instances in which the Talmudic rabbis saw themselves authorized to decree the taking of another human life despite the principle of *pikuach nefesh*. How can the inalienable right to human life be reconciled with these various laws that allow the court to execute a criminal?

The Talmudic authorities were themselves well aware of this tension. Their solution was to acknowledge their right to effect capital punishment in principle while at the same time making the halachic practicalities of carrying out such an execution so stringent as to render performing the execution impossible in actuality. One discussion of this matter, for example, gets around the problem by demanding that the cross-examination of the witnesses be such that a self-contradiction is eventually elicited and so an acquittal must be reached (Babylonian Talmud Makkot 7a).[18] Other discussions on this topic, appearing in several places in the Talmud (Babylonian Sanhedrin 129a, for example, and Babylonian Yoma 83a–84b, et al.) conclude that in any case of doubt, even if there is no actual acquittal, one should rather break the law (i.e., not execute the defendant) than risk taking a life wrongly. Another good example along these lines is the parents' right to have a rebellious son stoned in accordance with Exod. 21:15. The Talmud all but revokes this rule through a discussion in Sanhedrin 37b which, after a lengthy deliberation on what such a son would be, comes to the conclusion that given the proper definition of the term, "the rebellious son never was and never will be in the future." The stoning of such a son can happen then only in theory, never in practice.

The general attitude might find its best summation in Mishnah Makkot 1:10, which asserts that "A Sanhedrin that puts a man to death once in seven years is called a murderous one. R. Eleazar ben Azariah said, 'Even one in seventy years.' Rabbi Tarfon* and Rabbi Akiba said, 'If we had been in the Sanhedrin no death sentence would ever have been passed.'" This attitude prevailed even in the face of opposition from no less a figure than the patriarch Shimon ben Gamaliel, who argued that if such a lenient attitude were to be put into effect, then murderers would abound in Israel. Despite Shimon ben Gamaliel's pragmatic arguments, it does appear from the literature to be the case that the actual execution of criminals technically subject to capital punishment fell into complete abeyance.

This practical annulment of executions, however, led to other theoretical problems. What, for example, was to be the fate of those people who should have been executed but were not? The tractate Sanhedrin actually attempts to deal with this gap between theory and practice. Sanhedrin 37b notes that "From the day of the destruction of the Temple, even though the Sanhedrin suspended the four death penalties, they were not suspended [by the heavenly court]." The passage goes on to explain that this means, for example, that one who would have been sentenced to stoning will end up falling off of a roof or being stamped to death by a wild beast, and so suffer a kind of stoning, albeit not by human hands. But even this death was apparently a matter of ambivalence among the rabbis. Mishnah Makkot 3:15, for example, suggested that an offender subject to *kareth* (death at the hands of heaven) be sentenced instead to human flogging. The logic here is that by being punished once for the crime through flogging (accompanied it should be noted with due repentance) the miscreant would surely not be punished a second time by God.[19] All of this legal maneuvering to eliminate capital punishment in practice was justified in the law itself by reference to the biblical verse that one should live by the law, not die by it (Lev. 18:5, cited for example in Babylonian Talmud Yoma 85a, Babylonian Talmud Sanhedrin 74a, and Babylonian Talmud Avoda Zara 27b).

A rather interesting take on this attitude of the sanctity of life above all else is the question of martyrdom, or self-sacrifice, in the name of a higher cause. The rabbinic consensus is that on only three occasions must one allow oneself to be killed rather than engage in a prohibited act.

These three exceptions are illuminating because they, in effect, define the limits of the individual's otherwise absolute right to life. These three occasions are practicing idolatry in public (thereby possibly leading others to apostasy), committing incest in public, and killing another. In the first two instances the violation is a public desecration of God's name and so takes precedence over preserving the life of the individual. In essence the idea is that if one openly and willfully denies God, then one cannot claim the protection of life on the basis that all people are equal by virtue of being created in the image of that God. In the third case, the reason given is that no one has the right to determine that his or her own life is more worthy than another's, the point being that one should never take violent action against another because the other has an equal right to life. This principle is articulated several times in the Babylonian Talmud through the phrase: "[W]ho is to say your blood is redder; perhaps the blood of the other is redder?"[20] It follows that if you take another life (with malice aforethought), you thereby give up your own claim to protection (why is your blood deemed redder?) The only exception to this rule is when one kills an active attacker or pursuer (the Hebrew term is *rodef*) in self-defense. That is, one may kill another person only if the other person, as a *rodef*, presents a clear and immediate danger to one's own life.[21] There is considerable discussion as to whether or not this exception applies as well to the case in which a *rodef* threatens not your life but the life of a third person. In general, Talmudic law allows such a killing, provided that this is the only way to prevent the *rodef* from killing the third, innocent, party.

The notion that a *rodef* may be abdicating his own right to life by pursuing the life of another is taken up also in the case of dangerous pregnancies and abortions. There is general agreement that abortion in and of itself is an offense against Jewish law, although it is not generally regarded as an act of criminal homicide *simpliciter*. The usual biblical reference invoked in such cases is Exod. 21:22–23, in which two men are engaged in a fight and one of them hits a pregnant woman, thereby causing a miscarriage.[22] The punishment as prescribed by the Bible is parallel to that of damage done to the husband's goods, not that meted out to a murderer. The penalty is more severe (life for life, eye for eye, and so forth) only in case "other damage ensues" (i.e., bodily harm or death suffered by the woman). But more to the issue at hand, what if the continued existence of the fetus is threatening the very life of the pregnant woman? Is it possible to consider the fetus to be a kind of *rodef* or pursuer? Mishnah Ohalot 7:6 addresses itself directly to this question. It states explicitly, "If a woman is having difficulty in giving birth, the fetus is cut up within her womb and extracted limb by limb inasmuch as her life takes precedence over the life of the fetus. If the majority of it (the fetus) has come out, they do not harm it for they do not set aside one life in favor of another." In other words, no human life can be judged expendable in favor of another's (whose blood is redder?), so once the fetus is born it is deemed a viable person and has as equal a claim to life as the mother. But before that time, the fetus is not yet a present living person and so the living mother, as a present full human life, does take precedence. An abortion to save her life is permissible (even demanded) and is usually justified by reference to the case of the *rodef* mentioned above, namely, that one can regard the fetus as a pursuer whose continued existence in and of itself presents a real threat to the continued life of an innocent victim, namely, the mother.

There is another angle on this question, however, that is explored in the Babylonian Talmudic tractate Baba Metzia 62a. It involves a situation in which a person either has to let another die or both will die. The case is stated in theory as follows: "Two men are traveling on the road (in a desert and facing dehydration). One of them has a flask of water. If both drink of it they (both will have insufficient liquid and both) will die; but if one drinks, he will (survive to) arrive at an inhabited place (but the other will die). Expounded ben Petura, 'It is better that both drink and die than one witness the death of the other.' This remained until R. Akiba came and taught, 'It is written 'That thy brother may live with thee (Lev. 35:36),' this means that thy life takes precedence over the life of they brother.'" This view, of course, would seem to contradict the principle adduced above that who can tell whose blood is redder. That there is no fully acceptable answer to this conundrum is shown by the fact that the argument continues to reverberate into the Middle Ages.[23] On the other hand, two early medieval authorities, Isaac ben Jacob al-Fasi* and Asher ben Yehiel,* both put forward the argument that the person who brought the water in the first place has the prior claim to it [since it is his water to begin with]. It is too complicated here to trace the history of this convoluted discussion through the literature. Suffice it to say that the moral and human rights issues raised by this legal conundrum in the Talmud have remained difficult and unsettled, the Talmud itself never arriving at a definitive answer.

A similar issue adduced by the rabbis is whether one life may be purposefully sacrificed to save many lives. The *locus classicus* for this discussion is usually taken to be Tosephta Terumot 7:20:

A company of people are [approached] by gentiles who say to them: "Give us one of your number; if not we will kill all of you." Let all of them be killed and let them not turn over to them a Jewish life. But if they [the Gentiles] themselves designate someone, for example, Sheba ben Bichri, then let them give him to them so that all of them not be killed.[24]

In the first case, the people are asked, in essence, to kill one of their own (or allow one of their own to be killed) for no particular crime but simply to protect their own lives. Since the proposed victim is innocent (i.e., not a *rodef*), his life is not to be sacrificed, for after all whose blood is redder? The second case is different in that a particular victim, Sheba ben Bichri, has already been singled out to die and it is he personally who has now put the entire group into danger. In these circumstances, his companions are under no legal obligation to become martyrs on his behalf. Since he is going to die anyway, turning him over is not a matter of actually deciding "whose blood is redder."

THE RIGHT TO HUMAN DIGNITY

NEXT IN IMPORTANCE to the right to life is the right to human dignity. A discussion on this very topic takes place in the Babylonian Talmud tractate Berachot 19b in connection with how one is to comport oneself for the dead. The Talmud takes special care to preserve the dignity of the dead since the deceased is obviously in no position to defend her- or himself. At one point in the discussion, the text says, "Come and hear, 'the dignity of humans is so great that it can set aside even a negative command of the Torah'"—that is, one may override a biblical command that prohibits some act if doing so is for the sake of preserving human dignity. This seems like an unusually far-reaching exemption and, not surprisingly, is met with some challenges. One challenge draws on Prov. 21:30, "No wisdom, no prudence, and no counsel / Can prevail against the Lord." In other words, no mere human reasoning can lead to one's deciding that a certain express command of God, or by extension of the sages speaking in the divine name, can be overridden (for, say, the sake of human dignity). But in the end, this resort to Proverbs is not allowed to be the last word in the matter of human dignity. The discussion is brought to a conclusion by Rav Kahana, who says, "We establish [the validity] of all the words of the sages on a negative, namely, 'you must not deviate (from the verdict that the sages announce to you either to the right or to the left,' Deut. 17:11), but because of his [i.e., human] dignity, the rabbis allow [deviations from their own rulings, albeit not from biblical laws]." So in the end, the Talmud holds that while the words of the Torah itself cannot be overridden by human wisdom, the rulings of the sages and rabbis can be and, in fact, should be in cases in which such an overriding is done in the interest of preserving human dignity.[25]

The concern with human dignity does not apply only to the dead. The example above is an extreme case, meant to show that human dignity is to be preserved, even in death. The Talmud is replete with examples of preserving human dignity in ordinary everyday life. For example, Talmud Baba Metzia 75b rules that if a person is a creditor and knows that a certain debtor does not have enough money to repay the loan, this creditor should avoid passing in front of the debtor, so as not to "act toward him as a creditor" (citing here Exod. 22:24), thereby causing him shame or embarrassment. Similarly, if an officer of the court or a debt collector shows up at one's house, he was to stand outside rather than enter the dwelling (Baba Metzia 113a, for example).[26] To be sure, other passages in the Talmud suggest a more practical reason for this rule. According to the Babylonia Talmud Baba Kamma 27b and the Jerusalem Talmud Baba Kamma 10:38, one should not enter a house of a debtor to seize a pledge or retrieve personal property without prior permission to avoid being thought a thief. As another example, a person is allowed to make a special accommodation for one who is unable to pay a debt rather than consign that person to debtor's prison. Similarly, one may make appropriate accommodation in assessing and collecting the Temple tax, a principle articulated in Talmud Baba Metzia 113b. In these and a variety of similar cases, the pauper is not to be exposed to public humiliation on account of his or her poverty. The operative principle is expressed succinctly, I think, in the Babylonian Talmud Sotah 8b, which bluntly asserts that "humiliation is worse than physical pain."

It is precisely to avoid this kind of humiliation that gossip also is roundly condemned. The Hebrew expression for gossip is *lashon hara*, literally "evil language." The school of Ishmael is reported in the Talmud Arachin 15b to have held that "gossip is more hideous than capital crime." The reason is that not only is one's name and reputation ruined, but there is no real defense against gossip. In such cases, the Talmudic sages were usually ready to impose some sanctions on the offender, even if these were only moral and social rather than judicial.[27]

To show the seriousness with which instances of humiliation were taken, a debate in Mishnah Baba Kamma 8:6 is instructive. A discussion takes place that deals with the compensation due to a person who has been humiliated in public. The opening discussion concludes with the general rule that the compensation all depends on the honor of the victim. At this point, Rabbi Akiba chimes in, "Even the poorest in Israel we regard them as though they were freedmen that have fallen on hard times, for they are children of Abraham, Isaac and Jacob." This did not sit well with Akiba's contemporaries, who proceeded to set up the following test case: They poured fine oil out on the street in front of a poor woman. She immediately loosened her hair right there in public and smeared on the oil. In triumph they brought witnesses to this event before Rabbi Akiba and asked him if he would still be willing to award her a full 400 zuz for being publically humiliated by another since she was obviously willing to publically humiliate herself. Akiba answered, "You have proven nothing. One who harms himself, even if he has no license to do so, is nonetheless exempt (from punishment) but if others cause this one harm, they are liable. [It is like] one who cuts down his plants. Even if he has no license to do so, he is exempt; but if others cut down his plants, they are liable." In short, Akiba's argument, which won the day, is that even though the woman in question is poor and is willing to humiliate herself in public, anyone else who humiliates her is liable to the same punishment as one who humiliates in public a person who is rich or of high status.[28]

Human dignity is understood in the Talmud to involve not just the right to be free of malicious gossip or public humiliation, but also the right to just and fair treatment. It is for this reason that the rights of workers are taken up with some regularity. A passage in the Talmud tractate Baba Kamma 116b (and see also Baba Metzia 10a), for example, concludes that a worker may choose to withdraw his service even in the middle of the day if he is dissatisfied with the work offered him. This authorization is justified by reference to Deut. 25:55, which notes that "For the Children of Israel are my servants." This verse is taken to mean that the Children of Israel are the servants of God, meaning not the servants of other people.[29] Thus, a worker may not be forced to do work he or she does not want to do. Baba Metzia 76b goes on to add that if a worker walks off in the middle of the job, he or she is still due payment for the work that was already accomplished. Later medieval law will take up the complementary case, in which the laborer was paid in advance and quit before the job was completed. In this case, the employer has the right to recover only the unearned portion of the advance pay.

In addition to the worker's right to quit the job at any time, the worker also had the right to certain expectations regarding pay and working conditions. For example, the worker could expect to be paid the customary amount for that particular kind of work in the place he is hired, unless arrangements for a lower wage were agreed to beforehand (Mishneh Baba Metzia 7:1). The Talmud carries the Mishnaic principle forward by discussing how this number is to be ascertained (Babylonian Talmud Baba Metzia 87a). The worker also had a right to receive pay on an agreed upon schedule, whether hourly, daily, weekly, or monthly (Mishnah Baba Metzia 9:11).[30] Local custom also set work hours, and no employer could force workers to labor beyond the customary limitations (Mishnah Baba Metzia 7:1), again unless other arrangements were mutually agreed upon (Baba Metzia 83a). In addition, the worker could not be forced to work on the Sabbath or during mourning periods, and was to be given regular meal breaks.[31]

One of the more severe forms of public humiliation was incarceration. Talmudic authorities accordingly seem generally to have tried to avoid imprisonment whenever possible, preferring instead punishments such as fines or flogging. This brings up the much stickier issue of whether authorities are allowed to arrest and detain a suspect before that suspect has been judged guilty. On the one hand, the mere arrest of the suspect is a matter of embarrassment and humiliation. On the other hand, there is the fear that the suspect will disappear before the trial gets underway. A discussion around this issue is recorded in the Jerusalem Talmud Sanhedrin 7:10. There it was agreed that the detention of a suspect could only take place if there was fear that the suspect would flee before the witnesses could be brought to court. The Babylonian Talmud in Menahot 99b and in Baba Metzia 58b also warns against publicly degrading a suspect.[32] In the end, imprisonment was usually applied only to recidivists whose freedom posed a public threat. In such cases imprisonment was deemed preferable to execution.[33] Once in custody, there were certain rules for the treatment of the prisoner both during the imprisonment and after release.[34] Among these considerations was that a prisoner, Jewish or non-Jewish, who was released or escaped could not be overcharged for transportation (Yevamot 106a). In a similar vein, the Talmud reasoned that a slave who escaped would not have to be returned to slavery but would have to be set free (Gittin 38a).[35]

WOMEN

WOMEN OCCUPIED AN anomalous place in the rabbinic mind. In some regards, women were seen as only the property of men, first of their fathers and then of their husbands. Thus, women, in the phrase of Judith Romney Wegner, author of *Chattel or Person: The Status of Women in the Mishnah*, were sometimes chattel and sometimes people. A daughter, for example, was given in marriage by her father and acquired by the husband.[36] On the other hand, the Talmud is clear that no woman could be given away in marriage without her permission (Kiddushin 2b). A grown woman who was widowed or divorced became, however, a free agent in this regard and could arrange her own affairs, including marriage. In terms of marriage, a few limiting cases applied. A divorced woman could not marry a priest, for example, whose purity of lineage seems to have always been of central concern. The other category of unmarriageables was that of the *mamzer*, essentially an illegitimate child, meaning, in Jewish law, one born out of an adulterous relationship in which at least one party was married to someone else. Such people had no official lineage and so, whether male or female, were only allowed to marry among themselves.[37]

The other side of a woman's free agency was that she was considered responsible, and so criminally liable, for any sexual offense committed with her consent (Mishnah Keritot 1:4). Once married, however, the woman reverted back to being the chattel of her husband and all of her assets reverted to him. In fact, Mishnah Shavuot 7:8 ruled that the husband was under no obligation to pay off the woman's debts even out of the property she herself brought into the marriage unless the debt was incurred with his explicit consent.[38] This is not to say, however, that women were without any rights once married. Marriage contracts stipulated that the husband had an obligation to provide his wife with food, clothing, and sexual gratification (based on Exod. 21:10). His failure to provide these were grounds for her to demand a divorce. The marriage contract gave her in this case a right to a fixed sum of alimony. There were also certain kinds of properties a woman could bring into a marriage that were to be returned to her at their original value if the marriage ended, although the husband had the use of the income from that property during the marriage (so-called *tzon barzel* or "iron sheep" property; see Talmud Baba Metzia 69a, for example).[39] Women enjoyed other rights as well: They had prior claims to charity over men, for example, and a woman in debt could not be sold into bondage as could a man (Mishnah Sotah 3:8), nor could she sell herself into bondage. On the other hand, she was not allowed to acquire a male slave.[40]

It is very possible that the complex and at times internally inconsistent status of women in Talmudic law was influenced by norms operative in the surrounding Roman or Persian cultures. Whatever the reason, women did constitute a category of their own, sometimes to their good and sometimes to their detriment. This confusion is evident in the diverse and contradictory justifications given for one law or another. Some rabbis, for example, regarded women as light-minded. (Talmud Bavli Shabbat 33b and Kiddushin 80b, for example) while others, in different circumstances, ascribed extra wisdom to women. For example, in Talmud Niddah 45b, Rabbi Hisda* asks about the opinion of [Rabbi Judah Ha-Nasi] (Gen. 2:22), "'and God fashioned [yiben] the rib that He had taken from the man into a woman'; thus coming to teach us that the Holy One Blessed be He gave extra wisdom (binah) to the woman over that of a man." In this later case, Resh Lakish,* a greater authority, immediately finds another explanation for the Genesis verse. In all events, this back and forth argument about the character of women shows that the Talmudic rabbis hardly shared a single view of women, whether positive or misogynist.

More recent archaeological discoveries combined with other evidence suggest that in fact women may have had a much higher social status and played a much more significant role in the Jewish communities of the time than one would conclude from reading the rabbinic literature alone. It has long been assumed, for example, that in the synagogue women were relegated to at best a spectator role, if that. This was, after all, the medieval model and so was assumed to be true for ancient times as well. Recent archaeological evidence from synagogues of the second through fifth centuries c.e. have revealed a somewhat different picture. It now appears that there was no separation of men and women in these early synagogues and in fact inscriptions refer with some regularity to women as donors, leaders (archisynagogissa), and even officeholders. This archaeological evidence suggests that it is possible that, in practice, women had more power and authority over their own lives than the Talmud seems to suggest.[41]

Adducing the real life social role of women in late antiquity is beyond the scope of this book, and is at any rate only now beginning to be examined on the basis of extra-Talmudic evidence. What is clear is that as the Talmud and its class of (male) scholars and judiciary functionaries became the definers of normative Judaism in the seventh century c.e. and beyond, women became relegated to a second-class status, at least with respect to rabbinic law. This development will become clearer in the chapters that follow.

CONCLUSION

IN CONCLUDING THIS chapter, it is probably worth saying a few words about how these rights applied to others. The fact is that Talmudic law rarely touches on obligations and rights as regards non-Jews. It might thus be legitimately asked whether the human rights established by the Talmud are "natural" and so apply to all humans, or are specific to members of the covenanted community, that is, Israel. Certain passages certainly seem to assume the latter to be the case, addressing only other Israelites. Recall the citation from Mishnah Sanhedrin 4:5 above, which tells us that witnesses in capital cases are to be reminded that "as regards anyone who wastes a single soul in Israel, the Scripture applies as though he had destroyed an entire world; and as regards anyone who preserves a single soul in Israel, the Scripture applies as though he had preserved an entire world." Yet even here matters are not so clear. The same mishnah goes on to remind the witness that all people are descended from Adam and Eve: "the common descent from Adam serves [to promote] peaceful relations among people, so that no one might say to his fellow, 'my ancestors are greater than yours,'" thus implying a natural human right that extends beyond "souls in Israel." It seems to me from the repeated reference to the common ancestry of all humans from Adam and to the universal covenant made with Noah, that in fact these rights are in the end deemed to be part of natural law, that is, applying to all peoples as creatures of God. The reason that the application of these rights to non-Jews is rarely taken up in the Talmudic literature is due to the fact that the sages saw themselves as addressing only cases that fell under their own jurisdiction, that is, relationships between Jews. Relationships with outsiders were considered at times in delimited situations, but were rarely the subject of true Talmudic law, since these relationships lay beyond its legal competence and experience.

The one major exception to this general rule is comprised of the several peoples mentioned in the Bible who earned the eternal enmity of the early Israelites (or more accurately, of the Israelite God) because they oppressed the Israelite people or fought them in their struggle to reach the Holy Land. Such people—including the Egyptians, Edomites, Moabites,

Ammonites, and the Amalekites—are not deemed to have the natural rights assumed to apply to non-Jews in general. They may not marry into the community and in some cases are to be attacked, killed, and despoiled. Yet not even these people are universally written out of the human race and its rights, with the single exception of the Amalekites, who were destined for complete annihilation.[42] As regards the other peoples, Deut. 23:8–9 subsequently warns:

> You shall not abhor an Edomite, for he is your kinsman. You shall not abhor an Egyptian, for you were a stranger in his land. 9. Children born to them may be admitted into the congregation of the LORD in the third generation.

As for the others, Deut. 23:4 declares that:

> No Ammonite or Moabite shall be admitted into the congregation of the LORD; none of their descendants, even in the tenth generation, shall ever be admitted into the congregation of the LORD.

But even the biblical restrictions on Moabites and Ammonites were gradually abolished, or eroded away. The Book of Ruth, for example, not only has Boaz marry a Moabite woman (Ruth), but has the couple become the progenitors of King David. Mishnah Yevabot 8:3, no doubt with the Book of Ruth in mind, restricts the prohibition of Moabites (and by implication, Ammonites) entering Israel only to males (thus, Ruth presents no problem). Later, even this restriction was removed: In a dispute reported in Talmud Berachot 28a between Rabbi Gamliel and Rabbi Joshua ben Hananiah in the second century, the latter argued successfully for the acceptance of an Ammonite groom into the community of Israel on the grounds that the populations were now so intermingled that there were no longer any pure Ammonites (or by implication, Moabites) around anymore anyway. In short, anybody, even the biblically declared enemies named above, could enter the community and be fully accepted.

In fact, most authorities cited in the Talmud concede that all peoples can store up merits in the eyes of God.[43] The operative assumptions here, as noted above, are first, that all people are descended from common ancestors—Adam and Eve—and second, that all peoples fall under, at a minimum, the covenant made between God and Noah. This Noachide covenant, as noted earlier, set forth the basic principles of human morality.

Any non-Jew who adheres to this minimum morality is to be considered a *righteous gentile* and enjoys basic natural human rights and can even enter heaven. So even in the face of biblical statements to the contrary, the clear tendency in the Talmudic literature is to extend human rights beyond the covenanted community of Jews to all peoples.

This conclusion is strengthened by the treatment of non-Israelites in other areas of Jewish law. An interesting discussion on this point occurs in Talmud Baba Kamma 113b, pivoting around the requirement in Deut. 22 to return lost articles to their rightful owners. The Talmudic discussion concerns whether or not this holds even for returning the property of non-Israelites. Most of the participants argue that since scripture requires only returning the lost object "to your brother," the obligation is to return lost items only to fellow Israelites, but not necessarily to Canaanites (or by extension other outsiders). The last word, however, is given to Rabbi Pinhas ben Yair,* who says, "When there exists the possibility of bringing shame upon God's name, even lost objects are forbidden (i.e., to be kept by Israelites but must be returned)." He establishes his point by invoking the glory of the God who created all people, thus establishing the principle that the protections of the halachah should be extended to everyone.

By the seventh century C.E., the Talmud, with its particular structure of Jewish law, had come to define normative Judaism. Embedded in this law is a deep concern with preserving the rights and dignity of all humans as creatures of the same God and descendants of the same ancestors (Adam, Eve, and Noah). Over the next thousand years, the social life of Jews changed radically, but the basic legal principles laid out by the Talmud continued to define right and wrong for members of the rabbinic community. How this system was taken over, fleshed out, and applied to the new realities of the Middle Ages is the subject of chapter 5.

5

HUMAN RIGHTS
IN THE MEDIEVAL HALACHAH

I N ABOUT THE NINTH CENTURY C.E., the Talmudic academies of
Babylonia entered a period of gradual but inexorable decline,
with the result that local Jewish communities in the Middle East, North
Africa, and Central Europe found themselves more and more left to their
own devices. The decline of the Babylonian academies and their leaders
(the *Geonim*) was due to a number of developments. Among the most important of these was the Islamization of the region. The government of
the exilarch and the office of the Geonate were developed within the political structure of Sassanian Iran. As the region came under the control
of the Islamic caliphate, the political substructure supporting the academies shifted significantly. In addition, the Abbasid caliphate itself began
to crumble as the eighth century C.E. progressed (Spain broke away as
early as the 750s; Morocco broke with Baghdad in the 780s; Tunisia in
800; and Egypt in the mid-ninth century).[1] In this climate, the Babylonian Jewish intellectual centers did not so much suddenly disappear as
gradually fade into impotence, in accessibility, and finally into irrele-
vance. This demise corresponded more or less with the beginning of the
Crusades, first preached in the Western Church in the late eleventh century. These military incursions had the result not only of disrupting the
caliphate even further, but also of cutting off the Jewish communities of
Europe (i.e., those that survived Christian onslaughts) from the Muslim
world and whatever surviving Geonic academic activity remained.

There was an attempt to revive the Geonate and its academy by the Abbasids in Baghdad around 1170, but the effort seems to have survived barely a century, its last known leader being appointed in the late thirteenth century.[2] It thus turned out that the far-flung Jewish communities of Europe, North Africa, and even the Middle East found themselves, over a period of several centuries, forced to develop their own indigenous intellectual resources. It is in this context that local rabbinic authorities arose to fill the gap. Needless to say, the emergence of such local authorities combined with the growth of the diaspora and the loss of central institutions, led to a highly variegated rabbinic Judaism in the medieval period. To be sure, the Talmud (especially the Babylonian one) provided a common canonical text and body of law, but the interpretation and application of this legal tradition depended heavily on local political and social realities, as will become clear in the following discussion. The spread of printed texts from the fifteenth century on helped to some extent to overcome this fractionalization, but local and regional variations persisted well into the nineteenth and even twentieth centuries.

A word needs to be said at this point about how this change will effect the analysis in this chapter. The emergence of the local rabbinate as surrogates for the erstwhile Babylonian Talmudic academies was hardly an organized or planned process, but rather the result of the emergence over time and in various places of individual scholars (rabbis) who gained a reputation for their knowledge and wisdom and who, as a consequence, began to receive from local community leaders the queries that once were addressed to the academies in Babylonia. As a rule, a rabbi of a local community faced with a difficult question would write to another rabbi whom he regarded as an authority. These questions (*sheelot*) elicited a response (*teshuva* or *responsum*) that would provide an answer and a rationale, and, as time progressed, the argument behind the rationale. By the tenth and eleventh centuries, resorting to such local resources had reached a level of functional maturity so that certain rabbis appeared to have such wide-ranging credibility that their answers were routinely sought.

Such legal briefs have survived in their tens and hundreds of thousands from about the ninth century. Because they deal with the minutiae of everyday life, and with every conceivable circumstance, these rescripts are invaluable resources for reconstructing the popular history, folkways, and halachah of Jewish communities over the last millennium.[3] Here, the interest is of course in the notion (or notions) of human rights that operated in the laws, customs, and norms presupposed by this vast corpus of re-scripts that made up what can best be described as medieval Jewish common law. It is thus this literature that will form the basis of this chapter's investigation into the idea of human rights as it functioned in the medieval communities of Judaism. Although the Jewish communities of both the West and the East underwent massive changes beginning in the mid-eighteenth century with the Enlightenment and the beginning of Jewish emancipation (a topic taken up in chapter 6), traditional Jews have continued writing *responsa* up to the present day. In fact, even liberal and post-Enlightenment Judaisms, such as Reform, have taken up the practice and in the last half century produced a virtual library of their own *responsa*. Consequently, only a relative handful of texts can be used in what follows to adduce what were broadly held values. It should be kept in mind that local variations were myriad and often in flux.

Before delving into this material itself, a few general principles should be set forth. First, all of these *responsa* relied heavily on the Talmud, that is, they claim to carry forward Talmudic lines of thought and reasoning and, when they cited any source, it was most often the Talmud, although as the Middle Ages progressed, *responsa* tended more and more to cite other, earlier *responsa* as well. To establish and maintain their authority, the myth developed that the local rabbis were saying nothing different than their Geonic predecessors had said, or at least would have said, in the circumstance under consideration. Thus, the rabbis struggled to maintain the sense that they stood in a direct line of inheritance to their Geonic predecessors. The general attitude is captured well by Moses Maimonides, the great medieval philosopher and legalist.

> It is explicitly and clearly laid down in the Written Law that its norms stand forever and evermore: the Law suffers no change, no diminution and no addition: for it is written, "Ye shall not add unto the word which I command you, neither shall ye diminish aught from it;" and it is written, "Those things which are revealed belong unto us and our children for ever, that we may do all the words of this law" (Deut. 29:29)—hence you learn that all the words of the law are binding on us in eternity.[4]

The point is that in theory, the law that was being promulgated in the diverse variety of medieval *responsa* was all part of the same coherent system revealed by God at Sinai and worked out in its detail by the Talmudic, Geonic, and now rabbinic sages. In actuality, of course, the range of interpretation and application varied widely. There were in the medieval ages a variety of ways of dealing with these divergences and differences, but the overall truth and inner cogency of the halachic system as a whole was never questioned. Scholars who gave apparently different answers to the same question were nonetheless held to be articulating the word of the living God.

Looking back from our perspective, of course, it is clear that medieval rabbinic law is not merely an elaboration of Talmudic law taken in its simple sense. The answers given by a variety of local authorities who made up the medieval rabbinate depended not only on the Talmud, but also on the specifics of the issue at hand, and of course on the author's own social location, that is, the time and place in which he lived and wrote. As Haim Cohen, former justice of the Israeli Supreme Court, put it:

> Most talmudical human rights pronouncements are . . . clothed with divine (or quasi-divine) authority, they are but normative expressions of their authors' humanitarian creeds (as, indeed, pronouncements denying human rights may well serve as indications of their authors' neglect of, or indifference to, humanitarian concerns). The "divinity" of Jewish law is in actual practice achieved, and freely admitted to be conditioned, by human agencies operating for human ends with human methods and from human motives.[5]

One more methodological point should be made before proceeding to the texts themselves. Because Jewish communities in both the Islamic and the Christian worlds were left by and large to run their own internal communal affairs, *responsa* tended to deal mostly with matters of religious practice and ritual, matters of Jewish personal status (marriage, divorce, inheritance, burial), and matters of internal Jewish communal administration (especially the collection of taxes and aid to the poor). Legal issues between Jews and others usually ended up in non-Jewish courts, whether Christian or Islamic. These very practical and community-focused concerns limited discussions of such broad themes as human rights. The result is, as will become clear, that attitudes toward human rights have to be teased out of the details of the law. This makes adducing broad characterizations of medieval Judaism and its law impossible. While it is true that the Talmud provided a kind of common basis, it is also the case that even in these highly focused internal matters, the traditions, practices, laws, and interests of the outside world found their way into Jewish thought. These differences, especially between the Islamic world and the Christian world, lead to some differences in the web of moral and legal assumptions emanating from these two respective blocs of Jewish communities. So each *responsum* finds its own compromise between centrifugal, local, and centripetal forces.

A few examples may make this clearer. The following discussion begins with the larger question of authority in the Jewish world in the wake of the collapse of the Talmudic academies and how that authority interacted with the surrounding rulership. In the Islamic world, for example, a kind of microcosm of the old Sassanian exilarchate continued to operate, yielding a more centralized community answerable to the imperial ruling elite. This gave the organized Jewish community of the Islamic Empire a measure of legally recognized status, albeit of a lower rank (*dhimmi*) than was true for Muslims. Thus, Isidore Epstein, former principal of Jews College, London, notes as one rather dramatic example that the Jewish community in Northern Africa in the fourteenth century "was most undemocratic. The administration was in the hands of a kind of sheik . . . who derived power from the government and whose authority—supported at times by a large retinue—in the community was supreme."[6] But this centralization offered a certain status as well. A wonderful description of the closeness of the exilarch in Babylonia to the ruling caliph is given in the travelogue of Benjamin of Tudela,* who visited Baghdad in around 1168:

> And every Thursday when he goes to pay a visit to the great Calif, horsemen, non-Jews as well as Jews—escort him, and heralds proclaim in advance: "Make way before our Lord, the son of David as is due unto him." . . . Then he appears before the Calif and kisses his hand, and the Calif rises and places him on a throne which Mohammed had ordered to be made in honor of him, and the Mohammedan princes who attend the court of the Calif rise up before him.[7]

The situation was different in Christendom. In Europe, the division of territories among a plethora of rival kings, princes, barons, and landlords of various sorts led to much less coherency and much more regional variation in how Jewish communities were founded, organized, and overseen. Not only did each community have its own particular charter, but the Jewish communities often found themselves answerable to rival masters.

In some cases, Jews were caught up in the struggle between emerging secular authorities and the Church as to which was the proper defender of the Christian faith. For example, a report from France noted that in the year 1270, a dispute broke out between a knight and a Jew in the monastery of Cluny. The Jew, asked about his view of the Virgin Mary being the mother of God, responded that he believed none of it. He was thereupon beaten up by his adversary and eventually died of his wounds. This case of murder came before the king, Louis IX, who seemed to have fully approved the murder. The king reportedly claimed "that a layman, when he hears the Christian law mis-said, should not defend the Christian law, unless it be with his sword, and with that he should pierce the mis-sayer in the midriff, so far as the sword will enter."[8] This incident is interesting on two counts. First, it is noteworthy that the case of a confrontation in a monastery should end up in a royal court. Second, it says something about the status of Jews in this period that the murder should have been deemed justified by the royal (secular) court on the basis of theological considerations.

Another document from about the same period, this time from Central Europe, shows that in some cases the exact opposite attitude prevailed and that the ruling authorities in fact went out of their way to ensure fairness to their Jewish subjects, even in royal courts. One such example is the charter drawn up for the Jews in the Duchy of Austria in July 1244. Among other stipulations, the charter required that in any monetary case between a Christian and a Jew that came before the royal court and for which there was a Christian witness, there must be a Jewish witness as well. There were also stipulations to protect Jewish life and wealth, although the concern here may well have been that both the Jew and his wealth belonged, in some sense, to the ruler.[9] Nonetheless, there was a measure of protection afforded to the Jews here that did not seem to obtain in France at the same time. In short, it can only be said that given this variety of circumstances, it is hardly surprising that there was no uniformity in the medieval Jewish conception of human rights. With each respondent having to work within the given legal framework of his time and place, it is impossible to make hard and fast generalizations about medieval Jewish-life attitudes about virtually any topic, despite the shared legacy of the Talmud.

In this welter of material, Moses Maimonides stands out as model of clarity. Drawing on his experience as a rabbi, philosopher, and practicing physician, Maimonides tried to develop not only a comprehensive commentary on the Mishnah, but a systematic code of Jewish law (the Mishnah Torah, often called the Yad) and wrote a major philosophical work on Judaism, the *Guide for the Perplexed*. His idea in all three projects was that in the wake of the collapse of the Geonate, there needed to be a coherent exposition of Jewish law that could serve as a universal source of reference for *responsa* writers. Thus, in the process of putting together his code of Jewish law, and later in writing the *Guide*, Maimonides also paid attention to adducing and articulating the basic presumptions and core values that underlay all of the halachah and that gave it structure. Although Maimonides could in the end hardly encompass all of medieval Jewish law and in fact sparked significant criticism from other rabbinic authorities, his influence was such that his work has to be regarded as a major expression of early medieval Jewish jurisprudential thinking.

In his *Guide*, Maimonides articulates what must be the first clear statement of a philosophy of Jewish law. The whole point of Jewish law, he wrote, is to protect and extend the life of each individual person. This was true not only of the dietary laws (a subject he knew particularly well from his experience as a physician), but also of the moral laws, and even of the ritual and civil laws. These later laws in particular were designed to promote the exercise of the rational faculty of the human mind and so create a basis for good health and a lengthened life.[10] This was not to deny the older theory that ones's "length of days" was a function of divine grace or blessing. But it did translate the notion of the divine promise of long life for the faithful and law-abiding person into a natural or scientific explanation, namely, that human action in accordance with the rational law of Sinai (good diet, regular exercise, living by the golden mean, and so forth) could itself preserve life or delay death in line with the divine scheme of things.

To conclude this discussion of methodological considerations, it is important to reemphasize the fact that despite Maimonides' pioneering synthesis, the fact remains that variety was the order of the day. Even with the advent of printing in the late fifteenth century, which made a standard canon of literature more universally available, local variation and coloration always remained, and to this day remain, the rule. Given the sheer vastness of the literature, it is necessary in any study such as this to limit the investigation to those authorities who seem to be the most prominent and who answer questions that seem most pertinent to the topic at hand. Also, in the following discussion, the *Shulkhan Arukh*, a virtually complete compendium of the agreed upon halachah at the time of its publication in the mid-sixth century, will be cited regularly.[11] It should thus be kept in mind that this chapter will be able to give little more than an impressionistic overview of the larger trends within medieval, and more specifically Western, Jewry.

JUDICIAL PROCEDURE

OUR CONSIDERATION OF human rights in medieval Judaism begins with a look at judicial procedure. As noted, Jewish communities, even before the formal legal imposition of ghettoes in the sixteenth century, were largely self-governing, at least with respect to personal and civil matters. Thus, a certain portion of the halachic discourse of the time dealt with the hows and wherefores of resolving civil disputes. In this regard, it is important to note at the outset that it was taken largely for granted that all members of the community had the right to an appearance before a court and to a fair hearing. The authoritarian rule of the sheik (*zaken* in Hebrew) that was noted in Benjamin of Tudela's previously cited report, seems to have been more the exception than the rule, and was always imposed from the outside. Within Jewish communities themselves it was assumed that a fair trial was a basic right. Given the generally small size of the community, the judge or judges were also likely to have been community leaders in other areas and so were responsive to the needs of the community and its population.

Before proceeding it needs to be pointed out how the Jewish judicial system worked in practice. The jury system as developed in English common law was unknown. Rather, medieval Jewish legal proceedings, based in most cases on the Talmudic system, was a matter of appearing before either a single community leader (who might or might not be a formally trained judge) or before a panel of such judges (three judges constituted an official court, termed a *bet din*). In either case there was no jury and the judge or judges had full authority to hear testimony, examine evidence, question the litigants and witnesses, render a decision, and determine the penalty. Consequently, a good deal of effort was expended in medieval Jewish law in addressing how such judges were to be chosen— qualifications, mechanisms for their appointment, and the rules of evidence they were to follow. This topic opened up broader questions of communal governance and the rights of the community members in general as regards the selection and empowerment of the ruling body within the community. The details are less important here than the fact that this was an issue of ongoing concern and attention. A few examples should serve to give a flavor of this area in medieval Jewish law.

One example regarding overall governance is a *responsum* of Meir of Rothenburg,* a major central European authority of the thirteenth century. He was confronted with the following situation. In one particular community, a group of prominent members had decided among themselves to band together, appoint from among their number a presiding officer, and take over the governance of the community. The question addressed to Meir concerned the legality and legitimacy of this move. Meir's answer was unequivocal and extremely important at this early stage of the expansion and constitution of Jewish communities in Central Europe: "They are not (legally) masters in this matter. They are not permitted to make any new enactments without the consent of all (i.e., the entire community)."[12] Meir further cited the Talmud (Baba Batra 8b) that only the community as a whole can tax itself. He took this to mean that only people chosen by the community had the right to make decisions about taxes, and by extension, about anything else regarding communal government. In other words, the power of the community lay in its members, not just the rich or the rabbis or some aristocratic elite. Meir's *responsum* clearly upholds unequivocally the right of the community to choose democratically its own leadership.

A good example of how this might work out, and some of the complexities involved, is found in a *responsum* of Judah ben Eliezer of Minz* (1408–1508), who was consulted about a dispute that was tearing apart the community in Treviso (in what is now Northern Italy). In his answer, he quoted Rabbi Meir of Rothenberg as follows:

[I]f there is a quarrel in your community and they are unable to come to an agreement in choosing officers with everyone's consent, . . . and because of this division of hearts, study of the Torah is neglected and there is no truth and judgment and peace in your city, . . . It seems to me that they should gather together in a meeting all the taxpayers of the community, who should promise on oath that everyone will give his opinion in the Name of God and for the good of the community; and that they should follow the decision of the majority as to choosing officers, appointing cantors, and fixing the treasury for charity. . . . In brief, all the needs of the community shall be decided by the majority. . . . If the minority refuses and stand off at a distance . . . then the majority shall have the power to appoint heads, to compel and to exert pressure.

This *responsum* adds an interesting twist at the end. After citing Meir in apparent agreement, Eliezer of Minz concluded by taking away what he has just given by saying that if the community in fact had a different tradition for solving such issues, they should follow that tradition rather than his "outside" ruling.[13] In light of this qualification it is possible to read the *responsum* of Meir as not so much upholding democracy in its simple sense as upholding a community's traditional way of doing things. The social clique that chose itself as the governing body may have been wrong not because it was acting undemocratically (in our sense) but because it violated the expectations and norms of the community. In either case, both respondents agreed that the community was self-governing and was to rely on its own internal traditions when it came to choosing its leaders. In short, it is clear that both *responsa* carry forward the principle that legitimacy of leadership depended in some way or another on the consent of the governed.

Of at least as much importance as the overall governance of the community was how it dealt with internal disputes. Each community had at least one judge who handled such cases. It should be kept in mind that not all Jewish communities were as large and as organized as the ones Meir and Eliezer of Minz were addressing. In parts of Central and most of Eastern Europe, a community might be established by the ruling prince for a specific purpose (lumber trade, for example) and be explicitly limited to only a few dozen families or so. In such a case, there may not really have been a ruling counsel per se, but only a single communal leader who served as liaison with the ruler, tax collector, magistrate, and judge. In such a case it is only natural that some dissatisfaction might grow up around the judge and his decisions. How was this kind of internal tension to be solved? A good example of how this worked in one of these smaller communities of the medieval Jewish world, as well as the problems this could create, can be found in an answer given by Rabbi Joseph ibn Migash* in *responsum* no. 114 to a question about a local man who ended up filling the role of judge for a certain community. The problem was that the local man (allegedly) had no rabbinic or judicial training and so simply cited and enforced the decisions of earlier Geonic texts rather than produce thoughtful decisions on the basis of his own careful deliberation of the facts before him.[14] The questioner was concerned that the judge did not know what he was doing since he seemed to select Geonic *responsa* arbitrarily when rendering decisions. Rabbi Migash's answer is worth quoting at length:

> Know that this man is more fit to act as a judge than many nowadays who have appointed themselves as judges. Most of (these "modern" judges) do not even have one of these two qualifications: knowledge of the law and a foundation of legal knowledge based upon geonic opinion. Those who presume to render judgment on the basis of speculative reasoning on the law, and on the strength of their deliberations on the Talmud, are the ones who should be restrained from acting as judges. . . . However one who renders judgments on the basis of geonic *responsa* and relies on the geonim, even though he is unable to understand the Talmud fully is more suitable and more praiseworthy than one who thinks he knows Talmud and relies on himself. The man who depends on the geonic legal tradition, even though he judges on the basis of a possibly flawed line of reasoning from geonic precedents, does not thereby commit an error since he does what he does on the precedent of a decision from a major and authoritative Jewish court of law.[15]

The case can be read on several levels. It might simply be the complaint of a defendant or plaintiff who lost his case and so is bringing the judge's abilities into question. On another level, the question can be seen as part of a larger philosophical issue regarding any judge's role in making legal decisions. Does a judge have the right (or even duty) to interpret and so in a sense make law, or does a judge merely apply the law as given? The local judge in question seems to hold the former position, namely, that the work of the judge is merely to decide which law governs the situation at hand and then apply that law. In this view, Jewish law is based on precedent, and so is highly predictable; the judges discretion, at least in theory, is severely limited. This is of course perfectly consistent with the covenant notion of the community and it affords a certain mood of legal stability and predictability to the law since matters do not depend on the judge's arbitrary decision.[16]

The questioner, on the other hand, wanted a more activist judge. He wanted local law to reflect local values and conditions. For him, the judge's reluctance to use judicial discretion and to make new law was a detriment. It is clear from the *responsa* that ibn Migash, at least, sided with the judicial positivists. Better to have a conservative judge who ruled by the letter of the law than an activist judge who did not really know what he was doing. This is certainly a question with which many in the Jewish community are still struggling today. The case shows, however, that common members of the community had a stake in this debate and could give expression to their concern and be taken seriously.

So much for the broader issues of community governance. It is now necessary to turn to some more specific matters of process and procedure. In general, the *responsa* literature wanted to keep the judicial process as fair and transparent as possible. Case no. 111 brought before Rabbi Israel ben Haim of Brunn* can serve as a general example. A renter, Simeon, was asked to vacate a building belonging to Reuben. (Reuben and Simeon are pseudonyms commonly used in medieval Jewish legal discussion.) Simeon countered that he had a document showing that he could live in said building until his death. Reuben asked to see the document before the trial and Simeon refused. The questioner wanted to know whether Simeon was right in his refusal to turn over documents to the plantiff before the trial. The answer offered by Israel ben Haim is sharp and to the point: "Simeon shall give the copy to Reuben. My colleagues agree."[17] Disputes were to be handled openly and without secrecy. This was essential for the development of an appropriate rule of law within the Jewish community.

The importance attached to this openness is illustrated in another ruling of Joseph ibn Migash, cited above, in his *responsum* no. 715. In this case, he argued that a person had a right to appeal a court ruling and even to sue the judge if he thought that the judge had rendered a wrong decision. The importance of this latter clause cannot be overstated. For Talmudic law, the opinion of a single judge was not valid, only the rulings of a three-judge court. Technically, then, the decisions of a single judge were invalid by Talmudic law, *ab initio*. Yet ibn Migash noted that at the present time the situation is such that at times one had to rely on only a single judge and so the judgments of a single authority have to be deemed valid. But the other side of the coin is that such a judge was to be held liable for his decisions and could be made either to reverse his decision or pay indemnity if and as appropriate. Judges, then, were hardly communal dictators and each individual had a right to his day in open court in front of a judge who was answerable to the community.

PUNISHMENT

GIVEN THAT THE internal court system was designed to be fair and equi-table, the question arises as to its powers vis-à-vis the individual. A good example of the community's rights over that of the individual is case no. 1016 that came before Rabbi Meir of Rothenberg. The question was as follows: "In a town where there are only ten Jews [a quorum of ten men, called a *minyan*, is required for a prayer service] and one wants to leave the synagogue, can the others force him to stay?" Rabbi Meir's response was to affirm that they could:

> It seems to me that if they have no *minyan* without him, the others can force him either to stay or to hire someone to take his place. Tosefta Baba Metzia 11:12 states that the people of a community have the right to compel one another to pay for building a synagogue or burying a Torah scroll. This is clear evidence that we may use coercion in order to satisfy the needs of the community. It is the universal custom to hire people when a community is short one or two men to complete the *minyan* on [The holidays].[18]

Another example of the power of the community over that of the in-dividual is demonstrated in a *responsum* of Rabbi Joseph Colon.* Appar-ently an agreement had been signed with the local duke that a tax of 13,000 florins would be paid by the community. Two members of the community had subsequently moved to a different principality and were claiming exemption from the tax, the amount of which was apparently fixed while they had still been members of the community. The ruling as to their liability is clear: "The halachah states that those who move away to avoid paying a tax are not exempt from paying that tax. They are still linked to their former community. They were partners in the tax from the start. They are still partners and surely must pay their share."[19]

For some medieval decision makers, the community had almost com-plete power of punishment over miscreants. In this regard, a basic posi-tion is staked out by Jacob ben Asher,* one of the founders of the medieval Ashkenazic legal tradition. In his fourteenth-century com-pendium *Arba'ah Turim, Hoshen Mishpat*, chapter 2, he wrote:

> Even though they do not impose the penalty of death or of flogging or fines outside the Land of Israel, if the court sees that the need has arisen,

inasmuch as the people have become unrestrained in sin, they may impose the death penalty, monetary fines, or any other kind of punishments. . . . We see in what Maimonides wrote that the court may flog one who does not deserve flogging or kill one who does not deserve death, not as a matter of transgressing Torah, but to build a fence around it. If the court sees that the people have become unrestrained in some matter they have the power to define and strengthen the matter as they see fit. But all this is only an injunction for the moment (*hora'at sha'ah*) and not to be taken as establishing halakhah for future generations.

In light of the overwhelming reluctance of the Talmudic leadership to impose the death penalty, the readiness of Jacob ben Asher to impose this punishment in the name of the common good is surprising. Yet, it should be noted, he concluded his discussion on a cautionary note: "But in all matters he should act for the sake of Heaven, and he should not take human dignity lightly." In our discussion of human dignity, it will become clear that this is no small concession. In essence, Jacob ben Asher had authorized even the death penalty in theory, but by referencing human dignity he had taken it away in practice, just as the Talmud did, as discussed in chapter 4.

This brief passage from the *Arba'ah Turim* catches at least three major themes of medieval Jewish law. First, the court has full authority to rule as it must to maintain public order. An extension of this is stated succinctly in a *responsum* of Asher ben Yehiel, no. 6:5:

Your question is whether two or three ordinary inhabitants of the town may exclude themselves from enactments agreed to by the community or from a decree enforced by a ban concerning any matter. Know that as to matters involving the public, the Torah states, "Follow the majority." The majority governs in all matters of public enactment; and the minority must abide by all that is agreed to by the majority, because otherwise, if a few individuals could veto the enactment, the community would never be able to legislate. Therefore, the Torah declared, "Follow the majority" with reference to all communal enactments.

In short, the welfare of the community was always to take precedence over the right of the individual to dissent.

Second, the court could even violate an individual's rights to the maximum degree ("flog one who does not deserve flogging or kill one who does not deserve death"). The latitude given here to governing authorities has to be understood not only in terms of the general temper of the times, but also the increasingly precarious position of the Jewish communities, especially in Christian Europe. To be sure, as will be noted more fully below, there was a basic recognition of human rights in medieval Jewish law, but the *responsum* made it clear that at least in some extraordinary circumstances exceptions were sanctioned for the preservation of the community and its welfare.[20]

In this context, there is actually an interesting take on the imposition of flogging on one who would not normally be subject to such punishment. One punishment that was prescribed by the Bible was that of *karet*, literally, "cutting off." This was considered such a horrendous possibility that often the human court was advised to flog the offender instead. This advice was based on the assumption that no individual should be punished twice for the same crime. It was thus thought that if the offender were flogged by the human court, maybe the eternal divine punishment of *karet* would be forestalled. This was a view stated explicitly, for example, by Maimonides in his commentary on Mishnah Makkot 3:1. He also opined that the offender, being flogged and doing repentance is also free from the penalty of death by divine act.[21] This view seems to have been maintained even over the opposition of some who argued that it is presumptuous for humans to think that acts ordained by a human court could contravene the decree of the Almighty.

Along these lines, it should be mentioned that medieval Jewish law was more comfortable with imprisonment than its Talmudic predecessors. Thus, various authorities allowed imprisonment for offenses like sexual misconduct (for example, Isaac ben Sheshet Perfet* in *responsum* no. 351) and certain property offenses (for example, in Yom Tov ben Abraham Ishbili,* *responsa* no. 159), and even for nonpayment of taxes.[22] Maimonides even went so far as to say that if one was observed entering a dwelling and leaving with certain goods and then claimed he was only seizing a pledge for an unpaid debt or retrieving his own goods, he was to be considered a thief until proven otherwise (*Mishneh Torah* "Gezila vaAveida" 4:12).[23] Along with the increased use of imprisonment were considerations of the rights of the imprisoned and of those newly released from incarceration, drawn largely from Talmudic discussions.[24]

The third point emerging from the passage cited from the *Arba'ah Turim* returns to the issue of human dignity mentioned at the end. What is clear is that this must always to be a consideration. While such extraordinary punishments as flogging or death may indeed be carried out (at least in theory), they are only to be done so in unusual circumstances and never to be taken as precedents. In short, the court (or communal leadership structure) can do whatever it deems necessary for the welfare of the community, but the basic notion of human rights must not be permanently undercut or taken lightly. It is within these parameters that medieval European Jewish law takes shape.

In light of this more theoretical discussion, it is interesting to see how Asher ben Yehiel actually handled a case of a person who in fact posed a physical danger to the whole community. Just such a case came before Rabbi Asher ben Yehiel. *Responsum* 17:1, for example, concerns a Jew who had "become a notorious informer against, and defamer of, Jews and the Jewish community. He terrorizes (the Jews) daily because he might go to the secular government to inform against individuals or communities in matters that could result in economic loss or physical danger to them. The community is very frightened of this man who is in regular attendance at the court of one of the most powerful men of the gentile world." After detailing the investigation and determinations so far, the questioner went on to ask whether or not this person may be tried as a "pursuer," that is, one who may be prevented from killing another innocent victim by being killed himself! Several precedents are cited, including Talmud Baba Qamma 117a.

The answer is long and complex, as the seriousness of the case would certainly warrant. After noting that death sentences could no longer be passed once the Sanhedrin passed out of existence, Rabbi Asher ben Yehiel went on to say that "in cases where a person is not on trial for past misdeeds, but in order to save a potential victim from his pursuer, the death sentence may still be carried out if the local government permits it. For we apply the verse, 'Do not stand still when your neighbor's life is in danger'" (Lev. 19:16). The sages equate an informer who causes Jewish property to fall into the hands of oppressors with a *rodeif* who threatens to kill.[25] The legal distinction here was a neat one. The offender may not be executed as a punishment for a crime, as noted earlier, but a pursuer could be killed either in self-defense or for the protection of an innocent victim who would certainly be put into physical danger, or even killed, without our intervention. It is this later case on which the *responsum* based its permission to execute the death penalty. The following is the concluding argument to Asher ben Yehiel's rather involved discussion:

Therefore the custom has arisen throughout the Diaspora that we seek advice and counsel in order to remove an informer from the world as an extraordinary procedure for curbing lawless acts, it having been first established that the informer has on at least three occasions caused a Jew, or Jewish property, harm. This is done as a deterrent against the proliferation of informers; and also to rescue all Israel "the pursued" from his power. In this case under notice, three witnesses have established that the man is a known informer, and whereas this is a situation involving the actual time of the commission of the crime, they have done well to return the decision that he be hanged.[26]

A few items need to be noted here. First, the case was deemed to be highly unusual. It is also noteworthy that the (alleged) informer had to be established as such by three separate and witnessed events. Only then was he considered a habitual informer and thus a pursuer whose life could be taken. The reason for requiring three separate witnessed acts surely went back to a Talmudic precedent that an ox's owner was regarded as fully liable for the damage caused by his animal only if the animal was a known problem, and that status was established after three incidents. But Asher ben Yehiel pointed to another reason, namely, to deter this person (and presumably others) from doing further acts against the community. In effect, the offender was to be given three chances before he could be prosecuted as a pursuer. That is, he could be tried and executed only if caught in the actual act of informing the *fourth* time, it now being clear that he was a habitual and unrepentant informer. The legal basis for execution is not that of punishment, but rather that of stopping a known homicidal pursuer in the process of committing a further act.

Even ben Yehiel's relatively benign and delimited approval of the death penalty did not stand unchallenged. Consider the discussion of this very same situation by the fourteenth-century rabbi, Isaac ben Sheshet Perfet in no. 239. His argument was that "even if he did inform or defame in such a way as to cause mortal danger to someone, and a criminal act done as a direct consequence of his utterance, such a one is not executed. . . . A murderer cannot lawfully be put to death by the court except when he himself committed the murder." In this ruling, Perfet did not accept the legal fiction of the informer as pursuer. Execution, in his view, was to be carried out only as punishment for an actual crime, not as a preventive measure. Execution as a punishment was, however, not allowable any more under Talmudic law. The bottom line for Perfet was that the person may well deserve the death penalty, but that this would have to come at the hands of the heavenly court, not the earthly one.[27]

HUMAN DIGNITY

SINCE THE ISSUE of human dignity has come up, it is worthwhile to look at this concept more closely. As in Talmudic times, the preservation of human dignity was considered a social priority. It will be recalled that the Talmudic authorities considered gossip to be one of the most pernicious of social offenses. Talmud Arachin 15b, cited in chapter 4, even declared gossip to be worse than capital punishment. This principle was carried forward and expanded in the Middle Ages. Numbers Rabbah, a post-Talmudic commentary on the biblical book of Numbers, cites Samuel ben Nahman* in noting that gossip actually kills three people: the speaker, the listener, and the subject (thus explaining why it was worse than capital punishment, which only kills one victim, namely the convicted criminal). Eliezer ben Isaac* in his *Orhot Hayyim* from the middle of the eleventh century admonished his readers, "Be not like a fly, seeking sore spots; cover up your neighbor's flaws, and reveal them not to the world." By medieval times, several precedents had been established to deal with socially damaging libel and slander. Maimonides in the *Mishneh Torah* Talmud Torah 6:14 listed a number of cases in which a form of banishment (*niddui*) could be imposed for reckless speech. These included insulting a scholar, calling a free man a slave, invoking the divine name for trivial purposes, and any activity that could bring Jewish scholarship into question or disrepute.[28] Various local customs established other forms of slander and the punishment appropriate for each, including even flogging. Needless to say, gossip and the damage it causes was a common theme in the *responsa* literature, the variety of responses being too great to be easily summarized.[29] This is because even in this area, with strong Talmudic precedence, the power of local custom should not be underestimated. Asher ben Yehiel ruled in no. 101:1:

[I]t is true that TB Kiddushin 28a states that one who calls his fellow a *mamzer* [illegitimate] received forty lashes. However, in this country, we do not apply this rule where there is an enactment and a custom to fine such a person. Custom overrides the strict law. . . . If it becomes evident that enactments have been instituted in the town regarding slander, one should follow the enactment rather than the law found in the Talmud.[30]

Human dignity, while taken into account, could be overridden if the community's welfare is at stake, as previously noted. The complementary attitude was that if the safety of the community was not at stake, there were certain limits on how much compulsion might be used against an individual by the governing authorities or the courts. The reason for this restraint was almost universally acknowledged to be the need to prevent the public humiliation of the offender. One of the leading proponents of this view was Rabbi Isaac ben Sheshet Perfet, who tended in general to be concerned with the rights of the accused and tried to place limits on the power of the court. In one of his *responsa*, no. 484, he addressed the case of a man facing confinement in a debtor's prison. Specifically, Simeon had loaned money to Reuben with the condition that he (Reuben) could be seized if he did not repay the debt. It later turned out that Reuben could not repay the loan. As he was about to be thrown into prison, he argued that his prior agreement to be arrested was invalid. Rabbi Isaac ben Sheshet Perfet agreed, writing a lengthy *responsum* that argued that Reuben is, in fact, correct. The *responsum* quoted many of the Talmudic dicta already cited in this chapter (for example, a worker may quit in the middle of the day because he is not *your* servant) and concluded matters as follows:

> If, however, the debtor is a poor man and has no means to pay, it is clear that one may not seize his person or oppress him, even if he consented to these measures in the loan document. His consent is legally invalid, because even to pass in front of him in order to embarrass him is forbidden, as we read in TB Bava Mezi'a 75b.[31]

A somewhat similar situation was discussed by Moses Sofer (Hoshen Mishpat 11). The case involved an insolvent homeowner, whose creditors were demanding to take possession of his house. The debtor's son-in-law used local gentile law to take the house himself and then let his father-in-law remain in the house in the hopes that his financial situation would improve. The neighbor, another creditor, then went to the rabbinic court to claim that he (the neighbor) had a right to take over the property. The Jewish court threw out the case. What is interesting here is the reasoning of the Jewish court:

Because of this principle, the Talmud (Baba Metzia 35a) grants the right to
redeem property which has been awarded to his creditors in satisfaction of
his debts. This is so despite the fact that according to strict Biblical law, the
creditor obtains an unrestricted absolute interest in the property upon ac-
quiring the property through a writ of execution. This right of redemption
may be exercised during the entire period that the creditor is in possession
of the property.

The rabbis based this right on their view that the foreclosure of the
debtor's property was an extremely traumatic experience for the debtor, and
that it would be cruel to permit the creditor to preclude the debtor from re-
gaining possession of the foreclosed property. The rabbis held, therefore,
that this right of redemption was included within the intent of the biblical injunction, "Do what is right and good."[32]

In short, absent a threat to the community, the argument to protect
the human dignity of the accused or debtor enjoyed considerable weight.
This is not so different from the previous case in which a pauper faced
being sent to debtor's prison. An even more interesting example appeared in a *responsum* of Rabbi Joseph Chaim al-Chakkam, who lived in
Baghdad from 1834 to 1909. At issue was a man who wished to test the
honesty of one of his servants by leaving some money lying around and
sending the man into the room. If the money turned up missing, then
the master would know that the servant was a thief and not to be trusted.
But is it permissible to test a servant in this way? The answer was that "it
is forbidden to do tests of this kind. If the servant succumbs to the temp-
tation and steals, the employer is guilty of placing a stumbling block in
his path (cf. Lev. 19:14), causing him to sin. . . . Therefore it is surely
forbidden to entrap someone and to lure his evil inclination into committing a sin."[33]

An even more dramatic example was a decision on the part of Moses
ben Isserles (who annotated the *Shulkhan Arukh*) to authorize a wedding
on the Sabbath, a custom that runs counter to all norms of Jewish practice, and so this was especially surprising for a rabbi of Isserles's stature
and visibility. The case came about in the following way. A young girl was
betrothed to be married. During the long engagement the father died and
left her an orphan without any financial means. She was eventually taken
in by relatives, who encouraged her to go ahead with the wedding plans.
At the last moment the relatives refused to deliver the promised amount
for the dowry and the groom thereupon refused to move forward with the

wedding, despite the pleas of everyone. Finally, late on Friday, he relented and Isserles thereupon immediately performed the ceremony. He explained in the *responsum* that although the performance of religious ceremonies that change one's status is prohibited on the Sabbath, these prohibitions, being rabbinic, can be broken in the case of an emergency. He went on to say:

> [I]t is clear that, in a great emergency, we may permit such a marriage. There can be no greater emergency than this case in which a grown orphan girl was being put to shame. It would be a lifelong disgrace for her, enough to set her apart from all other girls. Great indeed is the commandment to be considerate of the honor of human beings. It sets aside the negative commandment [of Deut. 17:11, on which obedience to rabbinic authority is based], "Turn not aside from all that they teach you."

Just as one was permitted, even required, to violate the Sabbath rest to save a life, so was one permitted (or even required) to violate the Sabbath to save a person from humiliation. Causing a person humiliation was deemed equivalent to causing that person's death.

Another fruitful topic for the examination of human rights is the treatment of workers. It has already been pointed out that workers as early as Talmudic times had a right to certain wages, regular pay, and the right to quit. Medieval law systematically expanded on these laws in a number of ways, although again the diversity of local variations and customs make generalizing hazardous. One area of labor law can serve here as a general example. It was assumed for the most part that if a person entered into a contract to perform a particular service, the contract could be terminated by the employer with reasonable notice. The length of reasonable notice, however, never received universal definition and so usually ended up being decided by local custom. Gradually, attempts were made to regularize the terms of employment. The same Moses Sofer (discussed in the case of the insolvent homeowner), went so far as to argue that as regards public office, a person's appointment was to be considered valid for life unless otherwise stipulated.[34] In a few cases, *responsa* addressed the situation in which a public officeholder died, leaving his surviving family without income. Several halachic authorities, including the nineteenth-century Joseph Saul Nathanson in *Sho'el Umeshiv* 3:1 no. 154, for example, ruled that in this case the son, if qualified, may take over his father's position in order to secure the financial position of the family. Payment was assumed from Talmudic times to be in coin. Rabbi Meir of Rothenburg in his commentary (Mordekhai to the Babylonian Talmud Baba Kamma 1) allowed payment in kind, say food, if the worker was in need of that. A *responsum* of Simon ben Zemach Duran,* 3:109, even allowed for annual paid vacations for teachers and rabbis.[35] It was precisely this persistent concern for the welfare of the laborer that has led so many Jews in the modern period into socialist and other liberal movements that backed the rights of the proletariat.

This same concern for the preservation of human dignity carried over even after death. A variety of Jewish funerary and burial customs were designed both to protect the honor of the deceased—*yeqara dishkhiva* in Talmudic Aramaic; *kavod hamet* in Hebrew—and the dignity of the mourners. In basic terms, the dying were not to be left alone, but were to have members of the family, and even of the community, around them at the time of death. In fact, a special holy brotherhood—usually called the Hevra Kadisha—existed in virtually every community specifically to fulfill this and other funerary functions. At the time of death, the eyes and mouth of the deceased were closed and the body was immediately bathed, dressed in a shroud, and placed in the coffin (usually by members of the Hevra Kadisha, who were familiar with all of the proper procedures). There was to be no viewing or wake, as both practices were held to be disrespectful to the deceased, who, after all, could not look back or participate. It was also customary to leave anything attached to the body (i.e., limbs or organs) with it at burial, but to add nothing, so that everyone was more or less equal in death.

The *Shulkhan Arukh* in Yoreh Deah 352:1 even disallowed the use of fancy shrouds, "even for a prince (*nasi*) among Israel." The *Shulkhan Arukh* Yoreh Deah 353:1 also noted that at one point the faces of the rich were covered while the faces of the poor were left uncovered. When this turned out to cause embarrassment to the living poor during times of famine (when the face of the deceased reflected the poverty of the family), the practice was changed to cover all faces. In accord with similar logic, the dead person was not removed from the house on a bed, according to Yoreh Deah 353:7, unless the head and body were intact. In all these cases, the reasoning was to prevent embarrassment or disgrace to the deceased or to his or her family.

Once the body of the deceased was prepared for burial, it was not to be left unattended, because, of course, it could not fend for itself. The burial was to take place as quickly as possible, even on the same day, but certainly within two or three days. If there were a delay it would only be for the honor of the deceased—awaiting a shroud, for example—or for family members.[36] When the body was brought to the grave, even students studying Torah were to stop and participate in the procession (Yoreh Deah 361). Embalming and other tampering with the body, sometimes even including autopsies, were not allowed, again for reasons of preserving the honor of the dead. The question of autopsies has become an issue of contention more recently, especially with the argument that nowadays an autopsy may help with medical discoveries that might eventually preserve other lives. In this case, the principle of *yeqara dishkhiva* (dignity due to the dead) collides with the principle of *pikuach nefesh* (saving human life). Without getting involved in the detailed discussion of Jewish law on this point, suffice it to say that in most cases, the possibility of saving future human lives takes precedence provided the autopsy is done with due concern for the dignity of the deceased.

After death the immediate family (usually children, siblings, and parents) went through a mourning ritual that was most stringent during the first week, moderately stringent for the rest of the first month, and then continued until the first anniversary of the death. A special mourners' prayer—the *kaddish*—was recited each day during the first year to help the soul gain final forgiveness of sins and enter heaven. It became customary to recite this prayer for only the first eleven months, lest praying the full twelve months be taken as an indication that the deceased was of such a character that he or she needed all possible help.

WOMEN

BEFORE CONCLUDING THIS chapter, it is important to say a few words about the position of women. As noted earlier, the Talmud in general seems to have held that a woman belonged to her husband, although it did acknowledge that an unmarried woman did have some status as an independent legal person. At the same time, it seems from other evidence that the actual situation of women in Jewish society may have been much better in practice during this period than what appears in the legal writings of the Talmud. Medieval Jewish law, being much more like common law than the academic law of the Talmud, took the actual role and position of women much more seriously. As a representative example, consider the case that came before Rabbi Simon ben Zemach Duran in

Tashbatz no. 3:86. The question concerned a man who married a woman in Bejaia, Algeria, although all of his family lived in Algiers. At the wedding he agreed to live with his wife in Bejaia. Ten years later the man had new business opportunities in Algiers, and besides, the local people have been spreading evil rumors about his wife. He wants to move to Algiers. Can he compel her to move? The *responsum* began by noting that if she, in fact, agreed to a move after ten years, then she was bound by that promise, unless she swore under oath that such a promise was never made. Absent such a promise, Duran ruled that the husband could force her to move. His argument was based on three grounds. First, which was clearly minor, was that it was best to remove his wife from their evil and gossipy neighbors. Second, and more important, was the fact that her life in all events would be no worse in Algiers than in Bejaia. Third, and apparently the central point, Duran relied on a passage from Maimonides' code (*Laws of Matrimony* 13:17) that reads, "If a man marries a woman in a given country and he is a citizen of that country, he cannot force her to move to a different country, but he can make her move from one village to another or from one region to another within the same country." The passage in Maimonides goes on to state that "he can not bring her from a town to a village or a village to a city for there are advantages [respectively] to living in a town [rather than a village] and advantages to living in a village [rather than a city]." The principle behind Maimonides' ruling, which Duran clearly accepted, was that a wife could be compelled to move by her husband, but only to a place that would not aversely affect her comfort or standard of living. So the woman was understood to be under her husband's control, but his control was limited by certain considerations for her rights and welfare.[37]

That this was not an unusual or restricted view can be shown from the response to a similar situation that came before Rabbi Moshe Alshekh,* *responsum* no. 55 some two hundred years later. The question involved a husband from Cavalia (a small village of about a thousand in European Turkey) who married a woman from Adrianople (a city of several thousand inhabitants). The couple set up house in Adrianople, but the husband now wanted to move back to his hometown of Cavalia. The problem was that his wife refused to move on the grounds that the water in the village was bad, the land there was said to cause miscarriages, and besides, it was a dangerous place. To make matters worse, residents once there could not, by governmental decree, move away. The husband, for his part, argued that she had, in fact, agreed to such a move at the time of the marriage. Alshekh concludes his *responsum* by declaring that "even if she agreed to join him and took an oath to that effect, since she was not informed at the time of the drawbacks of Cavalia, her oath was not given with full knowledge of these negative factors. . . . Therefore Dinah's [a legal pseudonym like Simeon and Reuben] refusal to move to her own detriment prevails. Her husband cannot make her move away from her hometown."[38]

A rather more interesting case was brought before Rabbi Nissim ben Reuben Gerondi,* *responsum* no. 38. In this case, Simeon, along with two compatriots had taken a solemn oath to migrate to the Land of Israel. Moving to the Holy Land in Jewish law was always considered a positive commandment, the fulfillment of which was incumbent upon all pious Jews who could afford to do so. Correspondingly, a Jew living in the Land of Israel was not supposed to leave and "go down," that is, live back in the lands of exile. But Simeon now found that his wife, urged on by her family, not only refused to accompany him, but also refused to accept a divorce from him on these grounds, an act that would free him to make the move. Simeon, apparently a good and loving husband, now felt he had no choice but to violate his sacred oath and abandon his plans to "go up" to the Holy Land. His question to Gerondi was whether or not the oath may be revoked, and if so, how. Gerondi's answer was that while an oath to migrate to the Land of Israel could not be revoked, there were nonetheless grounds for saying that the oath was never really valid in the first place because it involved abandoning his wife and that went against the teachings of the Torah. As to the argument that the wife should be compelled to accompany her husband, he cited arguments similar to those above, that one cannot force a wife to move to a place that will aversely affect her.[39] These three cases seem to indicate that there was a persistent tendency in medieval *responsa* to respect a woman's right to demand to live in a certain place and to refuse moving to another place, even for the benefit of her husband, if she felt such a move was a detriment to her own situation.

This view persisted into modern times. For example, Rabbi Shalom Mordechai Schwadron* addressed almost the exact same case in his *responsum* Maharsham no. 1:116. It should be kept in mind at this point that this is a legal ruling from a very traditional Polish rabbi of the nineteenth century, when Orthodoxy was in the process of hardening its positions in light of the rise of alternatives, including Hasidism in Eastern Europe and Reform Judaism in the West. This was also a time when the fulfillment of the important command of going to the Holy Land was both much more possible and, given the rising anti-Semitism in Poland, not nearly so major a deterioration in the wife's safety as would have been the case earlier. Yet Schwadron ruled that the husband could not force such a move on his wife. Moreover, he could not divorce her in order to make the move on his own. So even for the Orthodox Schwadron, the wife had what amounted to a full veto over her husbands move, even to the Holy Land.[40]

But these rulings did not mean that the wife had full control over her husband in all aspects of life. On other matters that might affect her, she had more limited options. There is, for example, a case from the eighteenth-century rabbi Yechezkel Katzenellenbogen,* who ruled in Teshuvot Kennest Yechezkel no. 74, for example, that a wife could not prevent her husband from starting a new profession that she found loath-some. In the case at hand, the man wanted to become a religious scribe. This job involved not only the actual writing of documents, but also the preparation and tanning of the parchment, an extremely smelly process. One implication of his career change was a Jewish law that allowed a husband with a disgusting profession not to have sexual relations with his wife as often as he might otherwise.[41] So this husband's change in profession had negative implications for the wife's marital rights. Katzenellenbogen ruled in this case that the wife had no right to prevent the husband from entering a profession in which he might be successful, especially in these times of "bitter exile."[42]

What is interesting to note here is not so much that the wife lost the case in the end, but that it was a case to begin with. The husband could not simply impose his change of profession, which would have an impact on her rights, just as he could not forcibly make his wife move to another city. That Katzenellenbogen took the time and energy to write a *responsum* on this situation indicates that the woman's claim was taken with some seriousness. She was hardly the mere chattel of the husband.

One interesting insight into the social role of women within late medieval Jewish society is the remarkable diary published by Glueckel of Hameln. Glueckel was born to an apparently prosperous family in Hamburg, Germany, in 1645. Her diary was written as an exercise in self-therapy after her husband died, leaving her to raise their twelve children. Her diary shows her to be a well-educated woman who knew at least some Talmudic literature and who had some familiarity with the Bible and with other Jewish moral literature of the day. In the diary, she described how she successfully raised her children, arranged appropriate marriages, and managed the family business until her remarriage several years later. While she often had to work through or rely on men, it is also clear that she was very often the one in control, that is, she worked "with" or "through" men, but not "under" them. It is of course impossible to know how representative Glueckel was of all Jewish women of the time, or even of Jewish women in Northern Germany, but she was from a relatively small Jewish town and clearly enjoyed a quality education. Her diary suggests that women, at least in the early modern period in Western Europe, were hardly uniformly uneducated and powerless.

CONCLUSION

THIS CHAPTER HAS presented only the tiniest tip of the iceberg of the richness and variety of medieval Jewish law. Despite limited space, the description of medieval Jewish law has drawn on *responsa* written by major figures. They are therefore a fair reflection of trends that held generally true throughout the Jewish world, whether in the lands of Islam or in Christian Europe. From the analyses, several conclusions can be drawn. First, Jewish law functioned very much like a common law tradition in which the discretion of the judges and arbitrators was limited by local customs and the consent of the governed. Judges whose qualifications or fairness fell into question could be challenged and their positions appealed. Second, while the Talmud was highly respected and even considered part of the divine Torah (the Oral Law), it could be overridden by the needs of justice and the preservation of human dignity. Several *responsa* cited above show that medieval jurists were willing to set the letter of Talmudic law aside when the rights or dignity of the litigants were at stake. Third, the rights of laborers were protected and even expanded in the medieval period. That is, despite the hierarchical and class-based structure of medieval society in general, Jewish law carried forward the Talmud's concern with the workaday laborer. Finally, women, while of secondary status, were hardly powerless or devoid of legal status and voice. Their concerns appeared regularly in the *responsa* literature, which often ruled in their favor.

It also has to be conceded that medieval Jewish society, while governed by the rule of law more often than was true of the surrounding world, nonetheless was medieval. It was governed by the rabbinic elite and individual rights could be quashed in the face of communal needs. As the modern period dawns, these governing structures and assumptions came under greater challenge. New realities such as the Enlightenment, full legal emancipation of Jews in Europe and especially America, and of course, Jewish sovereignty in the state of Israel, all provoked new understanding of the rights of the individual, the relationship of Jews to non-Jews, and the very principles upon which Jewish self-governance was based. It is these themes that the remaining chapters of this book address.

6

Jews as Europeans and the Adoption of the Enlightenment

THE ENLIGHTENMENT INTRODUCED profound changes in European Jewry. Through the process generally called the "emancipation," Jews were gradually allowed, region by region and country by country, to live legally outside the medieval ghettoes, to practice crafts and professions formerly closed to them, and in general to become part of mainstream European society. This process of Jewish emancipation was part of a larger intellectual and social change sweeping through Europe as the old coalition of Aristotle and the Church gave way to the Renaissance and then modern secular sciences and philosophies. These in turn produced the Industrial Revolution with its attendant changes, including the creation of secular civil societies.

All of the contemporary forms of Judaism, from American Reform to Zionism, are products of this process of Western modernization. These changes not only created the modern concept of universal human rights, but also forced the European Jewish communities to adopt this idea as well so as to define its place in the new world of the modern West. It should be noted that this process had only limited entry into and impact on the Islamic world until well after World War I. In fact, the process of introducing European modernity (or, as it is now called, globalization) into the traditional societies in the East is still ongoing and has been the cause of much of the unrest and instability of the region. For the Jews of the Middle East, the acceptance into posttraditional Islamic society has been made even more complex with the introduction of Zionism and the creation of the secular state of Israel, a topic that will be taken up in chapter 7. It is to these revolutionary changes in mental outlook in Europe and their effects on Western Jewry that this chapter turns.

The profound changes bunched together under the term Enlightenment worked on every level of Western society: intellectually (the Enlightenment proper), socially (the end of the feudal system), politically (the transition of people from being royal subjects to enjoying national citizenship), economically (the Industrial Revolution), and religiously (the Reformation and secularization). All of these changes had their effect over time on the social, political, and eventually, religious character of Europe's Jews. To be sure, during this process, the traditional life and social status of Jews in Europe did not change suddenly or completely, or always for the good. The actual process of Jewish emancipation was in fact a long, drawn-out business, deeply intertwined with local politics and economics, and it differed widely over time and place, sometimes even progressing and then ebbing within the same area. Further, even as emancipation occurred, it took on many different legal forms and was received socially in a variety of contradictory ways, ranging from goodwill, to reluctance, and to outright hostility. Nor was emancipation unanimously greeted with joy within the Jewish communities of Europe. Debates within these communities raged as to whether emancipation and Enlightenment ideas were "good for the Jews" and what they might mean for the correct fulfillment of God's covenant. These internal Jewish debates eventually became part of the political and rhetorical battles surrounding these matters, often ironically pitting pro-emancipation gentiles against anti-emancipation Jews. Overall, however, the advance of Enlightenment ideals and the emancipation of the Jews proved inexorable, progressing and broadening throughout the nineteenth century and, in parts of Eastern Europe, well into the twentieth century and was only beginning to penetrate the Middle East in the wake of World War I. But in all cases, myriad and interlocking changes brought about by the process of emancipation had profound effects on the Jewish community, resulting in the creation of a variety of ways of understanding and practicing Judaism in the modern world. These changes involved both Jewish self-perceptions as well as perceptions of Jews by others. The concept of natural or human rights was very much a part of the vocabulary of the day and had its reflection within Jewish discourse as well.

The new realities with which European Jewish thinkers were faced require some spelling out. In general, these changes amounted to what was at the time sometimes called "the civic betterment of the Jews" (which was actually incorporated into the title of an eighteenth-century pamphlet written by Christian Wilhelm von Dohm*). As the legal structure of medieval Europe gave way to new political, social, and economic arrangements, the position of the Jews came quickly into discussion. The vast majority of the general non-Jewish population at every level continued to hold the inherited attitude that conceived of Judaism as an inferior religion, rejected by God, and that its people, the Jews, were stuck in religious blindness, venality, and misanthropy. These attitudes, as noted in chapter 3, went straight back to Roman times and remained part of Church teaching for the next 1,500 years. But a few new thinkers, influenced by secular, even anticlerical Enlightenment ideas began to question these old basic assumptions. If human reason could break the hold of the Church and the old sciences and lead to social and political progress, maybe human reason could work to the improvement of Jews as well. The writer, Christian Wilhelm von Dohm, in his tract, *Ueber die burgerliche Verbesserung der Juden* (Concerning the Civic Betterment of the Jews), acknowledged up front all of the common prejudices against the Jews, but then suggested that the reason for these failings was precisely the tangle of medieval laws and restrictions that the governments and the Church had imposed on them. Dohm further proclaimed that "if this reasoning is correct, then we have found in the oppression and in the restricted occupation of the Jews the true source of their corruption. Then we have discovered also at the same time the means of healing this corruption and of making the Jews better men and useful citizens."[1] Dohm concluded that if the Jews were released from the network of medieval restrictions placed upon them and if they were allowed to live like all other citizens in the modern state, with full human rights and dignity, then they would naturally improve. The theory was that if Jews were given a chance to participate fully in their society as equals, they would respond to their new conditions and become decent, law-abiding, and productive citizens. In short, the decrepitude of Jewry was due not to some innate characteristic of the religion or its people, but to its environment.

Although this argument grew straight out of Enlightenment scientific optimism, it did not receive enthusiastic support, either from the general population or from the Jewish community. From the point of view of the outside population, emancipation meant new competition and loss of political power and social status. From the point of view of the Jews, this call for change presented both promises and challenges. There is absolutely no question that as European society modernized, the Jews were being left behind to stagnate in ghettoes, that is, in pockets of poverty, overcrowding, and intellectual obscurantism. Many younger Jews were more than anxious to see the call of Dohm and others implemented so that they could leave the cramped quarters of the ghetto, be freed of medieval restrictions, and be allowed to participate in the alluring and modern world of the eighteenth and nineteenth centuries. But it was also clear that there was going to be a price to pay. Along with the rights of citizenship came the obligations of citizenship. Jews would have to give up their "Judaic" character and become Europeans, even model Europeans, of various sorts—Frenchmen, Austrians, Germans, and so forth.

For example, in his Toleranzpatent (Decree of Toleration) of 1782, the Hapsburg emperor, Joseph II abolished many of the old medieval restrictions on Jews, such as the requirement to wear special badges and the obligation to pay a special poll tax. But the decree also enacted rules designed to encourage the newly emancipated Jews to assimilate into Austrian society. These rules included discouraging the use of Hebrew and Yiddish in communal affairs in favor of using German, abolishing Jewish schools in favor of Jewish attendance at public schools, abolishing Jewish judicial autonomy in favor of accepting the judicial competence of imperial courts, and opening up trades and professions once closed to Jews while making them subject to civil obligations such as the military draft. While for individual Jews these early reforms opened up whole new worlds of possibilities and promises, they also wreaked havoc on the Jewish communal structure.

So from the very beginning, it was clear that civic emancipation was going to involve a serious tradeoff: The Jews were expected to stop being "Jewish" and to become instead full-fledged (even Christian?) Austrians. This general attitude may be best summed up by a statement given by the count of Clermont-Tonnerre a few years later at the revolutionary French National Assembly of December 23, 1789. On that occasion, in which the "Jewish Question" was being debated, he announced, that as far as he was concerned, "[T]he Jews should be denied everything as a nation, but granted everything as individuals."[2] In other words, Jews cold enjoy the full rights of Frenchmen, but only if they *became* Frenchmen and stopped being Jews.

There could hardly be a more dramatic example of the logic that drove this internal debate than the Sanhedrin that Napoleon convened in 1806. At issue was the still unsettled question of the legal status of the

Jews of postrevolutionary France. The Revolution had, of course, dissolved all the old medieval legal structures on which the monarchy and aristocracy were based. It had also disestablished the Roman Catholic Church, thus creating a secular society, at least in name. But the Jewish community living on French soil was still anomalous. Were these people Frenchmen in the same way as their neighbors, or did their separate religion, history, social structure, and so forth, mean that they were not French at all and had no intention (or ability?) of being so? Were they, in other words, a separate and distinct nation living within France, as the Zionists would later assert? The conundrum presented by the Jews remained unresolved for over a decade.

Finally, in 1806, Napoleon decided to cut the Gordian knot, as it were, and make a determination once and for all about the status of the Jews living on French territory: Either the Jews would have to give up their exclusivism and become French in all regards and thereby earn the right to be accorded all the privileges and duties of French citizenship, or they could chose to maintain their own corporate (or national) identity, with the consequence that they could not be eligible for French citizenship. To make this determination, a representative group of Jewish leaders was convened in Paris on July 29, 1806, to answer a number of questions, the answers to which would guide Napoleon in his decision. The choice of the name Sanhedrin was not accidental, but it showed Napoleon's deeper logic. Just as a counsel of rabbis in ancient times had declared Judaism a separate people within Christian Rome, so now another Sanhedrin would be needed to undo that decision.

The questions posed to the group clearly showed that the price of French citizenship would be the complete dismantlement of Jewish self-government as decreed supposedly by the ancient Sandhedrin. The questions to be decided included: Is divorce allowed by the Jewish religion? Is divorce valid, when not pronounced by courts of justice and by virtue of laws in contradiction with the French code? Can a Jewess marry a Christian, or a Jew a Christian woman? In the eyes of Jews, are Frenchmen considered brethren or strangers? Do the Jews born in France, and treated by the law as French citizens, consider France their country? What kind of police jurisdiction do rabbis have among Jews?[3] By providing the answers that Napoleon made it clear he wanted to hear, the Sanhedrin would gain full civil rights for the Jews of France, but in the process it would dismantle rabbinic Judaism. Here, in its most explicit form, the delegates had to face head on the logic of emancipation.

The logic of the Sanhedrin, if not its dramatic form, was playing itself out all over Europe throughout the nineteenth century. Jewish responses to these initiatives and their implications can be divided into three, broad, though hardly homogeneous, categories. First, there were those Jews who found it inconceivable to ignore the new opportunities being opened up to them. The younger generation in particular was powerfully drawn to the seductions of the outside world. Leaving Judaism with its medieval legal, social, and religious traditions and restrictions was a price they were more than ready to pay to enter European society. A second approach went in exactly the opposite direction, rejecting the Enlightenment and the emancipation and all that went with it precisely to hold on to the covenant with God and avoid apostasy. The third option tried to find a middle way, a compromise that would allow Jews to leave the ghetto in all its manifestations and yet forge a way of being Jewish that maintained the core values of the religion. Each of these strategies had its own view of human rights, which will be examined below.

The Paris Sanhedrin illustrates the first Jewish communal response to the Enlightenment. Ultimately, the assembled Jewish notables in Paris crafted answers that gave Napoleon what he wanted to hear and so cleared the way for extending legal emancipation, citizenship, to the Jews of France. Given the choice of Judaism or French citizenship, the notables of the Sanhedrin had chosen French citizenship! The Jews represented by the Sanhedrin seem to have accepted the situation with little further ado. Non-Jews, too, saw the Sanhedrin and its aftermath as a crucial turning point for the future direction of Europe. For the conservatives (the old aristocracy, the landed gentry, the Church) it was of course a catastrophe, while for the liberals and secular modernists, it was a victory.

The readiness to leave the world of medieval Judaism behind was illustrated again and again by the Jews of Central Europe. The poet Heinrich Heine, justifying his conversion to Christianity, summed up nicely the attitude of many of his fellow Jews by noting that "the baptismal certificate is the admission ticket into European civilization."[4] Virtually a whole generation of Jews chose this route out of the ghetto, some with formal conversion to Christianity as was the case with Heine, some without formal conversion but with nonetheless benign abandonment of most, if not all, of Jewish religious and cultural practices.

Then, there were those Jews who saw the outside world as the allurement of the devil, designed to draw Jews away from the covenant and from their longed-for redemption. In this view, the Enlightenment was nothing other than a modern-day Babylon, intent on the destruction of the Jews, if not by war, than by promoting apostasy and assimilation. For them, the Sanhedrin was their worst nightmare and showed starkly what was at stake. The Sanhedrin, in their eyes, had sold out the covenant with God for the blandishments of the world. This group, comprising maybe 10 percent of the Jewish population including nearly all of the rabbis, fought emancipation with the vigor of the Maccabees fighting off Greek culture two thousand years before. For them, the offers of Joseph II, Napoleon, and others represented nothing more than a switch in tactics. Traditionalist rabbis warned their communities over and over that even the slightest acceptance of emancipation was nothing less than the first step down the slippery slope into apostasy. As one German Orthodox rabbi, Moshe Sofer* (also known as the Hatam Sofer), is reputed to have said, citing Talmud, "all what is new is forbidden," no matter how halachically unimportant.[5] Granted that this was, and is, an extreme view, it captures the central spirit of the reaction to the Enlightenment and an appreciation of the dangers inherent in the emancipation. In light of the massive abandonment of the Jewish tradition as illustrated by the Paris Sanhedrin and Heine, the traditionalist community found itself forced to act on to the defensive, having to exert tighter control on the remaining Jews in order to preserve some sort of faithful remnant.

The price of emancipation was rejected not only on religious grounds, but also, ironically, on national grounds. Unlike the Orthodox, many Jews saw the danger of emancipation not as a threat to the Jewish *religion*, but as a threat to the existence of the Jewish *people*. What resonated with this group of thinkers was the nineteenth-century Romantic notion of the *volk* or the "nation." That is, many Jews may have been perfectly willing to give up traditionalist rabbinic religion on the grounds of Enlightenment thinking, but at the same time they could not see themselves as French, German, Russian, or Polish nationals in the enlightenment sense of that term. Their problem with the Sanhedrin was not its displacement of traditional Judaism, but its turning of Jews into Frenchmen. In this view, if the Jews were to accept emancipation, they had to insist on their right to do so as *Jews*, not on the basis of being absorbed into some other nationality. It is this stance that gave rise of Zionism, which will be examined more closely in chapter 7. Moses Hess,* an early Zionist thinker, captured this stance precisely when he wrote in 1862, nearly a century after Joseph II's edict, that "If it be true that the emancipation of the Jews in exile is incompatible with Jewish nationality, then Jews ought to forego [emancipation]."⁶ It is surely one of the ironies of the time that an ideology opposed to emancipation was framed in concepts and terms that grew directly out of the Enlightenment itself—the Enlightenment idea of the nation-state.

These two options—accepting emancipation even if it meant giving up Judaism, and rejecting emancipation in order to preserve Judaism, or the Jewish people—represent the two extremes. There was a third way—that of compromise—that was taking shape, especially in the German-speaking lands. This third group wanted to be free from the ghettoes and the melange of humiliating medieval restrictions they imposed, but it also wanted citizenship in their lands of residence while preserving the right to remain faithful and practicing Jews (whatever that might now mean). How to accomplish this (assuming it is possible at all) was, and still is, a central existential question for the modern Jew. One answer, of course, was Zionism, the creation of a Jewish homeland in which one could be free, modern, and Jewish all at the same time. Another much more practical solution was to find a way to redefine, or reform, the Jewish religion in such a way that one could continue practicing Judaism in one's private life while openly participating in the larger surrounding culture in the public sphere. Judah Leb Gordon* expressed this sentiment in *Hakitza Ammi* (Wake up, O my People) in 1863: "Be a Jew in your tent, and a man outside."

This third approach, which eventually became the foundation for a variety of modern Judaisms (Reform, Conservative, Reconstructionism, even modern Orthodoxy to an extent, to name the most prominent), had to face a double, and in some sense internally inconsistent, challenge. On the one hand it had to fashion a form of Jewish life that was arguably consistent with the covenant, albeit stripped of its medieval trappings. On the other hand, it had to present the skeptical outside world with an individual who remained Jewish "in his tent" but was nonetheless a model citizen of the state and the world in public (as, say, the response of the Paris Sanhedrin demanded). To this end, a whole movement of modern Jewish religious thought developed, especially in the German-speaking lands, to articulate just what such a modern Judaism should be like. Given the slow, often incomplete, and tentative nature of the emancipation process throughout the nineteenth century and into the twentieth century, the task faced by these thinkers was an ongoing, urgent, complex, and controversial enterprise. Nonetheless, these thinkers, who often had both rabbinic and secular university training, were able to fashion a variety of modern Judaisms that have succeeded in claiming the bulk of practicing Jews to this day. It is to these people, and their views on human rights in particular, that we consider in the rest of this chapter.

Human Rights in Modern Judaism

Modernist Jewish thinkers had to address two audiences at once. To the outside world, they had to present a Judaism that was ready, willing, and able to promote good citizenship, as Dohm had insisted was possible, and to which the Paris Sanhedrin had committed the Jews of France. To this end, they had to overcome an attitude toward Jewry that was deeply ingrained in Western Europe through two thousand years of Church teaching. The roots of this attitude were already established in the writings of Roman conservatives such as Tacitus and Apion, as was pointed out in chapter 3, concerning the Greco-Roman world. This train of thought had been carried forward into the New Testament by the early Church Fathers and so had become part and parcel of Christian teaching and culture. Aversion to Judaism, and thus to Jews—and to Jewish emancipation—persisted right through the Enlightenment process, although along the way it transmogrified from theological anti-Judaism to secular, racial, and national anti-Semitism.

Even such major Enlightenment figures and advocates as François-Marie Arouet (Voltaire), who was bitterly critical of Christianity, did not hesitate to defame Jews and Judaism as well. Although he did much to pave the way intellectually for the emancipation of Jews on rational grounds, he also regarded Jews as superstitiously religious and having an "invincible aversion" to others. He concludes one essay with: "[W]e find in them only an ignorant and barbarous people, who have long united the most sordid avarice with the most detestable superstition and the most invincible hatred for every people by whom they are tolerated and enriched. Still, we ought not to burn them."[7] In short, there were many writers like Voltaire who were deeply committed to the Enlightenment and its values, but who still held traditional attitudes when it came to the Jews. It was this long tradition, then, taken for granted by even the most ardent Enlightenment thinkers, that presented Jewish theologians and philosophers of the nineteenth and twentieth centuries with one audience that they had to counter. In response, they had to show that Judaism did not preach hatred of all others but in fact had a deep regard for the sanctity of human life, dignity, and rights, for Jews and non-Jews alike. This had to be done, of course, in the language of rationality and reason that was the common currency of the Enlightenment. It short, Judaism had to be made into a modern, rational religion that preached a universal ethic.

The other audience was, of course, the Jewish community itself. It was hardly sufficient to convince the outside world to accept Jews on equal terms if Jews were not prepared to live this theory in practice. If Jews refused the emancipation out of "hatred of mankind," as the Orthodox were seen as doing, or if they saw acceptance of the Enlightenment as possible only through the abandonment of Judaism, as Heine did, or if they insisted on maintaining their own national and exclusivist identity, as the early Zionists did, then all the arguments of this third way would be revealed as hollow theory and meaningless rhetoric. The Jews themselves had to be convinced that there was a Judaism other than the traditional one, one that was able to accept emancipation without giving up its essence. The fashioners of a modern Judaism certainly had their work cut out for them.

It is nearly impossible to talk about such religious debates and choices in the Jewish world without mentioning Baruch Spinoza.* Spinoza was part of the vibrant, seventeenth-century Sephardic community of Amsterdam, a community made up of the descendants of Jews expelled from the Iberian peninsula in the late fifteenth and early sixteenth centuries. Seventeenth-century Amsterdam was caught up in its own way in the European-wide struggle—military, intellectual, and theological—between the forces of Protestant Reformation on one side and the Counter-Reformation of Roman Catholicism on the other. Although Jews were attracted to the Netherlands because of its religious tolerance, their presence only added fuel to the religious arguments already being waged, especially since the refugee Spanish Jews had already been heavily influenced by Catholicism. It was into this maelstrom—rife with theological debates not only between Catholics and Protestants, and of course between Catholics and Protestants and the Jews, but also within the Jewish community itself (between the Sephardic and the Ashkenazic traditions)—that Spinoza was born in 1632. He was an outstanding student and somewhere in his training, whether with Jesuits or dissident members of the Jewish community, Spinoza came to question the truths of religion altogether, and of Judaism in particular.[8] In his major opus, The *Tractatus Theologico-Politicus* (published in 1670), Spinoza argued forcefully that the Bible could not have been divinely revealed. In particular, he denied the Mosaic authorship of the Bible, repudiated the validity of biblical prophecy, and contended that all the miracles recorded in the Bible and subsequent Jewish literature were not to be taken as supernatural events at all, but as natural occurrences (if they happened at all!), subject to rational explanations. This led him, finally, to a comprehensive critique of all Jewish ritual and ceremonial law and a call for all religious life to be examined and shaped on the basis of reason alone. Obviously none of this was accepted passively by the leadership of the Amsterdam Jewish community. Spinoza's thought was well known, and he had in fact been excommunicated in 1656, more than a dozen years before the *Tractatus* even appeared. A good example of his attitude is contained in a letter written to a friend, Albert Burgh, who had converted to Roman Catholicism. Baruch Spinoza's writing reverberates with his disdain for the rationality of all religion in general:

> But you, who presume that you have at last found the best religion, or rather the best men, on whom you have pinned our credulity, you *"who know that they are the best among all who have taught, do now teach, or shall in the future teach other religions. Have you examined all religions, ancient as well as modern, taught, here and in India and everywhere throughout the world? And, if you have duly examined them, how do you know that you have chosen the best"* since you can <u>Give No Reason for the Faith that Is In You</u>? But you will say, that you acquiesce in the inward testimony of the Spirit of God, while the rest of mankind are ensnared and deceived by the prince of evil spirits. But all those outside the pale of the Roman Catholic Church can with equal right proclaim of their own creed what you proclaim of yours.[9]

Baruch Spinoza went on to argue that one could lead a fully moral life on the basis of reason alone, and, in fact, he tried to make his own life living proof of that. Obviously Spinoza's attack on religious coercion and triumphalism in favor of purely rational inquiry, while an important forerunner of the Enlightenment, was hardly of use for a Jewish community concerned with its own survival. In fact, so powerful and thoroughgoing were Spinoza's critiques that there has been some discussion as to whether, in the end, he can really be considered a *Jewish* thinker at all.

Spinoza is important in this discussion because his thoughts and writings were both a precedent and a bane for later nineteenth-century reformers. His critique of the credulity of rabbinic authorities was an important forerunner and even precedent for later attempts to reform traditional (that is, rabbinic) Jewish ritual practice. The strategy of German reformers was to show that the Talmudic law of rabbinic Judaism was not the essence of Judaism, but merely a layer of medieval incrustations, forced on the community by its social situation. Thus, Judaism could drop rabbinic law (as the Paris Sanhedrin had) without destroying the essence of Judaism. So Spinoza's critique of rabbinic legalisms was welcomed. But the reformers also had to convince the Jewish community that Judaism without the Talmud was still authentic Judaism, and for this they returned to the very foundation of the Jewish tradition, namely, the basic moral law of the Bible as revealed by Moses and encapsulated in the Ten Commandments. But Spinoza's attacks on the Bible and all "revealed" (as opposed to rational) religion proved to be troublesome. So while reformers admired Spinoza for his attacks on "Rabbinism," they could hardly celebrate his attacks on the Bible and revelation. Spinoza, in essence, showed how delicate an operation it would be to eliminate Talmud on rational grounds without also bringing the Bible, a lesson not lost on either the promoters or the opponents of reform.

Despite Voltaire's and Spinoza's deep antireligious sentiments, it is important to keep in mind that there was room within the Enlightenment for religion, assuming that the religion in question was appropriately "rational." The challenge was to give this religion expression. The first Jewish writer after Spinoza to take up this challenge in a serious and public way was Moses Mendelssohn.* Born in Dessau, Germany, in 1729, he reached young adulthood as the matter of Jewish emancipation began genuinely to surface in Central Europe, as the first tentative regulations allowing limited Jewish participation in civic life in certain areas began to appear in the 1750s.[10] Mendelssohn emerged as an ardent champion of Jewish civil rights while at the same time advocating within the Jewish community for the abandonment of Jewish separatism. Yet, unlike Spinoza, he remained loyal to rabbinic Judaism and maintained a traditional Jewish lifestyle until his death. He thus showed that "civic betterment" and adherence to traditional Judaism were not incompatible but could coexist. Later in life he became friends with one of the leading Enlightenment literary figures of Germany, Gotthold Ephraim Lessing. For Lessing, Mendelssohn was a model of the "perfect" Jew: true to his religion, yet a rational, compassionate, and community-spirited man. It is widely assumed that Mendelssohn was, in fact, the inspiration for the praiseworthy Jew, Nathan, in Lessing's play, *Nathan the Wise*. For the Jews, Mendelssohn served as a kind of role model of how one could be German and Jewish at the same time.

Mendelssohn worked hard to bring his unique synthesis to the German Jewish masses. One strategy was to translate the Bible into (proper, contemporary) German as a way to help the Jews of Germany assimilate linguistically into the world around them while at the same time giving them greater access to their own (biblical) tradition. He also entered into conversation and correspondence with some of the leading Christian German thinkers of the day, with whom he constantly fought for the acceptance of Jews *as Jews*. Yet in many ways he also was a role model for the dangers of this approach. While Mendelssohn showed that it was possible to be a modern Enlightenment man and still remain a Jew, all of his children ended up converting to Christianity.

Part of Mendelssohn's program was to show, in a sense, that Dohm and others like him were right in claiming that if restrictions on Jews were removed, Jews could grow up to become model productive citizens, and he offered himself as a prime example. The terms in which he framed his argument were, as one might expect, very much those of the Enlightenment's concern with human rights. Mendelssohn warned at one point, "Concentrate on what men should or should not do; judge them wisely by their actions; and let us retain the freedom of thought and speech with which the Father of all mankind has endowed us as our inalienable heritage and immutable right."[11] The danger in this argument, of course, was that Jews would thus see this as an argument for abandoning Judaism entirely, either in favor of Christianity or in favor of Enlightenment secular rationality. To counter this possibility, Mendelssohn took pains to dissuade Jews from leaving their ancestral religion as part of the process of accepting emancipation. Maybe what can be regarded as his most significant statement in this regard is his book, *Jerusalem, or On Religious Power and Judaism*, which was published in 1783 in response to the public challenge of a Zurich pastor, John Lavater, for Mendelssohn either to justify on the basis of reason his decision to remain Jewish or to convert to Christianity. Mendelssohn's response was a model expression of early Enlightenment convictions about basic human rights, especially the right to freely exercise one's reason and to express one's thoughts. No religion, he argued, should use coercion to force its members to believe any particular way. In fact, the modern world requires just the opposite, namely, the mutual respect of all religions for each other since it was through reason alone that all people had equal access to truth. But that did not mean that Judaism was useless. In fact, what made Judaism a model, and maybe therefore even superior to Lavater's Christianity, was that Judaism does not force its adherents to accept certain doctrines or dogmas. Rather, its uniqueness lies in its divinely revealed code of legal, ritual, and moral law. That is, Judaism most closely fits the ideal that an enlightened society needs, a religion that supports social values but does not restrict intellectual inquiry. As he puts matters:

> Neither state nor church is authorized to judge in religious matters; for the members of society could not have granted that right to them by any contract whatsoever. The state, to be sure, is to see to it from afar that no doctrines are propagated which are inconsistent with the public welfare; doctrines which, like atheism and Epicureanism, undermine the foundation on which the felicity of social life is based. Let Plutarch and Bayle inquire ever so much whether a state might not be better off with atheism than with superstition. Let them count and compare ever so much the afflictions which have hitherto befallen and still threaten to befall the human race from these sources of misery. At bottom, there is nothing else than inquiring whether a slow fever is more fatal than a sudden one.[12]

In short, religious coercion by the government (or any other body, say, the Church) was to be avoided, but religion itself (freely and rationally adhered to) was still to be seen as an important part of the body politic. Thus, Jews were not only to maintain their religion while accepting emancipation, they were, in fact, in the position of being able to use their Judaism for the betterment of the social society altogether. In this they could serve as models for others as to what the Enlightenment was all about. "And even today, no better advice than this can be given to the House of Jacob: Adopt the mores and constitution of the country in which you find yourself, but be steadfast in upholding the religion of your fathers, too."[13]

So in the end, the enlightened civil society should allow religious people, including especially, of course, Jews, to have full civic rights while according them room to observe their own religious laws in accordance with their own reason and conscience. Mendelssohn was fully prepared to live with the consequences, namely a multiplicity of religions, provided all respected each other. What did reign supreme was freedom of human thought and expression, as Spinoza had already said, but in contrast to Spinoza, Mendelssohn maintained that freedom included the freedom to choose Judaism and all its ceremonial rules, even while one was free to raise questions about the revelatory basis of them all. In fact, religion, really contrary to Spinoza's thinking, had something crucial to contribute to the building of a modern civil society. For Mendelssohn, Enlightenment and Judaism not only could coexist, but should coexist, and were even able to reinforce each other.

The Mendelssohnian experience puts the theme addressed by this book into a certain perspective. In a way, the kinds of human rights that the Enlightenment was advocating were foreign to Judaism. Human rights in the sense used today is, after all, a *modern* conception. There is, for example, no real equivalent in either biblical or rabbinic Hebrew for the modern concept of human rights. To move to a theory of rights in the Enlightenment sense entails as a logical consequence giving up the Jewish communal tradition, as the discussion in chapters 4 and 5 has shown. The question Spinoza posed and Mendelssohn tried to answer was how one was to both adopt the new Enlightenment ideas of individual human rights while maintaining the halachic tradition, which up to this point had defined Judaism as a communal covenant of obligation?[14] An individual like Mendelssohn might be able to do this in his own life, but as the conversion of his children shows, the compromise was fragile and often unable to survive the transfer from one generation to the next. But the social and political situation of the Jews required that just such a transmission had to happen if Judaism was to avoid remaining a ghetto religion or becoming extinct within a generation or two.

By the beginning of the nineteenth century, emancipation at its various levels was fast becoming a legal and social reality in much of Central and Western Europe. For those committed to the Mendelssohnian strategy of accommodation, success depended on proper education of both children and adults. The need was to prepare Jews for life in the world outside the ghetto, yet with a sufficiently deep attachment and understanding of Judaism so that they were prepared to continue its traditions of their own free will. Mendelssohn's translation of the Hebrew Bible into German was the first step in this direction. Other schemes emerged as the process progressed. One strategy took the form of newspapers or magazines that were designed to educate newly emancipated Jews in the ways, wisdom, science, and etiquette of the modern world while encouraging them at the same time to maintain traditional Jewish values. One of the earliest such publications was *Shulamith*, which in its second edition (1808) announced that "Enlightenment offers us the correct vantage point from which we must view our obligation, which originate from these relationships. It teaches us that serving one's fellow also means serving God, that loving him also means loving God. . . . Enlightenment teaches us that we must think liberally and act humanely, not offend anyone who thinks differently or worships differently than we, but rather follow the example of the Creator, who embraces and preserves the entire host of Creation with the eternal bonds of love."[15] One can hardly find a clearer statement of Enlightenment religion, even among liberal Protestants. What this publication enunciates is what would later become the core theme of nineteenth- and twentieth-century liberal Judaism, namely, that just as emancipation demands that Jews be treated humanely and as equals, so it calls for Jews to adopt these same attitudes toward others. Further, in adopting these attitudes, Jews are not abandoning Judaism but are, in fact, fulfilling its highest calling. For *Shulamith* and its sister publications, Judaism emerged as the Enlightenment religion *par excellence*.

By the mid-nineteenth century this third way of Mendelssohnian accommodation had become the position of choice for the vast majority of Central and Western European Jews. A good example of how this approach unfolded can be found in the Second Zunz Lecture of the Menorah Society delivered at the University of Chicago in December 1920 by Louis Ginzberg.* Entitled "Jewish Thought as Reflected in the Halakah," the lecture looks at two arcane rulings in Jewish law to show that they, in fact, reflect broader humane values.[16] One is a discussion at the beginning of Mishnah Betzah between Shammai and Hillel on the question of whether an egg laid by a chicken on a holiday may be eaten. The point is that in traditional Talmudic law, food is not to be prepared on a holiday, but must be made ready ahead of time so as to preserve the holy sanctity of the day. Here the Talmud, in its inimitable way, finds a gray area to test the limits of the logic. What do we do about an egg that was laid (prepared?) on the holiday: Is it kosher (since no human labor was involved in preparing it) or is it not to be eaten because it was produced on that day? The ensuing discussion about the egg has been often used as an example of the casuistry and downright frivolity of the Talmud and its legalistic method.

Ginzberg argues that what is really at issue is the question of intention. Do we look only at the outcome of a certain action or do we look at the intent, into the heart of the agent. The latter view is really what wins out in the halacah. He backs up this reading with a second series of examples drawn from the laws of marriage (specifically Babylonian Talmud Kiddushin 49b). A man who marries on the condition that he is a just person is allowed to be married even if he is known to have acted unjustly. Why this allowance? Because we assume that in his heart the prospective groom is repentant and just, even if his past behavior seems to reveal him to be an unjust person. So, Ginzberg argues, the real point of the halacah is not in its details about this and that but its assessment about deeper human issues, and in particular, in these cases, how one is to judge our neighbors—according to their intentions or their actual deeds. The wedding case in particular shows that Jews must always start with the best assumptions; assuming that good intentions have gone awry. This, as Ginzberg would argue, is a lesson not in legal casuistry, but a moral lesson for all humankind.

Ginzberg's enlightened, and apologetic, view—that Jewish law teaches us that Jews are to assume the essential goodness of people even if their actions sometimes seem bad—hardly stands alone. As the century wore on, more systematic "theologies" of Judaism were written, all of which stressed the universal message of justice, love, and human rights that were understood to be inherent in Judaism, as the two Talmudic passages previously cited show, albeit in a clumsy way. One of the best examples of this is *Jewish Theology*, written by Kaufmann Kohler, a German-born rabbi who immigrated to the United States in 1869 and eventually became president of Hebrew Union College, the Reform Jewish seminary in Cincinnati, Ohio. In his book published in 1918, Kohler presented Judaism as a kind of liberal Protestantism without Jesus. He strongly believed in scientific progress and was even convinced that it was the task of the Jews to lead the world into the new, scientific messianic era that was dawning. In the decades that followed, Reform Jews in America continued to become assimilated and Americanized, to the point that many of the great synagogues of the day had their most popular religious services on Sunday (although they performed the daily, not the Sabbath, liturgy on those days). Yet these synagogues continued to raise a generation that regarded itself as Jewish, even if it regarded Jewishness as consisting in little more than participation in social action and fulfilling the call of the biblical prophets to construct a just and compassionate society.

"MODERN" JEWISH ORTHODOXY

To some within the Mendelssohnian tradition, developments within the Reform movement had gone so far as to bring their essential Judaism into question (Sunday services, removal of Hebrew from the prayer book, abandonment of the laws of keeping kosher). It was not clear at all that the next generation of such congregations would remain Jews (remember Mendelssohn's own children!), and in fact the rate of intermarriage was high and growing. To counter this, a kind of modern Orthodoxy took shape. This movement, associated with Samson Raphael Hirsch,* was opposed to the abandonment of rabbinic halachah by the Reform movement but was still open to the social and intellectual life of the day (as opposed to the separatist Orthodox who rejected the emancipation altogether). Hirsch, like Mendelssohn, put forth a spirited defense of both traditional Jewish practice and adherence to the covenant in its received rabbinic form, while still participating fully in modern (meaning German) life. One of his earliest works is *The Nineteen Letters*, published in 1836, which established him, at the age of only twenty-six, as one of the premier spokespersons of a kind of "enlightened" Orthodoxy.[17] The book is composed of a fictitious exchange of letters between a master (the young rabbi-philosopher Naphtali) and a young intellectual (Benjamin). In the letters, as in his later writings, Hirsch strongly upholds the rationality of following traditional Jewish halachah. What is interesting is that as early as the 1830s, even Orthodox Jewish thinkers had to use Enlightenment tools to speak to their audiences. His position is remarkably compatible with the much more secular *Shulamith*.

Of particular interest here is letter no. sixteen, in which Hirsch addressed the question of emancipation. Unlike nonmodern Orthodox rabbis, Hirsch saw the liberation of the Jews as a positive sign and a golden opportunity, not just for the Jews, but for all humankind, who could now see the covenant conceived of by God lived in its fullest glory:

> Summon up before your mental vision the picture of such an Israel, dwelling in freedom among the nations, and striving to attain to its ideal. Picture every son of Israel a respected and influential priest of righteousness and love, disseminating among the nations not specific Judaism—for proselytism is forbidden—but pure humanity. What a mighty impulse to progress, what a luminary and staff in the gloomy days of the Middle Ages would Israel have been then, if its own sin and the insanity of

the nations had not rendered such a *Galuth* impossible. How impressive, how sublime it would have been if, in the midst of a race that adored only power, possessions and enjoyment, there had lived quietly and publicly human beings for a different sort, who beheld in material possessions only the means for practicing justice and love towards all, a people whose minds, imbued with the wisdom and truth of the Law, maintained simple, straight-forward views, and emphasized them for themselves and others in expressive, vivid symbolic acts.[18]

The point that Hirsch was trying to make was that the specific covenant and its laws given to Israel were not for Israel alone but were to be a beacon for the rest of the world ("a light unto the nations" in Isaiah's phrase). In this interpretation, the emancipation of the Jews from the ghettoes was not to be seen as a chance for Israel to get out from under the "yoke of the law," but to the contrary, as a God-given opportunity for Israel to show that the law was really a model for human behavior toward one another. Thus, the Sabbath was not to be seen as an excuse for sloth, as the ancient Romans had described it, but as a sign of the dignity of the working man, who by rights was to have a day of rest.

In all of his letters, and especially in his later commentary on the Bible (*Horev*, published in Altona by J. F. Hammerich in 1838), Hirsch constantly stressed the symbolic value of the halachah for promoting human dignity and human rights. Leading a traditional Jewish life was a sign and symbol to all those around of the presence of the Creator and of the values of love and justice the Creator wished all mankind to embrace and practice. It is hard to imagine Mendelssohn taking issue with any of this. Judaism was about God, Revelation, covenant, and above all, human rights and dignity.

The more moderate form of Orthodoxy heralded by Hirsch continued to draw adherents. For this emerging community of modern or moderate Orthodox, the issue was not a simple Manichaean conflict between some pure halachah on the one hand and the vapid religion of Reform on the other. Rather, going back to Mendelssohn himself, the message was that the halachah had always to engage in constructive dialogue with the outside world. The two were always in interaction, a microcosm of God's incessant interaction with the Creation. Thus, the Jew was called on to live according to the principles of the halachah while interacting with the world. Through such interaction, the holiness of the halachah could be transmitted to the world and positively transform it while the outside

world with its science and philosophy could help the Jew better understand and carry out his halachic task. For such moderate Orthodox, human rights outside the Jewish community *did* exist. In fact, as the
reformers said, the Jews, with their inheritance of divine law, were charged
not only with living halachic values, but with also bringing these values
into the world. The difference was that the Hirschian Orthodox were
also prepared to learn lessons from the outside world and bring these lessons into their understanding of the halachah.

As the nineteenth century gave way to the twentieth, several alternative methods evolved for carrying forward this synthesis. A discussion
bringing some of these possibilities to the surface is contained in the report of a Israel-Diaspora conference on this theme published under the title, "Judaic Sources of Human Rights" (1989). One option, put forward
by Professor Avi Ravitzky of the Department of Jewish Thought at the
Hebrew University of Jerusalem, is to appeal to meta-halachic principles
within the halachah itself.[19] That is, in his view certain principles like
darchei shalom (in the interests of peace), *pikuach nefesh* (saving a human
life), and *kevod habriyot* (human dignity) can be invoked from within the
halachic system to enact a law or effect a change. Also, our understanding
of these principles, and how they are to be applied, can certainly be informed by the outside world. Another alternative is to allow outside values to play a role in rabbinic discussions. Thus, Professor Hava
Lazarus-Yafeh of Hebrew University's Department of Islamic Studies has
stated that "mechanisms exist within the halachah which enable it to in-
gest values that come from outside. This ingestion was done in the past,
during the period of the Second Temple and during the period when Jews
lived under the influence of Islam. This is seen also, for example, in the
writings of Rav Saadia Gaon* and the Ramban."[20]

Rabbi Irving Greenberg opened up a third possibility, namely, the overarching principle that we are all human beings and thus owe each other a
certain level of mutual respect. He refers in particular to the medieval
ban against Jews fraternizing with non-Jews. His argument is that this ban
reflects the specific realities and social structures of the Middle Ages but
is now out of date and in fact not helpful but dysfunctional. We simply
live in a world, says Greenberg, in which we have to interact with each
other, and not merely for reasons of expediency or *darchei shalom*.[21] The
halachah has to, as it were, respond to a kind of Kantian imperative.

The conference closed with Justice Menachen Elon noting that when
the Hatam Sofer allowed a Jewish doctor to treat a non-Jewish patient, he

did so on the basis of *darchei shalom*, by which he meant preventing hostility from the stronger Gentile community. Elon says he would make the same argument, but for him *darchei shalom* means that the Torah teaches that all people should be treated fairly and justly. So the same meta-halachic term is interpreted and given different meaning by different people at different times.[22] Elon's claim is that the outside world has helped those Jews within the halachic system better understand such meta-halachic concepts as *darchei shalom*. For these and like thinkers, Mendelssohn held the key to how Judaism should respond to modernity, Enlightenment and emancipation. The difference is the extent to which the halachah is still able to be maintained in an authentic manner.

Hirsch's synthesis took hold mostly in Western and Central Europe. Acceptance of the Western Enlightenment faded as one traveled into Eastern Europe. Nonetheless, it should be noted that even the Jews of Eastern Europe, while more traditionalist across the board than their West European coreligionists, were hardly a monolithic block, unaffected by developments in the West. While on the surface rabbinic Judaism continued to function in the eastern lands, in fact, a whole new approach to ethics and moral education was emerging in the Eastern European yeshivahs. The *Musar* movement (the Hebrew word *Musar* can mean both chastisement and ethics) took shape primarily around the teaching of Israel Lipkin Salanter* in the middle of the nineteenth century. His concern was that the traditional yeshivah education of Eastern Europe was turning out brilliant halachic scholars who had no sense of moral or spiritual virtue. There was, as it were, no fear of God, only halachic expertise. What Salanter wanted to do was find a way to renew the spiritual and moral traditions, and in so doing, halt the moral degeneration he detected in the traditional Jewish communities of Eastern Europe, a degeneration brought about by a deteriorating economic situation and the stultifying focus of education on halachic method alone. In short, he wanted to inject into the educational system an opportunity for moral reflection and growth. In this he was undoubtedly influenced by Enlightenment ideas (or *haskalah*, as it was known in Hebrew in Eastern Europe) although he rarely used the language of the Western Enlightenment.

His work began through a program of public lectures or sermons and then eventually to the founding of a school-like institution, the *Bet Musar*. But the older population seemed less receptive to these ideas than Salanter had hoped. He thus began to shift his focus to the younger, student population of the yeshivas, hoping to be able to shape the character of the students earlier on. Under his relentless prodding and leadership, and with some opposition from traditional yeshiva heads, the reading and discussion of traditional Jewish ethical literature were gradually introduced into the curricula of most traditional yeshivas. Over time, different approaches developed for nurturing moral development in these institutions. Many yeshivas set aside a regular time for communal reading and discussion of moral literature from the Jewish tradition (the *Slobodka* style). Other yeshivot adopted a more extreme method that often included strict rules of abstinence and even self-humiliation (the so-called *Navorodek* style). The two different styles obviously reflected different theories of the human self and how best it was to be shaped. In either case, the readings, discussions, and activities all took place within the confines of traditional Jewish texts and thought. Although these technical discussions were internal to the traditional side of the Jewish spectrum, they are nonetheless significant because they show how deeply Enlightenment sentiments had penetrated the Eastern European Jewish community, even its more traditional elements. The students of these yeshivot learned to think in broader terms about universal ethics and human rights, even if on the surface they never strayed beyond the bounds of the Jewish textual horizon. So in one way or another, it is clear that the Enlightenment and its principles had won the adherence of the vast majority of European Jews by the second half of the nineteenth century, whether they acknowledged it or not.

This discussion would be incomplete without mention of the fact that there still exist today segments of the Jewish community who find the Mendelssohnian synthesis total anathema. For some, even Samson Raphael Hirsch had gone too far. For ultra-Orthodox (*Haredi*) Jews, the halachah was binding and unchanging for the simple reason that it was a revelation of God. Finding good reasons or elevated sentiments in the halachah was, for them, entirely irrelevant. The revealed law is simply the revealed law, and any attempt to justify or explain it beyond that framework was to put something else in a position to judge God's law, and this the traditionalists were not prepared to do. As the Reform movement continued its growth both in Europe and America, the Orthodox wing of the community found itself forced on the defensive, and in response, progressively alienated itself more and more not only from the larger Jewish community, but from the increasingly secular and open host culture as well.

For many ultra-Orthodox leaders even the smallest deviation from the halachah came to be seen as the first steps down the slippery slope to assimilation or Reform. In practice this meant that leniencies that were once allowed or tolerated among traditional communities now had to be fully forbidden. This hardening and increased conservatism of the traditional halachah made the very practice of ultra-Orthodoxy in the modern world more difficult and isolationist. They have taken the Hatam Sofer quite literally at his word and continue to refuse any change at all. Such communities have cut themselves off entirely and live in isolation from the rest of the world in places like New Square, an hour north of New York City, Antwerp in Belgium, and B'nai Brak in Israel. They regard their neighbors, Jewish and non-Jewish alike, as seducers at best and at worst, modern manifestations of Amalek, dedicated to the destruction of the People of Israel in one way or another. For these groups, issues of universal human rights outside their own neighborhoods is not even a topic of consideration.

The Case of North America

In many ways, the liberal and even largely secular line of Jewish thinking reached a certain maturity early on in America. The Jews who came to the New World were of course immigrants like all other Europeans who arrived on these shores. But the Jewish immigrants did not come in quest of gold or military glory, as was the case of the Spanish conquistadors, but for religious freedom and economic opportunity, much like the Pilgrims. The first Jews who arrived in the new world settled largely in the Spanish colonies of Central and South America, away from the Inquisition raging in their homelands of Spain and Portugal. Unfortunately, over time, the Inquisition reached America as well and there were trials and burnings in many of the Spanish colonies from Peru to Mexico. This led to further immigration of Jews from the Spanish areas in the south and central parts of the continent to the northern colonies controlled by the more "enlightened" governments of France, England, and the Netherlands. This migration led to an incident that put into sharp historical focus how North America was forever going to be different from Europe, and how the Jews were going to position themselves as a religious community in the New World. The American experience, as already briefly alluded to, gave rise to a Jewish community that placed human rights at the very forefront of its concerns.

The story concerns the arrival of twenty-three Jewish refugees from Brazil in about 1654. Peter Stuyvesant, the local director of what was then called New Netherland, thereupon sent a petition (dated September 22, 1654) to the directors of the Dutch West Indies Company for permission to expel these members of "the deceitful race—such hateful enemies and blasphemers of the name of Christ" so that they "be not allowed to further infect and trouble this new colony."[23] So far there is nothing new or different in this from the standard treatment of Jews. But in an unprecedented move for the time, the Dutch West Indies Company wrote back denying Stuyvesant's petition, and in fact went on to explicitly instruct him to allow the Jews to trade and travel freely in the colony, "provided the poor among them shall not become a burden to the company or to the community."[24] Thus, America became one of the first places under European control in which Jews were accorded full legal rights. This turned out to set a precedent that held more or less universally, even as the colonies all gradually came under British sway and then broke away to form what was to become the United States of America. The British had after all already briefly offered full naturalization to Jews in its empire as early as the 1750s.

Needless to say, the principles of personal liberty and religious freedom that so much informed the framers of the Constitution, found deep resonance in the small North American Jewish community, which adopted these liberal attitudes as intrinsic to its own essence. This attitude found verbal expression in the very first years of the new republic. In a letter to George Washington on August 17, 1790, the Hebrew Congregation of Newport, Rhode Island, wrote, "Deprived as we have hitherto been of the invaluable rights of free citizens, we now, with a deep sense of gratitude to the Almighty Disposer of all events, behold a government, erected by the majesty of the people, a government which to bigotry gives no sanction, to persecution no assistance, but generously affording to all liberty of conscience and immunities of citizenship." Thus, some fifteen years before the Paris Sanhedrin, while the Jews of Western European could still only dream about the possibility of living in a context of religious toleration, the Jews of Newport found themselves in that very position. For them the argument no longer even had to be made because it was already won.

This is by no means to say that the problem was forever solved in North America. Local laws and prejudices continued to hold the minds of some. But as the various colonies with their diverse religious backgrounds gradually coalesced into a single nation, the Jews came to be seen more and more as one religious group among many, and so had the same rights as all other citizens, regardless of religious background. To be sure there were bumps along the way. The state of Maryland, with its strong Catholic tradition, did not fully emancipate its Jewish citizens until the passage of the so-called "Jew Bill" in 1826. Jewish separatism also continued in some quarters. Mordecai Manuel Noah, a member of a prominent Jewish family who once served as U.S. consul to Tunisia, bought Grand Island in the Niagara River in New York State in 1825 with the idea of setting up a Jewish territorial colony called "Ararat." Although the attempt caused much debate it never really developed beyond the embryonic stage and Noah eventually gave up on the project. Although he remained active in American and American Jewish politics, he was also an early supporter of a Jewish state in Palestine. Given this history of tolerance and openness, it comes as no surprise that it was only in America that Kaufmann Kohler could write and publish his *Jewish Theology* (1918) and find for it a receptive audience.

The important point is that following the lead of Moses Mendelssohn and other Enlightenment thinkers, the American revolutionaries regarded religion as at best a private matter and at worst a holdover from a discredited European past. The Jews who came to the United States during the years before the Civil War largely took this point of view as a matter of course. They regarded themselves as Americans of the "Mosaic persuasion" and showed no interest at all in setting up any kind of chief rabbinate or communal (*kehilla*) structure as was common in Europe. One's Jewishness was one's own private affair, and its practice was a private matter between the individual and his or her God. But it was equally clear that this right had to extend to all others as well. So American Jews came to see themselves as a religious community in which each person had full freedom, from the perspective of the state as well as other Jews, to determine what being Jewish meant and demanded. This freedom was a basic human right, extending to all believers of all faith traditions. It was enshrined in the Constitution and needed to be defended with all due diligence. So early on the American Jewish community that was taking shape in the decades after the Revolution saw itself situated at the forefront of liberal causes. While this was surely a matter of self-protection and self-preservation, it also represented the deep personal conviction of the majority of Americanized and Americanizing Jews.

CONCLUSION

IT SHOULD BE clear that the Enlightenment had a profound effect on Jews and their diverse Judaisms from about the mid-eighteenth century on. By the beginning of the twentieth century, the vast preponderance of Jews in the West had left the ghetto, both physically and psychologically, and entered the modern world. In the process some left Judaism behind entirely while others refused to make the transition at all. But most situated themselves somewhere in the middle, becoming modern Westerners and in the process transforming their Judaism into a liberal Western religion that preached a universal message of tolerance and social justice. The resulting transformations could take many shapes—from the *Musar* yeshiva of the Eastern European Orthodox, to the moderate Orthodoxy of Hirsch, to the liberal religion of the Reform movement, to the "civil religion" of the liberal Jew. In each case, the people involved drew their inspiration from the outside world to understand its Judaism and in turn tried to find in their Jewish tradition lessons in human rights and dignity that they could teach to the outside world. In nearly every case, Jews of course were working out of a measure of self-interest. They all understood that their own advancement, if not survival, depended on liberal attitudes of universal human rights, including the right to the free exercise of the religion of one's choice. But in all events, these attitudes became part of the very psyche of modern Western Judaism and its Jews. How this conviction has worked itself out in the twentieth and into the twenty-first centuries is the subject of the remainder of this book.

7

JEWS AS A SEPARATE PEOPLE
AND RIGHTS BASED
ON NATIONALITY

TWO STRANDS OF OPPOSITION developed to the Enlightenment and the associated Jewish emancipation within the Jewish communities of Western and Central Europe. One was a religious opposition, characterized most starkly by Moshe Sofer, as quoted in the previous chapter 6, that "all that is new is forbidden by Torah." His position, in essence, was that any innovation at all in any of the received practices of Judaism was a step toward assimilation and eventual abandonment of the covenant with God. For him, the Jews had to maintain their distinctiveness no matter what the social cost. The other strand was nationalistic, represented by Moses Hess. His argument was that the Jews comprised a separate nation and so deserved—in fact required—its own recognized national status, a nation-state, just like all the nations in Europe. For him, the problem with the Paris Sanhedrin was not that it required Jews to give up their religion; they were after all still technically allowed to practice Judaism in their private lives. The problem was that it required Jews to give up their *national* identity and to be "French" rather than "Jewish."

Before proceeding it might be helpful to state more precisely what was at stake, particularly with regard to human rights. In nineteenth- and early-twentieth-century thought, certain "Romantic" assumptions based on Social Darwinism were becoming widely accepted in contrast to the liberal "rational" Enlightenment theory.[1] These assumptions were centered around the notion that the different peoples of Europe (German,

French, Romanian, Jews, Gypsies, and so forth) were, in fact, separate races (or *nations*, to use the vocabulary of the time), parallel to the different animal and plant species in nature. Along these lines, it was further assumed that each of these nations or races had its own particular characteristics that were expressed in all aspects of its physical appearance and its culture—language, folktales, art, religion, and so forth.[2] As was the law in nature in general, it was these traits that provided the species with the assets it had at its disposal for competing for survival with its rivals and predators. It was also generally taken for granted by Social Darwinists that a nation could only achieve full expression of its innate genius, and thus compete successfully for its share of rare resources in the world, if it were able to control its own cultural and linguistic environment. In practical terms, this meant that each nation should be in a position to establish its own political entity, that is, a state.

Thus, Europe in the nineteenth and early twentieth centuries was deeply involved in the process of building a series of nation-states. Within this system, the nation-state gave its members the chance to develop its own genius in a natural way. A corollary of this was that the rights of the individual were "naturally" subordinated to the needs of the group as a whole. It was the survival of the nation, the group, that was important, and individuals were expected to subordinate themselves to the greater common good. This led to various political movements, whether on the right or the left (fascism or communism, for example), that supressed individual human rights in favor of national rights.

There was another important element in the creation of the nation-state. The nation-state performed the very important function of protecting its members who lived elsewhere from human rights abuses. Thus, for example, in this system, Germans living in Poland would be considered Germans and subject to certain protections by their state against abuses potentially aimed against them by the Polish state. Thus, such "foreign nationals" living in Poland might not have certain rights as part of the Polish nation but would be guaranteed certain legal and human rights by virtue of the fact that the German state could and would intervene on their behalf if necessary. The other side of this arrangement was that certain groups who did not have a state, often called "national minorities," were in a sense left out. Although in theory they may have had claims to basic human and legal rights, in practice, they were subject to the mercy and goodwill of the state in which they resided as "aliens" of some sort or another. Because of the anomalous situation of such populations, one of the persistent political questions of the time was what to do with such national minorities. European politicians struggled throughout the nineteenth century to deal with these groups in a number of ways, including the creation of a series of "minority treaties." Of particular interest to us here is that one of the largest and most difficult groups in this regard was, of course, the Jews. In essence, the spread of Social Darwinistic thinking left the Jews with one of two difficult options: either become assimilated into other nationalities and gain the rights therewith associated (Moses Hess's fear), or maintain their own particular identity (as Moshe Sofer wanted) but pay the price of having no guaranteed human rights in the European system of nation-states.

One more crucial aspect of the creation of the nation-state should be pointed out before turning our attention to how the Jews dealt with this conundrum. Before World War I, travel was deemed a natural right, a legal "fact" recorded already in the writings of Francisco de Vitoria, a Spanish theologian and legal scholar. "It was," he noted, "permissible from the beginning of the world . . . for any one to set forth and travel wheresoever he would."[3] This notion of free movement was also part of the natural law as codified by Hugo Grotius.[4] It was only with the creation of the modern state with unrestricted sovereignty over its territory that passports and travel restrictions came into being. People of a nationality that did not have its own state thus had to travel under the passport of the host state. Thus, passports of this era often indicated not only the citizenship of the bearer, but also his or her nationality. The logic of this legal situation played itself out in a devastating way during the Holocaust when German Jews lost their German citizenship. Without passports, they were illegal (and unwanted) immigrants wherever they went. A further extension of this is the creation of the particularly modern tragedy of "displaced persons" and "refugees."

With these thoughts in mind, we turn to the Jewish community and the particular response generated therein that has become known as Zionism. Although numerous national minorities in Europe found themselves in this awkward situation, the position of the Jews in this context presented particularly difficult problems. To begin with, there were many Jews, something like 8 to 9 million in Europe by the late nineteenth century. Second, the Jews were scattered throughout Europe, and so, like the Gypsies for example, they had no obvious place within European national geography to have their own state. Third, there were deep divisions among the Jews themselves as to whether they constituted a nation at all. On the one hand, the vast majority of Jews in the West saw themselves as fully part of the nation of the country in which they lived. The Jews of France had essentially declared themselves French at the 1806 Paris Sanhedrin, for example, and German Jews, who had spent most of the nineteenth century fighting for entrance into German society, regarded themselves right through the Nazi period as German nationals first and only secondarily (if at all) of the Jewish *religious* persuasion. On the other hand, Jews in many areas of Central and virtually all of Eastern Europe were only partially assimilated, if at all, and most had no desire to be assimilated. The mass of Jews in Russia, for example, never considered themselves to be Russian, and they were not considered such by non-Jewish Russians. Rather, they were deemed members of one of the various nationalities that made up the Russian Empire: Russians, Uzbeks, Georgians, and so forth. In short, there was much confusion on all sides throughout the nineteenth century as to whether Jews did or did not constitute a distinct nationality. In actual practice, they were treated (and saw themselves) as fully a distinct nationality in some places (as in Tsarist Russia) and less so in others (as in France).

It is in this context of rising nationalism (in the nineteenth-century sense) and dueling definitions of "Jewishness" that the rise of Zionism took place. To put matters at their most simple, Zionism hoped to preserve human rights for Jews in Europe (and elsewhere) by stressing their national character and so their natural rights as a nation among the nations. In light of the growing anti-Semitism across Europe, Jewish nationalism slowly and painfully became a serious topic of consideration (pro and con) among even the highly assimilated Jews of the West. What a small but growing minority of Jews undertook to argue is that Jews *as Jews* would never be accepted as local nationals by non-Jews, and therefore in order to have civil and human rights they needed a recognized national status, and even a "state" of their own, so as to have a presence on the international scene. The notion that this was something of a religious movement as well and so had to effect a "return" to the original Jewish national home in Western Palestine only emerged later. Zionism, in its earliest form, was a secular, Romantic nationalistic movement, responding to secular, Romantic nationalism and racial anti-Semitism.

THE RISE OF RACIAL ANTI-SEMITISM

THE FOUNDATION OF modern national or racial anti-Semitism, as opposed to traditional Christian theological anti-Judaism, began even as the Enlightenment-inspired and largely secular French emancipation was taking hold. Ten years after the Paris Sanhedrin, and shortly after the defeat of Napoleon at Waterloo, the German philosopher Jakob Friedrich Fries wrote:

> Judaism is the sickness of a people who are rapidly multiplying. Jewry will acquire power through money wherever despotism or distress engenders oppressive taxation; wherever oppressive, public ransoms become necessary; wherever the well-being of the citizen is so endangered that indebtedness on a small scale grows ever worse. Finally, the Jews also gain power where many unproductive countries are wasteful. The idle, stagnant capital of these countries is devoured by the Jews like worms gnawing on rotting matter.[5]

He even argued in a pamphlet written in 1815 entitled *Ueber die Anspruche der Juden an das deutsche Buergerrecht* that "Jews may be tolerated only as a subject nation and the medieval restrictions must be reapplied."[6] This view continued to become part of the thinking of even religious scholars. Consider the Protestant theologian and professor, Bruno Bauer, who wrote in 1843 that "Of the Jews it will at least be admitted that they suffered for their law, for their way of life and for their nationality, that they were martyred. They were thus themselves to blame for the oppression they suffered, because they provoked it by their adherence to their law, their language, to their whole way of life."[7] By 1879, this attitude had become so pervasive in Central Europe that Wilhelm Marr coined a new word for it: "Antisemitism."[8]

Thus, even among the highly assimilated Jews of the West, it was becoming clear that a full solution to what was widely known as the "Jewish Question" was not yet fully achieved and was even by some measure in remission by the late nineteenth century. The reactionary period of the 1840s in Central Europe was in many respects a period of liberal retreat and Romantic advance. Many of the gains made toward Jewish emancipation and integration were brought again into question and in some cases undone. More ominously, Enlightenment idealism was giving way to Romantic notions of the sacredness of the national "genius" and eventually to scientific racism and eugenics. These developments would eventually lead to the Nazi mythology of the Aryan superrace and the implementation of policies to find a "final solution" to the Jewish Question by systematically exterminating the Jews of Europe.

Of course, few Jews saw matters developing to this point. But they did sense that despite considerable outward progress, they were increasingly regarded by their Central and Western European neighbors of the later decades of the nineteenth century as racially Jewish, and so by the logic of matters, not "national" Germans or Austrians, and so forth. Thus, the simultaneous advancement of the Enlightenment (which backed full human rights on the basis of neutral reason) and romanticism (which promoted the idea of national rights based on membership in a certain "race" in Social Darwinistic terms) created two opposing attitudes, one accepting of the Jews as full citizens of the state, and the other seeing them as essentially members of a foreign "nationality." The rise of political anti-Semitism in Western and Central Europe by the late nineteenth century indicated to at least some Jews that the legal emancipation and civic betterment for which their predecessors had worked so hard were only skin deep; social acceptance did not follow. The situation in the East (Poland, the Balkans, Russia) was, in fact, even starker. As Enlightenment ideas did seep into these areas, the Jews and their neighbors found themselves largely in agreement that the Jews were indeed a distinct nation among the various nationalities of the Russian Empire.

Jewish reaction to this rising intellectual and popular anti-Semitism took three forms. The first was to ignore it as the rantings of a radical fringe. The second was to refute it, either through public media such as speeches, pamphlets, and other written materials, or through the private examples of exemplary citizenship. These were by far the most common reactions in Western and Central Europe because most Jews in these areas thought (more or less correctly) that legal emancipation in the West was a fait accompli. The third reaction, that of Jewish nationalism, was more common in Eastern Europe but slowly built up a following in the West, as well. This peripheral segment of the Jewish community took the rise of anti-Semitism seriously. They saw it as the tip of an immense iceberg signaling that assimilation into other nation-states was not really working and that Jews were, in fact, everywhere regarded (in their view, correctly) as a separate nation, a *volk* in its own right, and as such one that would not, could not, and should not, be assimilated into the foreign host cultures in which they lived. For these early Jewish nationalists, the only real and permanent answer to the Jewish Question was the establishment of a Jewish national home. As nation-states formed in Europe in the nineteenth century—France for the French, Germany for the Germans, Italy for the Italians, and so forth—it made more and more sense that there should be a Jewish state for the Jews. Only in this way could Jews as Jews enjoy national and not just minority rights. The issue was nicely stated by the American Zionist thinker, Horace Kallen,* who wrote in a 1919 essay on Judaism and liberalism that "The Jews are a historic People among other peoples, neither better nor worse." He went on to say, "Whether races or nationalities are of 'pure' breed or not, they exist as associations deriving from a real or credited predominant inheritance, and intimate sameness of background, tradition, custom, and expression as for the individual." The question was when, where, and especially how to carry this out.[9]

A crucial distinction needs to be made at this point. The idea that the Jews were a special people among the nations was hardly new in the nineteenth century. The notion of Jewish distinctiveness goes back to biblical times and in classical Judaism, Jews did, in fact, constitute a nation apart, seeing itself living in exile among the other nations of the world. With the very formation of rabbinic Judaism in late antiquity came the idea of a return to Zion and a rebuilding of Jerusalem and the Temple. But this was a matter of religious faith, something brought about by God, through a messianic act of salvation. Pious Jews prayed for the rebuilding of Jerusalem three times a day, and some even immigrated to the Holy Land, but none doubted that the return was to be an act of divine intervention. A considerable population of pious Jews was already living in the Holy Land, primarily in the four holy cities of Jerusalem, Hebron, Tiberias, and Safed. They lived lives steeped in prayer, writing Torah scrolls or holy books, and living largely off charity. It was only now, in the late nineteenth century, that the return of Jews to the Holy Land took on a concrete and *secular* political form. Modern Zionism was not about pious Jews returning to a renewed Kingdom of David to offer sacrifices once again on the sacred altar. It was about the creation of a national, secular homeland for one of Europe's racial minorities that needed a state to guarantee its national rights.

Given this history, it is somewhat ironic that the first stirrings of this movement came from religious thinkers. In 1843, Rabbi Yehudah Alkalai,* in a Hebrew pamphlet, called for a collective return to the Land of Israel:

It is written in the Bible: "Return O Lord unto the tens and thousands of the families of Israel." On this verse the rabbis commented in the Talmud as follows: it proves that the Divine Presence can be felt only if there are at least two thousands and two tens of thousand of Israelites together. Yet we pray every day: "Let our eyes behold Thy return in mercy unto Zion." Upon whom should the Divine Presence rest? On sticks and stones? Therefore, as the first step in the redemption of our souls, we must cause at least twenty-two thousand to return to the Holy land. This is the necessary preparation for a descent of the Divine Presence among us; afterward, He will grant us and all Israel further signs of His favor.[10]

In short, the prayed-for religious return would not happen until the Jews themselves took the first step and created a Jewish population of critical mass in the Holy Land. The same point was made in 1862 by another rabbi, Zvi Hirsch Kalischer,* who wrote:

My dear reader! Cast aside the conventional view that Messiah will suddenly sound a blast on the great trumpet and cause all the inhabitants of the earth to tremble. On the contrary, the Redemption will begin by awakening support among the philanthropists and by gaining the consent of the nations to the gathering of some of the scattered of Israel into the Holy Land.[11]

But both Alkalai and Kalischer were rabbis still speaking in essentially religious discourse. By the late nineteenth century, Zionism had become a secular movement aimed at securing national (not messianic) rights for the Jewish people. What can be regarded as the first manifesto along these lines was issued by a group called BILU (an acronym for the Hebrew expression *Bet Yaakov Lechu V-nelcha* [O House of Jacob, Come Let us go]), a collection of mostly Russian university students who had given up on life in Tsarist Russia, which had just passed a series of extraordinarily restrictive anti-Semitic laws, the so-called May Laws of 1881. For these students, the need to leave Russia was now clear, but settling in another foreign land (like America) ruled by non-Jews would just be continuing subjugation of the Jewish people to foreign nations led by foreign rulers. For members of BILU, and the more extensive Hibbat Zion (Lovers of Zion) movement that emerged at the same time, the only way to guarantee their natural human rights was to achieve national self-determination and that meant establishing a Jewish state.

Their manifesto began with a saying drawn from the ancient rabbinic sage, Hillel: "If I help not myself, who will help me?" However, for this group it was already clear that this was not going to happen in Europe and so they set their eyes on Zion. Near the end of the manifesto are explicit calls for what it wants, namely, "A Home in our country. It was given to us by the mercy of God, it is ours as registered in the archives of history."[12] There is no doubt that the land they had in mind was Palestine. Exactly what they knew about the area and its inhabitants is unclear, but they were at a minimum aware that it was under the control of the Turkish sultan (they mention this in the manifesto); and that it was, in fact, largely a backwater of the rapidly deteriorating Turkish Empire. There is no hint, however, that the authors of the BILU manifesto were aware of a local population or that they would have to displace anyone to reach their own dreams. It is also clear that they had little idea of the dimensions of the project they had naively undertaken. These were, after all, Russian university students, not Middle Eastern herders and farmers. Nonetheless, by the mid-1890s, some tens of thousands of young and idealistic Russians had made their way by hook or by crook to Turkish Palestine, where they struggled, largely without success, to eke out a living in their few agricultural settlements, such as BILU's *Gederah*. More often, they ended up as paid laborers for philanthropic enterprises set up by wealthy Jews (like the Rothschilds*) in places like Rishon LeZion (which means literally First to Zion).

But Hibbat Zion (including BILU) was a fringe movement established and loosely run by a marginalized group of Russian students. By the mid-1890s it had clearly run aground on the shoals of reality and was little more than a failure in progress. What made the struggle for a Jewish homeland into a matter of serious consideration among the larger and more mainstream Jewish public was the Dreyfus Case of 1894 and the ensuing "Affair," which lasted until 1906. Alfred Dreyfus, a Jew, was a captain in the French Army's General Staff. In 1894, he was accused of treason (transmitting classified artillery information to the Germans) and in a secret hearing was sentenced to life imprisonment. He was publicly humiliated by having his rank ripped off in front of a military formation and was then sent to Devil's Island to serve his prison term. Then, in 1896, new documents came to light that made it clear that the real spy had been Ferdinand Walsin Esterhazy and furthermore that it was his handwriting on the documents that had been used to convict Dreyfus. It also came to light that not only was the prosecution aware of this, but it had produced its own forged evidence to bolster the case.

To confound matters even more, many of these forgeries were produced by the then head of French Intelligence, Major H. J. Henry. When the new head of French Intelligence, Lt. Col. Georges Picquart, brought all this to the government's attention, he was promptly relieved of duty and sent to a diplomatic post in far-off Africa. The army clearly meant to keep matters undercover. Before leaving, however, Picquart turned over his findings to a liberal senator, Auguste Scheurer-Kestner, who immediately went public with the facts. This was followed by Emile Zola's* famous essay "J'accuse," which appeared in the January 13, 1898, edition of the Paris newspaper L'Aurore. In the essay, really an open letter to the president of the French Republic, Zola brought the whole sordid affair to light, accusing by name those responsible, and thereby sparked a bitter public debate. On the one side stood the liberals outraged over the government's duplicity and cover-up. On the other side stood the pillars of old France, in particular the Church and the army.

In light of these developments and the huge public outcries (on both sides) that ensued, the government was forced to arrest Henry and call for a retrial. Henry proceeded to commit suicide in jail. But by then, public passion on both sides had been raised to fever pitch and actual rioting broke out, generating a torrent of rabid anti-Semitism unequaled in Europe until the Nazi regime. It was in this atmosphere that a new trial in 1899 examined the evidence, noted the forgeries, and was formally asked by the government to annul the previous verdict. Instead, the military trial found Dreyfus guilty, but because of "extenuating circumstances" reduced his sentence to ten years, five of which had by now been served. This judicial compromise hardly satisfied either side. The struggle over Dreyfus continued and led eventually to the fall of the government. The details need not detain us here. Suffice it to say that Dreyfus, now a broken man, was finally granted a full pardon in 1904, and in 1906, a Court of Appeals finally overthrew the convictions. In the process the French Right felt that it had been thoroughly humiliated and defeated by "the liberal Jewish press."

The Dreyfus Affair had two important outcomes that are relevant to the rise of Zionism. One was a deepening of the Jewish Question among European Jewry. France, after all, had been the homeland of "Liberty, Equality, and Fraternity" and had been the first country to officially offer full emancipation to its Jews in the wake of the Paris Sanhedrin nearly ninety years earlier. The fact that such rabid anti-Semitism could emerge so quickly in France raised serious questions as to how deeply emancipation had really penetrated into society and if assimilation was really possible anywhere. The Dreyfus Affair, seen in conjunction with the growth of Jewish oppression and violence in Russia, the slow pace of Jewish social acceptance in Germany, and the continued reelection of the avowed anti-Semitic Karl Lueger as mayor of Vienna from 1897 to 1910, combined to cause even assimilated middle-class Jews to begin to see the logic of BILU and other Jewish nationalistic groups.

The second important outcome grew out of the mind of a newspaper reporter, Theodor Herzl,* who was covering the Dreyfus Affair for the Viennese paper *Die Neue Freie Presse*. Herzl, like so many others who watched the Dreyfus Affair unfold, became convinced that emancipation had failed, that Jews would never be accepted in foreign nation-states, and that therefore the only way to insure their national and human rights was the establishment of a Jewish national homeland. In an 1896 short novel entitled *The Jewish State: Quest for a Modern Solution of the Jewish Question*, Herzl, the product of an assimilated middle-class Jewish family, called for the establishment of a Jewish nation-state. A plea from this sort of person carried much more weight in the West than the idealism of some Russian Jewish radicals. Herzl concluded his essay with a rallying cry: "This is my message, fellow Jews! Neither fable nor fraud! Every man may test its truth for himself, for every man will carry with him a portion of the Promised Land—one in his head, another in his arms, another in his acquired possessions. We shall live at last, as free men, on our own soil, and die peacefully in our own home."[13]

Herzl spent some time trying to convince the imperial leaders of Germany, France, Turkey, and so forth, to provide a place for such a Jewish homeland. His argument was that this was not only good for the Jews, but would solve Europe's Jewish Question. Except for a British proposal to donate part of Uganda, he came up empty-handed. Obviously a change in tactics was called for, so he decided on a more dramatic public step. In 1897, he convened in Basle, Switzerland, the First Zionist Congress. In some psychological way, the actuality of the Congress—of hundreds of Jewish representatives meeting in the open to discuss the establishment of a Jewish national home—galvanized the Jewish public and provoked the establishment of an organized movement dedicated to actually building a Jewish national home.[14] While opposition among Western Jewish leaders was spirited, the movement did gain growing acceptance, especially among the younger generation. As a result of Herzl's initiative, Zionist Congresses continued to meet each year, financial resources were organized, land was purchased, local institutions were established (such as a field office in Palestine in 1908), the systematic training of immigrants began, and the work of creating a Jewish national home took on a professional character. By World War I, some 50 to 60,000 new Jewish immigrants were living in a variety of settlements, Tel Aviv had been founded, and the foundations of a civic society were beginning to appear: a rudimentary government, a school system, a technical college, newspapers, the start of a paved highway system, and so forth.

Even while this work was going on, the debate raged as to both the necessity and the character of the new homeland. Just about the only point on which all Jews could agree (albeit to varying degrees) was that Jews in Europe were facing severe and deep-seated obstacles to full social acceptance and human rights, especially in the East. The question was whether Zionism was the best way to address the problem. Widespread opposition to Herzlian Zionism came from lay people, who felt that stressing Jewish nationalism would work against their efforts to gain acceptance as equals in the states of Europe, and from the rabbinic leadership of Europe, who struggled to remind their flocks that Jews were united by the religion revealed at Sinai, not by secular nationalism. For these people, respectively, rights were best guaranteed either by holding their host states to the Enlightenment ideals of human dignity and equality or by trusting in God.

Those thinkers who did support Zionism did so out of a variety of motives and with a range of differing and even divergent agendas. The British intellectual Israel Zangwill, for example, had been a staunch supporter of the Uganda scheme. For him, the central issue was the "Wandering Jew," that is, the mass of Jewish refugees streaming out of Russia in the wake of the May Laws of 1881. By 1914, some 3 million Jews had fled Russian lands, many with little but the shirts on their backs. For Zangwill, this was a human tragedy in the making and some accommodation had to be found for these masses. He agreed with Herzl that finding a place for these stateless refugees must be a matter of diplomatic agreement, regardless of location. The Jewish Question had to be solved, but not at the expense of others. To make his point, he published his own manifesto in 1905. In it he noted:

But unless the settlement were made with the full cooperation of the Government of the particular country—and for the mutual advantage—the emigration would be attended with great local friction. The territory must be a publicly recognized, legally-secured home. In this one place of all the world the wanderer must feel himself received not grudgingly, but with the cry of "Peace be to you." Any other form of emigration is, we have seen inevitably destined to end in local antisemitism. And without a certain measure of self-government the better class of patriotic emigrant will not be attracted. Moreover, we have not the right to burden any other nation with the problem of governing our emigrants.[15]

Another view was expressed in 1905 and 1906 by Ber Borochov,* who conceived of the initiative to establish a Jewish homeland as an occasion not only to rescue Jews but as an opportunity to establish a true Marxist utopia. For him, the whole reason for anti-Semitism was economic. Anti-Semitism arose, he argued, because the Jews had not been allowed to establish a normal proletariat anywhere in Europe. Instead, they were forced into niches of the capitalistic system (banking, the press, the professions) in a way that skewered the economic basis of Jewish society and so distorted its national character. What was needed was not just a homeland, but a homeland that would provide a natural economy for the Jewish nation, an economy in which Jews would be not only bankers, doctors, and lawyers, but also policemen, garbage collectors, factory workers, and farmers—in short, a normal national economy. He saw in the Russian Jewish masses a new population now set adrift that could provide the foundation for just such a new society, one free to develop without the inherited cultural values, social structures, and intellectual prejudices of Europe. In his "Program for Proletarian Zionism," he noted that "The Party demands the democratization of the internal administration of the Jewish settlements in the land of Israel, based on principles of municipal autonomy and large-scale participation of workers in the self-governing institutions of the settlements. The Party demands that the settlements themselves regulate the relations between capital and labor within the jurisdiction without the intervention of the Turkish administration."[16] The new Jewish homeland, in essence, would create the economic basis for the creation of a new type of Jew—not the abnormal ghetto Jew of Europe, but a Jewish worker living off his own labor, as in every other normal nation. It is also clear, as was the case for many Eastern Europeans, that this would all be taking place in the biblical homeland of Zion, Turkish Palestine. In the event, much of the early Zionist settlement movement, the kibbutz movement in particular, was based on ideas close to those of Borochov. Land was bought from Arab landowners and then worked by Jewish settlers who, imbued with socialist ideas, refused to become capitalist landlords and have their work done by hired hands. This had the effect of squeezing Arab peasants off the land they had traditionally worked, and so leaving them without support for their families, creating the first serious clashes between Arabs and Jews.

A similar vision, though not nearly as radical, was taken up by Herzl himself in *Altneuland* (Old New Land), his 1902 novel that described his vision of the rebuilt Jewish homeland. In the book, the Jewish state is described as a kind of social democratic utopia in which there is private property, but all industry, including the press and utilities, are run by cooperatives. The spokesman for the Jewish State, David Litwak, points out to his two visitors, Friedrich Levinberg and his non-Jewish companion, Mr. Kingscourt, that the success of this cooperative organization in Palestine as opposed to its failure in Europe is due to the fact that the society was built anew, not with the baggage of the old regimes of the West. The prosperity that the new society brought to the region also benefitted the local Turkish and Arab inhabitants, who had by the 1920s turned into happy and prosperous participants in the enterprise.

But Herzl's vision in *Altneuland* went even further. On a visit to an industrial complex near Tiberias, the visitors are introduced to Dr. Steineck, a scientist who works with microbes. When asked what he is working on, the scientists answers, "On the development of Africa." He goes on to explain that by conquering malaria, he will be able to make Africa ready for modern development. After all, he notes, all people are entitled to their own homeland for only then will each person be at peace with his fellow man, because then each person will love his fellow man and understand him.[17] Clearly, Herzl is invoking the lingering European Romantic notion that human rights depended on membership in a nation that controlled its own territory. If this was true for the Jews, it must be equally true for Africans. It also captures the European notion that Europeans bore the possibility, and so the responsibility, of bringing civilization to the still primitive peoples of the globe. For Herzl, like Borochov, the new Jewish state was to be a microcosm of the ideal Europe.

The Zionist thinkers and organizers more connected with reality on the ground, however, were already beginning to worry about the situation of the indigenous Arab population. Would Zionism in the end create another national minority, in this case Arab, in somebody else's homeland, an anomalous situation that Zionism was meant, in the case of the Jews, to resolve? Was it not, in fact, an internal contradiction within Zionism to solve the Jewish Question by setting up a homeland that only created another problem in its place, namely, the Arab Question? One thinker who saw this potentiality early on was the Hebrew writer Yitzhak Epstein, who published an article in 1907 entitled "The Hidden Question." He begins right off by writing, "Among the difficult issues regarding the rebirth of our people in its homeland, one issue outweighs them all: our relations with the Arabs." He goes on to point out that there are some 500,000 to 600,000 Arab peasants on the land. To be sure, the land that is used to build Jewish settlements is being legally bought from the (largely absentee) landlords. But where does that leave the Arab peasant (*fellah*) who earned a living from the land?

> But let us leave justice and sensitivity aside for a moment and look at the question only from the point of view of feasibility. Let us assume that in the land of our forefathers we don't have to care about others and we are allowed—perhaps even obligated—to purchase all the lands obtainable. Can this type of land acquisition continue? Will those who are dispossessed remain silent and accept what is being done to them? In the end, they will wake up and return to us in blows what we have looted from them with our gold! . . . We must therefore enter into a covenant with the Arabs which will be productive to both sides and to humanity as a whole. We will certainly agree to this covenant, but it also requires the agreement of the other side; and that we shall gain gradually through practical deeds which are of benefit to the land, to us and to the Arabs. . . . Come let us teach them the right path, we shall build them up and we too shall be built.[18]

This seems to have been largely the assumption of American Zionists as well. The phrase "American Zionism" might at first seem to be an oxymoron. After all, the Jews who came to North America from 1880 on had the choice of going to Palestine, either under the auspices of Hibbat Zion or later under the umbrella of the World Zionist Organization. Yet the vast majority (some 2.5 million) had chosen to migrate not to the Jewish homeland but to America. What did it mean for these immigrants to then call themselves Zionists? The answer is that the bulk of the American Jewish community viewed Zionism as a massive humanitarian effort that would work to the benefit to everyone in the region. Although they had made a different personal choice, they saw it as their obligation to support their brethren who made the difficult decision to go to Palestine. In fact, they saw the creation and support of a Jewish democratic national homeland in Palestine not as contradictory to their choice to become

Americans, but as fully compatible with American ideals. Americanism and Zionism were not seen as contradictory or competitive but, on a deep level, as mutually supportive. Consider the words of Louis D. Brandeis,* a leader of American Zionism and later an appointed justice of the U.S. Supreme Court. In 1915 he penned a statement entitled "Zionism Is Consistent with American Patriotism." In this he notes that:

> America's fundamental law seeks to make real the brotherhood of man. That brotherhood became the Jewish fundamental law more than twenty-five hundred years ago. America's insistent demand in the twentieth century is for social justice. That also had been the Jews' striving for ages. Their affliction as well as their religion has prepared the Jews for effective democracy. . . . Indeed, loyalty to America demands rather that each American Jew become a Zionist. For only through the ennobling effect of its strivings can we develop the best that is in us and give to this country the full benefit of our great inheritance.[19]

This is a similar sentiment to that expressed by Horace Kallen.

Despite these dreams that Zionism would promote the growth of human rights globally, both for Jews and for others, harsh realities on the ground continued to intrude. Thus, by the mid-1920s, as the Zionist enterprise in Palestine had grown in number and sophistication, the problems that Yitzhak Epstein saw in embryonic form in 1907 had grown considerably. Yet, in the face of the increasing persecution of Jews in Eastern Europe and the rising anti-Semitism of Central and Western Europe in the 1920s and 1930s (Adolf Hitler came to power in January 1933), many Zionists saw themselves engaged in an immediate and real need to save the Jews of Europe. It was not so much that the indigenous Arab population was actively persecuted as that attention was focused elsewhere and the Arab peasants became the subject of benign neglect. With stunning optimism, some, like Herzl, perceived Zionism as a model for dealing with minority rights in Europe and across the globe and so just assumed the Arab Question would be resolved on its own. After all, Palestine was but a small slice of territory in a vast Arab continent that stretched from Morocco to India. The Jews, on the other hand, had nowhere else to turn. Even the United States closed its doors with the passage of a very restrictive immigration law in 1924. Thus, while other voices, like Epstein, were raising concerns, they were largely ignored.

In 1926, after an outburst of Arab violence against Jewish immigrants, Zionist thinkers began to take the problem of the Arabs much more seriously and urgently. Zeev Jabotinsky,* who went on to found Revisionist Zionism, openly called for the rejection of Herzl's diplomatic approach and demanded that Jews take it upon themselves to establish their homeland by force of arms if necessary. He even foresaw the need for a mass evacuation of Europe's Jews to Palestine. Yet despite his militance, he recognized that the human rights of the indigenous Arab population had to be taken into consideration. In his essay, "What the Zionist-Revisionists Want," he wrote:

> Our attitude toward the Palestinian Arabs is determined by the full recognition of an objective fact: even after the formation of a Jewish majority a considerable Arab population will always remain in Palestine. If things fare badly for this group of inhabitants then things will fare badly for the entire country. The political, economic and cultural welfare of the Arabs will thus always remain one of the main conditions for the well-being of the land of Israel. In the future Jewish state absolute equality will reign between residents of both peoples, both languages and all religions.

Jabotinsky realized that this goal was far from being accomplished. A few sentences later he notes:

> It is a dangerous falsehood, however, to present such a reconciliation as an already existing fact. Arab public opinion in Palestine is against the creation of a Jewish majority there. The Arabs will continue to fight for a long time—sometimes energetically and sometimes apathetically, sometimes with political means and sometimes with other means—against all that which leads to the creation of this majority.[20]

Ten years later the situation had only grown worse. Throughout the late 1920s and early 1930s, masses of Jewish immigrants from Europe were arriving in Palestine, increasing the Jewish population tenfold to some 400,000. At the same time the Arab population had risen by about 50 percent to nearly 900,000. Conflicts between the two populations led to widespread outbreaks of violence and riots by the Arab population in 1936. In his testimony to a British commission of enquiry set up in 1937 to investigate the violence between the two communities, David ben

Gurion,* later first prime minister of the state of Israel, still thought an accommodation with the Arab population was possible. In his testimony he refers at one point to the program articulated at the First Zionist Congress of 1897:

> We did not say to make in Palestine a Jewish State. We did not say it at that time, and we do not say it now and I will tell you why. There are three reasons. Our aim is to make the Jewish people masters of its own destiny, not subject to the will of mercy of others, as any other free people. But it is not part of our aim to dominate anybody else. If Palestine were an empty country we could say a Jewish State, because the Jewish State would consist of Jews only and our self-government in Palestine would not concern others. But there are other inhabitants in Palestine who are here and, as we do not want to be at the mercy others, they have a right not be at the mercy of the Jews.[21]

While ben Gurion was articulating Zionism in these fine abstract terms, the Revisionsists under Jabotinsky were doing on the ground precisely what ben Gurion seemed to be rejecting in diplomatic circles, namely setting up a Jewish state. So both Jewish immigration and militance, and corresponding Arab hostility, continued to grow unabated. The idealism and even romanticism of early Zionism was giving way to the harsh and violent realities of both Europe and of Western Palestine.

By 1945, the situation had altered considerably for the worse. On the Arab side was the betrayal of the British and French, who had promised to create an Arab empire on the ruins of the now defunct Ottoman Empire. Instead, the two powers had divided the area between them, creating in the region the melange of states that currently exist. With both the British and the French devastated by World War II, the Arab leadership saw an opportunity to throw off the Western colonialists and create the Arab empire they had been promised. As the French and then the British withdrew from the region, the Jewish colony in Western Palestine remained the sole significant Western presence in the House of Islam. Reasserting control of this crucial region became a priority in the rebuilding of the Arab world. Mixed in with this was rising hatred of Jews nurtured by the Nazis, who had established ties with the Arab leadership on the basis of combating the common enemy: the British, the French, and the Jews.

On the Jewish side was the massive genocide of the Holocaust and the refusal of all the Western democracies to take in Jewish refugees. The restrictive immigration policies of the Western world and the mass of postwar Jewish displaced persons (most of whom did not want, understandably, to return to Europe) made the need for a Jewish homeland a matter of urgency. This in turn only strengthened the arguments of Zionist militants like Jabotinsky's Revisionists that a Jewish state had to be created, by force if necessary. In this enterprise, little, if any, regard was paid to the needs of the indigenous population, which by now had, at any rate, shown itself, by its alliance with Hitler, to be the enemy of the Jewish people. Given the overwhelming humanitarian need to house and feed tens, even hundreds, of thousands of Jewish survivors and displaced persons, and given the rising ethnic violence in the region, the finer points of dealing with the Arab population were simply ignored. The immediate need to create a defensible Jewish state was now simply taken for granted.

But the question of what to do with an Arab population of more than a million people remained. As early as November 1945, even before the refugee problem had been fully sorted out and while the British mandate was still in effect, the Hashomer Hazair Worker's Party issued a memorandum on what seemed the logical solution: a binational state. The memorandum pointed out precedents to the Flemish and Walloons in Belgium and the English and Boers in South Africa (with no mention of the South African native population). The party called on the administration of the new state to "raise the standard of living and education of the Palestinian Arabs to approximately the present Jewish level during the same period" and to "promote and actively encourage Jewish-Arab cooperation in every field and by every legitimate means available as well as to encourage the gradual development of self-governing institutions, local and national, on bi-national lines, until the stage of full independence within the framework of a bi-national constitution is reached."[22]

Whether this idealistic vision would be amenable to the Arab leaders is questionable, and it is certain that not all Jewish leaders in British Mandatory Palestine thought that cooperation with the Arab population was possible, or even necessarily desirable. But in the end, events overtook whatever discussions along these lines might have taken place as to the future of the Jewish state. At the end of November 1947, the British requested, and received, United Nations permission to end the mandate and within six months the British army, the only force keeping the Jews and Arabs from each other's throats, was gone. Violence immediately broke out and increased in intensity until in May 1948, with the proclamation of the state of Israel, full warfare broke out. In the ensuing confusion and violence—five invading Arab armies, each with its own strategic interests, a brief civil war in the Zionist camp, and the struggle of local Arab politicians to maintain their own spheres of authority—some two-thirds of the local Arabs fled, ending up in refugee camps, where they and their descendants remain to this day.

It turns out that the idea of working with the local Arab population to ensure their human rights never died a formal death. In fact, in his Proclamation of the State of Israel of May 14, 1948, ben Gurion explicitly called for "the Arab inhabitants of the State of Israel to return to the ways of peace and play their part in the development of the State, with full and equal citizenship and representation in all its bodies and institutions, provisional or permanent." The document went on to add that "We offer peace and amity to all the neighboring states and their peoples, and invite them to cooperate with the independent Jewish nation for the common good of all."[23] To what extent this was a serious goal of the state of Israel as opposed to necessary diplomatic rhetoric remains a matter of considerably heated debate, as will become clear in chapter 8. But for the period in question (the late 1940s and early 1950s) the point was in any case moot.

The Israeli War of Independence of 1948–1949 ended not in peace but in a (temporary) cease-fire. None of the boundaries of the new state were recognized by any of its neighbors and the threat of renewed fighting from inside and from without remained constant. At the same time, the state, with a population of roughly 700,000, undertook the task of absorbing some 650,000 to 700,000 impoverished immigrants, more or less evenly divided between survivors of the Holocaust and exiles from Arab countries. Dealing with the simple humanitarian needs of these traumatized, often uneducated, and un-Westernized masses placed a virtually impossible burden on the rudimentary economy of the new state. Housing stock had to be doubled, schools and hospitals built, jobs created, and a reasonable defense force put together. In the minds of the Israeli authorities, these needs took precedence over worries about human rights for the Jews and certainly for the Arabs. Arab refugees were refused any right of return and their land and houses were taken over for the needs of the arriving Jewish immigrants. Thus, while Israel remained committed on paper to upholding the human rights of all its citizens, in actual practice this was often ignored in light of the exigencies and demands of the moment. Those Arabs who remained in Israel were granted citizenship but were then largely ignored. The Arab refugees, needless to say, were not even on the radar screen.

The high principles of human rights for Jews and Arabs that stood at the foundation of Zionism never entirely died, however. As the security situation was brought under some sort of control, as the economy developed, as the governmental and social institutions of the country matured, and especially as Israel has tried to become part of the developed Western world, attention to human rights has begun to resurface. Over the last few decades a bevy of human rights organizations and a flurry of court cases have made the issue of human rights very much a part of Israeli public discourse. While practical matters on the ground still leave much to be desired, the vigor of the debate offers some rays of hope. This discussion within Israel as to the type of society it wants to be and what role human rights will play for all of its citizens, Jew as well as Arab, is the topic of chapter 8.

8

HUMAN RIGHTS IN PRACTICE: THE LIBERAL JEWISH TRADITION IN NORTH AMERICA

L IKE ALL OTHER JEWISH COMMUNITIES examined in this book, American Jewish attitudes toward human rights have been deeply influenced by the community's experience within the larger society. What makes the American experience unique is both the extraordinarily high level of toleration extended toward Jews on the one hand, and the correspondingly high degree of assimilation by Jews into the social, economic, and political American scene on the other. Because of the values of Judaic culture and the Jewish immigrant experience, which will be examined in more detail below, the American Jewish community developed a very clear, socially progressive bent. This has meant in concrete terms that the American Jewish community has had a proportionally greater presence than its numbers would suggest on the American liberal Left and was particularly prominent in the civil rights movement. This political orientation was seen by American Jewish intellectuals as expressing not only the conjunction of Jewish and American values, but as expressing the best parts of both.

BEGINNINGS AND EARLY GROWTH

THE EARLIEST SETTLERS in North America were mainly Sephardic Jews, descendants of the medieval Spanish community that was expelled by the new Catholic monarchs in 1492. Many of these exiles found their way either to the Low Countries in Europe, where tolerance of religious differences was already being established, or to the Spanish colonies in the New World. From these Spanish colonies, Jews were forced to flee once again as the Inquisition was established in Latin America in the seventeenth century, and they moved mostly to the more religiously tolerant English or Dutch colonies of North America. Despite some religious prejudice, these arrivals generally found a level of acceptance, or at least tolerance, that was still rare in most of Europe. There were several reasons for this. First, many of the colonists already in North America had themselves come there to escape religious persecution, especially to what is now Rhode Island, and so shared this experience with the Jews. Second, many of the religious communities in the New World saw themselves as constituting in some sense the "New Israel" and so were open to welcoming "Old Israel" in their midst, often as part of their Protestant theology, which saw the ingathering of the Jews as part of the redemptive process leading up to the Second Coming of Christ. Adding to these religious elements was the fact that the entire social structure of the New World was being reconstituted without the established Church hierarchy and social class institutions that defined so much of Old World society. There was thus a place for non-Christians in the New World that had not really existed before in the West. In short, Jews, as fellow victims of religious persecution and as partners in colonizing and building a new society in the New World, found much greater readiness among the non-Jewish population to accept them as equals. The Jews, in turn, became dedicated to nurturing and promoting these American (and Protestant biblical) ideals.

These attitudes on both sides carried directly over into the American Revolution and beyond. One reason was of course that the American revolutionary movement itself was driven by Enlightenment idealism, including the primacy of reason and the existence of innate human rights. The patriots often cast their revolutionary rhetoric in precisely these terms. In addition, by the time of the Revolution, many of the Sephardic Jews in North America were locally born and already highly assimilated, and with their lack of ties to the British aristocracy, they were much more likely to be Whigs and thus supporters of the revolutionaries rather than sympathetic to the Tories. In fact, not only did Jews fight in local militias, but a few rose to high military rank. A handful of Jewish individuals were also involved in financing the Revolution, including Aaron Levy of Lancaster, Pennsylvania (Aaronsburg, Pensylvania, is named in his honor), Philip Minis of Georgia, who advanced money to pay troops in the

South, and the "Broker to the Office of Finance," Haym Solomon.[1] It was this reciprocal loyalty of the Jews to the revolutionary cause combined with the commitment of the patriots to Enlightenment ideals that prompted George Washington's letter to the Newport, Rhode Island, Jewish congregation in 1790, as previously mentioned in chapter 6 on the Enlightenment. This letter, remarkable for any Jewish community of its time, was already an indication of how deeply Jewish acceptance had become part of the American scene.

Despite the relatively progressive character of the early United States, as indicated by Washington's letter, the new country was still part of the eighteenth century. Thus, there still lingered a certain amount of European Christian prejudice, although what anti-Judaism persisted was small-scale and usually of little consequence. Of course, this also had something to do with the character of the Jewish community itself. To begin with, the community was largely Sephardic and so had a tradition of being aristocratic and socially flexible.[2] Second, the number of Jews in postrevolutionary North America was relatively small, numbering only about 4,000 to 5,000 in the year 1800. These Jews were mostly concentrated in, and highly assimilated into, the mercantile class of the eastern seaboard. While a few organized congregations did exist in some of the bigger cities, there was no national organization per se. As new states entered the Union, they simply granted equal rights to all citizens, making no specific mention of Jews or often even of religion; the one notable exception being the heavily Catholic state of Maryland, which did not extend equal citizenship to its Jewish inhabitants until the passage of the "Jew Bill" into law in 1826. The result was that Jews had a low profile and so remained largely invisible to most Americans and consequently only rarely faced anti-Jewish attitudes or social segregation. It could be said with a good deal of accuracy that this early Sephardic American Jewish community was really part of the emerging American establishment.

THE NINETEENTH CENTURY

THE CHARACTER OF this community underwent two radical changes in the nineteenth century, both connected to immigration, that had profound effects on its social and political profile. The first occurred during the decades prior to the Civil War (approximately 1830 to 1860). The previous chapters pointed out that the early years of the nineteenth century were tumultuous and even frightening ones for the Jews of Central Europe. With the fall of Napoleon and his political liberalism came the rise of nationalistic romanticism and eventually racial anti-Semitism. As liberals in the newly emerging middle class witnessed a retreat from the grand ideals of the Enlightenment and a turn toward reinstituting conservative (and often medieval) social structures and attitudes, many Europeans came to see America as a land of openness, religious toleration, and economic opportunity. The political and social turmoil involved in this retrenchment of conservative forces came to a head in a series of revolutions and counterrevolutions around 1848. The result was a considerable migration of Central Europeans of all types to America. Among these immigrants were of course many Jews, who after all had a good deal to lose in the reaction against liberalization on the continent. While the arrival of Jews to the United States in this period was not particularly heavy, it was steady, and so its cumulative effect was significant. By the outbreak of the Civil War in 1861, the Jewish community in the United States had grown to some 150,000–200,000 people. Unlike their Sephardic predecessors, these German Jews were much more conscious of their Jewish ethnic character. They were also generally from rural areas in the Old World and so did not settle comfortably into the American Eastern elite. Rather, they tended to migrate inland where financial opportunities for their modest skills seemed greater. Thus, these Central European Jews showed up particularly in the South and the West, often earning a living as traveling peddlers or small artisans and craftsmen serving the isolated farms and plantations of these regions. With the discovery of gold in the West, some more venturesome Jewish businessmen even made the trek to California, hoping to take advantage of the new economic possibilities opening up with the Gold Rush. Wherever they ended up, they knew that their future lay in the new American openness to cultural diversity and Enlightenment ideals, not the medieval hierarchies, social structures, and religious intolerance of the lands from which they fled.

Over time, a certain proportion of these traders, peddlers, and artisans earned enough capital to settle down and open shops and small stores, a few of which were successful enough to develop into larger concerns. Many eventually became prominent merchants in their hometowns and entered the new middle class of the American South and West. Because of their geographical dispersion, only rarely did enough Jews settle close enough to each other in any one area to create the critical mass needed to found a synagogue or other Jewish organizations (such as a burial society).

Cincinnati, Ohio, which had a large number of German immigrants alto-gether, saw one of the first Jewish congregations established outside the eastern seaboard, a German-speaking synagogue organized in the early 1840s. But this was an exception. In general, the patchwork of small, usu-ally unorganized clusters of Jews across the country made any effort to create regional or national organizations fruitless. The first truly national Jewish organization, the fraternal social-service society of the B'nai B'rith, was founded in New York in 1843, but it remained largely limited to New York and the surrounding areas until after the Civil War.[3] In sum-mary, the character of the American Jewish population by the beginning of the Civil War can be best summed up by saying that German Jews had come to vastly outnumber the older Sephardic community; that they were scattered in small pockets across the country from the Appalachians to the Ozarks to the Pacific; that they had a strong sense of their Jewish (or at least non-Christian) identities; and that they were generally ac-cepted as individuals in their local communities, but had established few organizations of any sort. It can also be said that although as individuals they had a deep commitment to the Enlightenment principles of liberal-ism and anti-clericalism, they displayed relatively little readiness to par-ticipation in political or social action beyond the local level. In many ways, then, it is premature to call this widely spread collection of individ-uals a community with any discernable policy. Jewish communal organi-zations that would take a stand on national issues and policies came into being only after the Civil War.

THE CIVIL WAR AND THE QUESTION OF SLAVERY

IT IS THIS situational reality that largely accounts for the silence of the Jewish community as regards the deepening debate over the issue of slav-ery. As noted above, there were no real national or regional organizations that could speak for the Jews, and local Jews, struggling to assimilate and make a living in their new homeland and communities rarely took public positions, especially on controversial issues. Their attitude is nicely and accurately summed up in the Annual Report of the American and For-eign Anti-Slavery Society in 1853:

The Jews of the United States have never taken any steps whatever with regard to the Slavery question. As citizens, they deem it their policy "to have every one choose which ever side he may deem best to promote his own interests and the welfare of the country." They have no organization of an ecclesiastical body to represent their general views; no General Assembly or its equivalent. The American Jews have two newspapers, but they do not interfere in any discussion which in not material to their religions.[4]

One notable exception to this silence was the well-known published debate of the time between two rabbis, Morris Raphall of New York, who took something of an anti-abolitionist stance, and Michael Heilprin (then one of the editors and contributors to *Appleton's New American Cyclopedia*), who argued in favor of abolitionism. Raphall's argument was based on the fact that slavery was part of the biblical legacy and so enjoyed the highest of authority. How, he asked, could Jews condemn slavery when Abraham, Isaac, and Jacob owned slaves? He did go on, however, to make a distinction between biblical slavery, which regarded the slave as "a *person* in whom the dignity of human nature is to be respected," and slavery as it had taken shape in the South, which regarded the slave as a *thing*.[5] Heilprin's response was to ask how the Jews, who had suffered slavery in Egypt, could allow these "Egyptian principles" to be fastened on others by Israelites themselves.[6] While neither writer could claim to represent any particular constituency, their exchange does highlight the differing attitudes within American Jewry. Raphall's support of slavery is interesting in that he seemed to accept the concept of slavery of a certain type (really more like indentured servitude) but did not express real support for the Southern style of slavery. It is also interesting to note that the only Jewish source he cited is the Bible, which would of course find resonance in the Christian community, and not Talmud or medieval halachic literature.

Another outstanding exception to the general silence of the Jewish community was Rabbi David Einhorn,* a well-known radical reformer. Einhorn gained notoriety for openly preaching abolitionism from his pulpit in Baltimore, Maryland. This created problems for him and his congregants since Maryland was a slaveholding state. He was subsequently forced by his congregation to leave his pulpit and flee to New York.

For the most part, however, Jewish leaders stayed on the sidelines, reflecting the ambivalent attitudes of the Jewish community at large. Jews had of course been involved in the institution of slavery from the very beginning. There were Jewish stockholders in the Dutch East India Company, and Jewish merchants in Newport, Rhode Island, were active in the "triangle trade," which was an important element for the import of slaves into North America. There were also a limited number of individual wealthy Jews who owned slaves, albeit mostly for use as house servants, there being very few Jewish farms, let alone plantations. But the vast majority of Jews, North or South, did not own slaves and many, especially in the North, were active in abolitionist activities.[7]

As the slavery issue heated up, it seems that many Southern Jewish slave owners, though not all, freed their slaves but did not actively join abolitionist movements. Jews in the North, however, were more ready to speak out against slavery and associate themselves with abolitionist movements. Thus, individual Jews generally conformed to the attitudes of the community in which they lived: Jews in the North tended to side with the abolitionists while Jews in the slaveholding states, who were mostly merchants dependent on the patronage of their neighbors for a living, generally supported the economic status quo, even if they did not own, or even if they had freed, slaves. It is precisely because of the prominence of Jews in the commercial life of the South that they were suspected by Union commanders, rightly or wrongly, of smuggling goods into the South through Union blockades. In one notorious case, the Union general Ulysses S. Grant actually issued an order (General Order No. 11) expelling all Jews from the Department of Tennessee (which included parts of Tennessee, Kentucky, and Mississippi) in order to shut down movement of goods through the Northern blockade. The order, it should be noted, was revoked at the insistence of President Lincoln.

The lack of a coherent Jewish attitude is also illustrated by the fact that Jews could be found on both sides of the conflict during the Civil War, enlisting in both the Union and the Confederate armies in support of their respective communities. Estimates are that some 10,000 Jewish soldiers fought in the Civil War, about 7,000 in the North and 3,000 in the South, suffering about 500 deaths overall.[8] Thus, as in Europe, Jews fought for their respective countries, even against other Jews.

Two significant developments in the immediate post–Civil War years changed the character and politics of the German Jewish community in the South. First, Jews in the South recovered relatively quickly from the war. Since few Jews were in any case plantation owners, but were mostly merchants and businessmen, they had an easier time adjusting to the new economic realities of the postwar South. This also meant that they had little incentive to see a return to slavery and correspondingly little impetus to persecute or oppress freed slaves. On the contrary, Southern Jews tended to see that the industrial and trade economy of the North represented the real future and they could also easily see African Americans as part of that future. In these attitudes they were joined and supported by coreligionists from the North who had come to the South either as part of Union forces or as carpetbaggers hoping to participate in the rebuilding of the economy. As Jewish communities grew, organized, and prospered after the war, they were thus more ready than many of their neighbors to move beyond the issue of slavery. It is likely that many in fact saw in the persecution of ex-slaves a reflection of just the kind of persecution they or their parents had faced in Europe, which had prompted them to come to America to begin with. Southern reactionary movements like the Ku Klux Klan found virtually no Jewish support and had no Jewish members, a circumstance that may have led such movements to become increasingly anti-Semitic.

Second, Jews, like other Americans, began to think of the United States as a single entity rather than as a loose conglomeration of independent states. A national identity began to emerge, making possible for the first time the growth of national Jewish organizations. The B'nai B'rith fraternal organization, which had been largely restricted to the New York area, led the way in this postwar national expansion to become the first national Jewish organization, but others soon followed. A landmark event in this regard was the founding, in 1875, of the first successful American seminary to train American rabbis for American Jewish congregations, Hebrew Union College in Cincinnati, Ohio. This and other institutional developments set the organizational stage for the creation and articulation of national Jewish policies on issues of Jewish and national concern. Northern Jews predominated in these organizations, and so these national groups took a much more progressive stand politically than was heretofore the case. A good example is the Pittsburgh Platform, issued on behalf of the Reform Jewish movement, a document that will be discussed further below.

THE EASTERN EUROPEAN MIGRATION

THE SECOND MAJOR change in the American Jewish community connected with immigration occurred in the final decades of the nineteenth century. Unlike the earlier German immigration, the Russian immigration of 1880–1915 had a profound, even revolutionary, effect on the American Jewish community. Beginning in about 1881, with the enactment of the harsh May Laws by the Russian government, a new migration of Jews to America began to make itself felt. Over the next thirty-five years or so, that is, until the outbreak of World War I, this immigration wave brought between 2 and 2.5 million Eastern European Jews to the United States. Unlike their predecessors from Germany, these Jewish immigrants were deeply Jewish in religion and culture, barely assimilated into Western ways, had virtually no marketable skills, and often arrived with little more than the shirts on their backs. Further, they spoke Yiddish, had never left Eastern European Orthodoxy, and had no immediate desire to do so. They were not interested in moving into the interior of the country (most did not have the financial resources to do so in any case), but preferred to stay in the large immigrant communities of the Northeast, where there were masses of fellow refugees from the Old Country (often organized into self-help clubs called *landsmanshaftn*) and a variety of synagogues, kosher butchers, Yiddish clubs, and other institutions catering to the needs of their traditional communal and religious way of life. Whole neighborhoods in eastern port cities became Yiddish-speaking enclaves, virtual reproductions of the Eastern European ghettoes. The most famous of these is New York's Lower East Side, but similar Yiddish ghettos appeared in Boston, Philadelphia, and even as far west as Memphis, Tennessee (the area known as the Pinch.) In these areas a lively Yiddish culture blossomed, with its own newspapers, book publishers, theaters, cafés, unions, and political parties.

These immigrants not only overwhelmed the institutional structure of the by now highly Americanized German Jewish community in America, but entirely reshaped its politics as well. Although many of the early arrivals were little more than semiliterate Jewish peasants from small rural villages (the *shtetlach*) of Eastern Europe, by the beginning of the twentieth century they were joined by highly politicized socialist, communist, anarchist, Zionist, and other political types who had been active in prerevolutionary Russian politics.[9] For this group of immigrants, the fight for human rights, which they so lacked in their home countries, was a central theme of their identity, often defining (if not indeed replacing) their relationship to the Jewish tradition. These activists immediately concluded that the terrible living and working conditions of the Jewish ghettoes, and the forced discrimination and exploitation of African Americans under Jim Crow, were the results of the very same capitalistic economic system that they had endangered their lives to overthrow back home. Thus, these newly arrived young Jewish radicals immediately became engaged with equal dedication to overthrowing capitalism and racism in order to set up the egalitarian, socialist economy they had struggled so hard and fruitlessly to create in Russia. What started as self-help actions for other Jews soon became a movement to change the very nature of American society and its treatment of all immigrants, all workers, and the poor more generally. The deep commitment to leftist political action gave the American Jewish community its disposition for liberal activism that characterized it for the rest of the twentieth century.

The way social activism and the fight for human rights took shape in America was a combination of the conditions found in Eastern Europe and of the immigrants' own experiences in coming to, and settling in, America. To understand the liberalism of American Judaism, then, it is worthwhile to take a second to look at these two elements. In Eastern Europe, as pointed out in chapter 7 (on Zionism), conditions deteriorated drastically with the passage of the 1881 May Laws. For some young Jews, exasperation and disillusionment ran so deep that they determined to be farmers in the Middle East, but for the vast majority of Eastern Europe's Jewish masses this was simply not an option. What did beckon them was the image of America as the Land of Opportunity (*Die Goldene Medina*, The Golden Country, as it was called in Yiddish). The migration itself began with a few poor Jews showing up hopelessly at the border stations of Western Europe, such as Brody in Austria. The dozens turned into hundreds and then thousands and then tens of thousands. Only gradually did the Jewish organizations of the West realize that they were not dealing with a few Jewish vagabonds, but with a population shift of massive proportions. But with the Western European Jews still unsure of their own status in Germany, France, Austria, and so forth, these hordes of exotic, un-Westernized, highly traditional Jews were hardly a welcome sight. They seemed in fact to ratify all of the European anti-Jewish stereotypes. Gradually, a network of Jewish social organizations did pull itself together to meet the refugees and to help them, but help usually took the form of taking care of their immediate needs and then hurrying them on their way out of Europe and on to America. At the receiving end, this was a migration for which the American German community—small, poorly organized, and highly assimilated—was hardly prepared.

By virtually all accounts, the trek across Europe and then the voyage across the Atlantic was one of unrelieved wretchedness. One immigrant recounts:

> On board the ship we became utterly dejected. We were all herded together in a dark, filthy compartment. . . . Wooden bunks had been put up in two tiers. . . . Seasickness broke out among us. Hundreds of people had vomiting fits, throwing up even their mother's milk.[10]

This story was repeated in its essential details 2 million times over. Unfortunately, the reception in the United States was at first hardly better. Virtually every immigrant Jewish family from this time has its Ellis Island story. The poor and bewildered immigrant peasant had to run a gauntlet of medical exams and official questions before admission to the United States. What made the whole experience more frightening was that it meant confronting uniformed officials, something most of these people feared more than anything. While most made it through, it would occasionally happen that one or more members of a family were refused entry for some reason or other, and so the family faced the choice of separation, returning to Europe, or going through the appeals process, guided by a lawyer they did not know and in a language they did not understand. Despite these harrowing experiences, most immigrants did walk out of Ellis Island into the free streets of New York, astounded, shaken, but also grateful for the comparative gentleness of the experience.

But walking out of Ellis Island was only the end of one phase and the beginning of a much more difficult one. Once in New York, the immigrant had to find food, shelter, and a job. Some already had family waiting, others searched for relatives or even a former villager (a *landsman*) from back home, but many had to fall back on their own resources or be taken in as wards by hastily put together relief agencies. The native American Jewish community only slowly grasped the magnitude of the problem and got itself organized to meet the needs of these masses. After a period of some trial and error, a network of organizations were put together that provided a fairly comprehensive system of aid. The Hebrew Immigrant Aid Society (HIAS), for example, would meet the immigrants at debarkation, shepherd them through the intricacies of Ellis Island, provide honest legal and medical advice when needed, and offer an array of social services once the immigrants made it through the process and found themselves on the street. Many of these agencies gained a good deal of experience in dealing with immigrants and providing social services in the community, and they became models for and partners with other non-Jewish social services agencies.

Given the arduous crossing and the transfer from the very traditional culture of Eastern Europe to the utterly unfamiliar culture of North America, it is not surprising that the social and psychological costs were significant. The conditions in which the new arrivals lived and worked were often of the meanest sort. Sweatshops in the garment district abounded, with men, women, and children laboring endless hours for minimal pay. The abysmal circumstances of these immigrants (and others from Eastern and Southern Europe) became a public issue in its own right in America at the turn of the nineteenth century. A number of social reformers, Jewish and non-Jewish, arose to document the human tragedy of this wave of immigration and to found organizations to address and ameliorate at least the worst abuses.[11] One such social reformer, Jacob Riis, a non-Jew, reporting on the Lower East Side, noted:

> Five men and a woman, two young girls, not fifteen and a boy, who says, unasked that he is fifteen and lies in saying it, are at the machines sewing "knee-pants." . . . The faces, hands, and arms to the elbows of everyone in the room are black with the color of the cloth on which they are working. . . . They are "learners" all of them, says the woman, who proves to be the wife of the boss, and have "come over" only a few weeks ago. They turn out 120 dozen "knee pants" a week. They work no longer than nine o'clock at night, from daybreak.[12]

The German Jewish community did not take long to respond to the burgeoning human needs of the immigrants. As early as 1893, one writer (Julia Richman) noted in a speech to the Jewish Woman's Congress (part of the Parliament of Religion, which was held in conjunction with the Chicago World's Fair) that:

> Almost all female immigrants who come to this shore, through lack of knowledge as to the means by which they can swing themselves above the discouraging conditions which face them, sink down into the moral and intellectual maelstrom of the American ghettos, becoming drudges, and then drifting into one of three channels: that of the careless slattern, of the giddy and all-too-frequently sinful gadabout, or of the weary, discontented wife.[13]

Although later in the speech, it is clear that Richman has Jewish women in mind, she is also certainly talking about the condition of women immigrants in general. This seems to have been a general pattern. The by now almost entirely native-born German Jewish community at first responded to the needs of the Eastern European Jews, but they soon came to the realization that this was part of a much larger problem connected with the mass immigration of Central and Eastern Europeans in general, and so became active in immigrant and human rights issues more broadly. This sentiment is wonderfully expressed in the so-called Pittsburgh Platform, a statement of principles adopted by a conference of Reform rabbis (almost all German) held in Pittsburgh in 1885. The platform's eighth, and final point, states:

> Eighth: In full accordance with the spirit of Mosaic legislation which strives to regulate the relation between rich and poor, we deem it our duty to participate in the great task of modern times, to solve on the basis of justice and righteousness the problems presented by the contrasts and evils of the present organization of society.[14]

It should be kept in mind that this platform represented the views of highly assimilated and relatively successful descendants of German Jewish immigrants of two or three generations earlier. This was not the manifesto of a newly arrived mass of socialist and communist activists from Russia. But it does show that the German Jewish religious community was profoundly affected by the human drama unfolding at its doorsteps.

The process of dealing with the needs of the immigrants gained considerable momentum by the beginning of the twentieth century as the immigrants themselves, or their children, began their own organizational and political efforts. Most significant, perhaps, was the changing character of the Jewish immigrants. By the turn of the century, the Jewish immigrants were made up of not only peasants with little education outside traditional Judaism, but of young, educated, socially radical, and politically active Jews belonging to a bewildering variety of socialist, anarchist, and communist groups. These young idealists and radicals (who often escaped one step ahead of the Tsarist police) saw the appalling working conditions of the Jewish immigrants on the Lower East Side and other Jewish ghettoes and, even worse, noted that many of the employers were German Jews. They began immediately to organize the Jewish workers along the same lines they had been working on in Russia. For many, the condition of the Jewish worker was nothing more than a microcosm of the plight of the proletariat in general.

One Russian-born social activist, Isaac Rubinow, wrote an article in 1905 titled "The Economic Condition of the Russian Jew in New York City." He took note of the fact that not all Russian immigrants had ended up in the needle (garment) trade, but many had found employment in other fields and a few even gained a certain prosperity. But when all was said and done, these lucky few were the clear exceptions. Most Russian Jews, in his felicitous phrasing, belong to the "masses" and not the "classes." He concluded by noting that "the vast majority of the newcomers also join this industrial army in this as well as other branches of manufacturing. The question of the economic condition of the Russian Jew in New York is therefore preeminently the question of wages, hours and conditions of labor in general."[15] In short, the problem of the Jewish immigrants could not be solved in isolation, but was only approachable through a change in the larger situation, a kind of economic revolution.

It thus comes as no surprise that by 1900, the combination of horrid working conditions, a network of high-minded but somewhat paternalistic German Jewish welfare organizations, and the arrival of political radicals led to a plethora of immigrant-organized political actions, usually focused on effecting a change in labor and working conditions along socialist lines. In 1900, one of the first trade unions in America, the Ladies' Garment Workers' Union, was organized. In membership and leadership it was almost entirely Jewish. By 1920, the union had organized garment workers not only in New York, but also in Cleveland, Chicago, and even Canada. At its 1920 convention, the leftist Yiddish paper, the *Forverts*, could claim that the I.L.G.W.U. (The "I" was added to indicate its International character) "stands now in the foremost ranks of the American labor movement, both materially and spiritually. It is one of the most important unions in the country."[16]

But there were other areas with their own injustices as well. In 1902, a rise in the price of kosher meat set off a kosher meat boycott, for example. In this case the action was organized mostly by women.[17] In 1909, the shirtwaist makers went on strike in what came to be called the "Uprising of the 20,000."[18] Labor action took on an even sharper edge after the infamous Triangle Shirtwaist Company fire of 1911, in which 146 garment workers (mostly female) were killed. Jewish labor organizations, with their associated calls for the respect of human rights and dignity, continued in ever-widening circles. Among the founders of the National Association for the Advancement of Colored People (NAACP) was a Jewish activist, Henry Moscowitz, and some of its earliest court battles in the first decade of the twentieth century were spearheaded by two Jewish brothers, Joel and Arthur Spingarn.

It should be pointed out that few of the leaders of these groups were religious in any traditional Jewish way, despite being thoroughly steeped in Eastern European Yiddish culture. Many, in fact, were atheists and secular socialists, with a few even seeing religion itself as the enemy (in accord with Marx's view that religion was the "opiate of the masses"). In fact, by the second decade of the twentieth century, the secular pursuits of social reform, economic justice, and upholding basic human rights was seen as the very essence of being Jewish, as opposed, say, to leading a halachic life in accordance with the will of God. The struggle for human rights was for many emerging American Jewish leaders precisely what Judaism and Americanism had in common. An eloquent testimony to this happy coincidence was penned by none other than Louis Brandeis, who became the first Jew appointed to the United States Supreme Court. In 1915, he wrote:

> America's fundamental law seeks to make the real brotherhood of man. That brotherhood became the Jewish fundamental law more than twenty-five hundred years ago. America's insistent demand in the twentieth century is for social justice. That also has been the Jews' striving for ages. Their affliction as well as their religion has prepared the Jews for effective democracy. Persecution broadened their sympathies. . . . It deepened the passion for righteousness.[19]

It should be noted that Brandeis, a leader in American Zionism, wrote this paragraph as part of his larger project arguing for the compatibility of being an American Jew and a Zionist, an argument referred to in chapter 7. For Brandeis, the goals of Judaism, both as a religion and as a culture, underlie the vision of Zionism and the promise of America, namely, a new society that in the light of modern reason and resources, would create a just and compassionate society offering refuge for the oppressed and the recognition of human rights in all sectors of society. In this view, the Jews settling in Palestine were doing in their way what the Jews in America were doing in theirs. In both places, the spirit of the ancient Jewish prophets was making itself felt. Isaiah's vision, the I.L.G.W.U., and the kibbutz were all facets of the same quintessential Jewish drive to bring out the best in humanity and human society. So for

Brandeis, being Jewish and American and a Zionist were not only compatible, but mutually reinforcing.

In fact, Zionism continued to be a major focus of Jewish philanthropy from the turn of the twentieth century. This focus seems to have grown out of a number of diverse motivations. Much had to do with the long tradition of the Jewish community taking responsibility for its own. This had been the case in Eastern Europe, and the tradition was brought over with the immigrants to North America. Another element may have been a sense of guilt for having the choice to go and help rebuild the Holy Land, but choosing to settle in America instead. Finally, of course, much of the work of Zionism was benefitting other Eastern European Jews, maybe even family members or inhabitants of the same former villages. For the masses, then, Brandeis' synthesis helped justify the decision to come to America while at the same time validated their desire to help fellow Russians. So at least in public discourse, American Jewish aid to the Zionist enterprise in Turkish and then British Palestine was always couched in philanthropic and human rights terms. It was in this way that Zionism could be made acceptable to these new American Jews.

It was also certainly the case that the needs of the Jews in Europe and in British mandatory Palestine were steadily growing. Germany underwent a severe economic crisis in the early 1920s, leading to the origin of radical right-wing and often anti-Semitic parties, including the German Workers Party, which a young Adolf Hitler joined in 1919, eventually turning it into the Nazi Party. In Eastern Europe, World War I saw not only the effective end of Jewish emigration, but also the Bolshevik Revolution. In 1924, the same year that the United States passed its restrictive immigration law, Lenin died in Moscow and was succeeded by Stalin. Stalin was not yet displaying the pathological Judeo-phobia that characterized the period after World War II, but clearly the humanitarian needs in the East were great. And in the Holy Land, a series of Arab attacks on Jewish settlers in 1921 killed scores of people. As the situation in Europe worsened, new waves of Jewish immigrants came to mandatory Palestine, where their resettlement and absorption into the presented a major humanitarian need. The American Jewish community, through organizations like the Joint Distribution Committee, active in Europe, or the United Palestine Appeal, became major donors to help the Jews overseas while fighting discrimination at home.

But by the 1930s, such prominent Jewish activity in the fight for social justice, humanitarian aid, and human rights had noticeably receded in

America. This occurred for a number of reasons. One was the ending of Jewish immigration and the more-or-less successful integration of the Eastern European Jews (or at least their children) into American society. By the outbreak of World War I, many of the children of immigrant Jews were native born and of military age. They fought alongside other American soldiers and came back after the war feeling ethnically Jewish and yet fully American. They had attended public schools, and after returning from the war, had enrolled in colleges or universities and moved out of the Yiddish ghettoes of their parents to close-in suburbs. They were achieving a measure of success and comfort (the essence of the American Dream), which tempered their radicalism.

At the same time, however, a significant segment of the non-Jewish, white American population was feeling threatened by the influx of immigrants and the changes that were rapidly developing in American society. In 1915, near Atlanta, Georgia, a revived Ku Klux Klan was organized. Its growth was fueled largely by rural white Protestants who felt threatened by the Bolshevik revolution in Russia and by the large-scale immigration that over the previous decades had so radically changed the demographic character of America. In 1924, this antiforeign sentiment led to the passage of a new immigration law that severely restricted the admission of immigrants from anywhere other than England and northern Europe. But that did nothing to address the mass of foreigners already in the United States. These people continued to be a source of suspicion and hatred, and so the Klan continued to grow, reaching a peak membership of some 4 million. In addition to its hostility toward Blacks, the Klan stood against Roman Catholics, Jews, foreigners, and organized labor (which was seen as Bolshevik). Thus, Jews returning home from the war found a country of growing discrimination and anti-Jewish sentiment. Many primary housing areas in the new suburbs were labeled "restricted," meaning Hebrews were not allowed. But this was not the time to attack these policies. Instead, Jews quietly moved into neighborhoods that would accept them, and when the local country clubs refused them membership, they founded their own community centers or Young Men's Hebrew Associations. Besides, there was much Jewish business to attend to with the rise of Nazism and anti-Jewish riots in the Middle East. All in all, the American Jewish community in the 1930s remained liberal in its politics, but maintained a low profile.

Of course, not everyone in the Jewish community agreed with Brandeis' synthesis. At the one extreme stood traditional or ultratraditional

Jews who were concerned only to maintain the halachic, "Torah-true," life that they knew from Europe. For them Americanism was just another form of assimilation, another Babylon beckoning Jews away from their covenant with God. So they rejected the America part of Brandeis' complex argument. For them, leading a halachic life was the beginning, middle, and end of Jewish concerns, whether in America, the Land of Israel, or anywhere else. At the other extreme were Jews who were so anxious to be undifferentiated Americans and to succeed that they gave up all connection with Jewish ethnicity or only regarded their Jewish ethnicity as secondary to their socialist beliefs. Many even converted out of Judaism, often joining Unitarian churches, one of the more socially liberal Protestant denominations. But most American Jews found a middle ground, a connection to Judaic culture and religion while still upholding the great liberal values of American democracy, human rights, and freedom. Many American Jews did not find these two poles to be in opposition, but rather to be opposite sides of the same coin, much as Brandeis had argued.

This quiescence changed dramatically in the wake of World War II. Again, a number of reasons can be cited. One was the Holocaust and a certain sense of "survivor's guilt" among American Jews. They had failed to speak out in the 1930s and now reaped the bitter harvest of their silence. A second reason was the attitude of Jewish war veterans. After returning from the war, they went to school on the GI bill and then wanted to move into the new suburbs springing up around American cities. Restricted neighborhoods persisted, but now Jewish veterans fought back openly in the courts. These challenges came in the wake of general public revulsion against the Nazis and against all forms of racial discrimination; this, after all, was precisely what Americans had fought and died for to eradicate in Europe. So one by one, restrictions against Jews in housing, university admissions, acceptance to civic groups, and so forth fell away. Jewish activists did not stop with the Jewish community, however, but became active in the broader civil rights debate. In 1954, the Supreme Court ruled in favor of desegregating schools. Jews, now well established and having won their own civil rights battles, were ready to push forward with this new agenda. As the African American civil rights movement took shape, Jews showed up in prominent numbers, often looking back with disdain at the silence of their parents in the 1930s. Some of the older groups founded by or for the earlier immigrants reemerged on the liberal scene. The American Jewish Committee, whose current motto is "Advancing Democracy, Pluralism and Mutual Under-standing," is one example of this phenomenon.

The list of Jewish activists in various radical groups that pushed for hu-man rights in the late 1960s is virtually endless. A few examples will have to suffice. Jews were a major part, maybe even on occasion a majority, of the radical group SDS (Students for a Democratic Society).[20] The Yippie! movement (the name is derived from the acronym of the Youth Interna-tional Party) was founded by three Jews (Abbie Hoffman,* Jerry Rubin,* and Paul Krassner).[21] Not all of these activists were necessarily connected to religious Judaism, but they saw their struggle as growing out of their Jewish roots and out of the Jewish experience and tradition they had in-herited. Julius Rosenberg, executed in 1953 as alleged spies for Russia wrote, "At Hebrew school I absorbed quite naturally the culture of my people, their struggle for freedom and slavery in Egypt." They went on to write that the Jewish "struggle for freedom from oppression and tyranny is a firm part of our heritage and buttresses our will to win our own free-dom."[22]

One of the most enduring symbols of this Jewish cooperation with the civil rights movement is Abraham Joshua Heschel. Heschel was a refugee from Hitler's Holocaust who went first to England in 1940 and eventually came to America. He was a scholar and teacher, first at Hebrew Union College in Cincinnati and then professor of Jewish Ethics and Mysticism at the Jewish Theological Seminary of America. In the 1960s he became an active figure in the civil rights movement. He is best remembered for walking side by side from Selma to Montgomery, Alabama, with the Rev. Martin Luther King, Jr. in 1965 to protest American racism. But this ac-tivism was not just for the leaders. During the Freedom Summer of 1964, it is estimated that Jews made up half of the young people who volun-teered in the effort to end segregation in Mississippi, and two of the three young activists who were killed in a notorious action by white extremists in Philadelphia, Mississippi, were Jewish.

This activism has gradually worked its way back into the religious com-munities. One striking example is the Freedom Haggadah published by Rabbi Arthur Waskow in 1969. Mixed in with the traditional Passover liturgy describing the Jews escape from ancient Egyptian slavery are state-ments calling on Jews to stop collaborating with those who are making slaves of others: "Jewish businessmen must stop buying grapes from farm-ers who exploit their hired laborers; Jewish organizations must not lend money to banks that oppress Black people; Jewish political leaders must not serve the military-industrial complex" and so forth. Today there are a range of radical Haggaddahs—feminist, lesbian, vegetarian—and many readings and prayers of similar sentiment have found their way into a variety of standard American prayerbooks, especially in the Reform and Reconstructionist branches.[23]

CONTEMPORARY AMERICAN JEWISH THOUGHT ON HUMAN RIGHTS

THE PHENOMENA MENTIONED above were not the result of isolated Jewish individuals, but represent at the street level a deep conviction along the lines laid out early in the century by Brandeis. His trilogy of ideas sunk deeply into the American Jewish psyche. As a result there have been a number of Jewish academic thinkers and writers who have addressed this "liberal agenda" as an integral part of American Jewish thought in the late twentieth century. Consider the similar sentiment expressed by Milton Konvitz in *Judaism and Human Rights*, published long after Brandeis' death. In his introduction, Konvitz notes that while the actual terminology of human rights is a product of the Enlightenment and has no exact Hebrew equivalent, the sentiment is nonetheless present and can be seen to be at work in the traditional Jewish literature, albeit never perfectly.

> There is no word or phrase for "human rights" in the Hebrew Scriptures or in other ancient Jewish texts. Nor is there in the Bible a word we would translate as "conscience." Nor is there mention of due process of law. Yet, as the essays in this book make clear, the absence of these and related words and phrases does not mean the nonexistence of the ideals and values for which they stand or to which they point.[24]

In the "Editor's Notes," Konvitz cites both Genesis (humans being created in the image of God) and Thomas Jefferson's words in the Declaration of Independence (all men "are endowed by their Creator with certain inalienable rights") to anchor his Jewish liberalism. There can hardly be a more striking example of the American Jewish idea that Judaism reflects the highest ideals of Americanism than the juxtaposition of these two moral authorities: the Bible and Thomas Jefferson. In fact, the entire book, which contains a number of essays, many by Konvitz himself, but also including others from Moses Mendelssohn, to Samuel Raphael Hirsch, to Emanuel Rackman* (a leader of American Orthodox Judaism), is designed to drive this point home. The thesis of the collection is best summed up by Konvitz himself at the end of his essay, "Judaism and the Democratic Ideal," where he says, "Not all democratic institutions were foreseen by the prophets and Rabbis; such agencies are evolved by societies of men as the need for them is felt to be irresistible. . . . But the spirit, the inner values, the energies of democracy are right at the very heart of Judaism."[25]

Nor is Zionism left out. In his introduction to the new and expanded edition of 2001, Konvitz refers to a number of events that have happened since the first edition. One is the passage, in 1992, by the Israeli Knesset of the Basic Law on Human Dignity and Freedom (discussed in chapter 9). Another is based on a 1999 ruling by the Israel Supreme Court that outlaws the use of torture on suspected terrorists, and also in that same year, limitis placed on the time a person could be held in jail before appearing in front of a judge. To bolster this point, the new edition contains an added section of almost one hundred pages entitled "Human Rights in An Israeli Context." These and other developments, Konvitz argues, only illustrate the theme of the book as first published in 1972, namely, that the struggle for human rights and dignity is always a work in progress but grows everywhere out of the center of Judaism's worldview. He concludes by saying that while there may be "concern about the future security of the State of Israel, . . . there need be no concern about its protection of human rights."[26] Whether this statement is true is not as important as the conviction it reflects, that, for Konvitz as well as for Brandeis, Judaism in its *essence* combines the best of Americanism and is (seen as well in the Zionist enterprise). So again Brandeis' formulation became a broad-based American Jewish creed: being Jewish also meant fighting for human rights at home and abroad and nurturing and supporting the growth of a Jewish national home (albeit, a home to which most American Jews would not themselves think of moving).

Unfortunately, the situation of the native Arab population of Palestine was hardly on the radar screen of these thinkers. Instead, the world's attention was directed to massive population disasters, the displaced persons in Europe, refugees from behind the Iron Curtain, the retreat of the Japanese, the huge number of deaths resulting from the partition of India and Pakistan, and so forth. In the massive need to take care of Jewish displaced persons, and then hundreds of thousands of Jews coming to Israel from Arab countries, it was simply assumed the Arab refugees would be settled in their new homes.

American Jewish involvement in liberal causes went beyond just individual choices and became part of the texture of American Jewish intellectual life. As American Jews became more secularized, in some ways it was Jewish professors and philosophers who became the intellectual engines of American Jewry. They became, as it were, the secular rabbis of the secular Jewish community. In nineteenth-century Germany, the leading source of moral thinking in the Reform community was Hegel. His thinking was translated into the Jewish community by such rabbis as Abraham Geiger and provided the basis for their program of reform. In the twentieth century there was a revival of Kantianism in Germany, especially under the leadership of Hermann Cohen. His reading of Kantian rationalism made sense to Jews who held on to a vision of Judaism as a kind of ethical monotheism. In addition, Kant stressed the importance of duty and law, principles that resonated within the Jewish community. Neo-Kantianism became the secular theology of Jews who could pride themselves on being members of a religious community that stressed rationality and ethical humanism.

This optimism in human reason and progress was dealt a heavy blow by World War I and was finished off in the wake of the Nazi death camps in World War II. The very notion of rationality fell apart under the attacks of Freud, Marx, anthropological studies of value systems, deconstructionism, feminism, womanism, and so forth. What people were looking for was authenticity in ethics. For the modern (and postmodern) American Jewish academic, this yielded a move back to the traditional sources, but mostly to glean their wisdom, not necessarily to readopt the halachah per se as a lifestyle.[27] What was important was rootedness in a tradition of wisdom that was both authentically Jewish and yet promoted liberal and progressive social activism. A number of Jewish academics rose to the challenge, seeking out ways of making Jewish law, or at least Jewish ethics, relevant without calling for a return to Orthodoxy and self-imposed isolationism. What they were hoping to find was a kind of reasonable Judaism without the romantic and discredited rationalism of a Hegel or a Kant.

One academic who has dedicated his life to articulating just such a synthesis is the professor and philosopher David Novak, who argues that the basis of Judaism is the Jewish polity and that that polity, in turn, is based on the covenant with God. In his book, *Covenantal Rights*, Novak asserts that despite the opinion of many, it is possible to draw a theory of human rights from the traditional halachic system. To be sure, as a system of norms, halachah really talks about duties, to God and to our fellow human beings. But duties, he notes, are really just the other side of rights. Once one recognizes this relationship, then it is easy to show that the concept of rights articulated in the Enlightenment really does also exist in Judaism, albeit in different language.[28]

One issue, of course, is that in the traditional rabbinic concept, social needs always stand in the forefront. The need, then, is to show how there can be such a thing as an individual human right over the demands of the community. For Novak, what the halachic tradition is all about, in the end, is the creation of the ideal polity, but it also has to be realized that this polity in its full form is possible only in messianic times. Only at that point will all people reach the fullness of their humanity. In the meantime, Jews must live among other peoples and societies that are also incomplete and imperfect. Thus, the situation of the modern Jew is one of struggle to make the Jewish tradition relevant in his or her life, while at the same time getting by in the real world of unrealized messianism.

One option is to give up on the Jewish tradition entirely, as did the children of Moses Mendelssohn. But Novak rejects this, for the Jewish tradition is the very thing that makes us Jewish. "Wherever Jews live together in a community that is self-consciously Jewish, there is a Jewish polity having to struggle with how it draws upon the Jewish tradition for its internal governance. As long as there are Jews who look to the Jewish tradition for authority, the covenant between God and Israel is still operative, however partially."[29] A second option is to secularize Jewish law, that is, to make it deal only with relationships among people. But Novak also rejects this because ultimately it negates the religious aspect of the Jewish tradition.[30] A third option is to take the ultra-Orthodox course and obey the halachah to the letter. But doing so means that you have to claim that you obey God because of God's power, not because what God says is right. For Novak this does not work either, because humankind is created in the image of God precisely to be able to make judgments and respond to God with will and understanding.[31]

Here is the problem, then: How can a Jew find a way of being true to the covenantal spirit of the halachah while still acknowledging human rights? In facing this dilemma, it is the notion of incompleteness or partiality that opens up a way for Novak to balance individual rights (the Enlightenment) with communal rights (the halachah). Because all societies are incomplete, they can have only a partial claims on an individual, or they become tyrannical. So when one talks about human rights and the comparative balance between the individual and the commonwealth, it has to be kept in mind that both are in a state of premessianic incompleteness. As Novak says in his closing argument, both:

> [T]he autonomy of the individual and the heteronomy of society are relative to each other, hence limited per se. What is not limited is the divine sanction that shines between the claims of both the individual and society. It is this divine source that is the final source of all claims, individual or communal.

> [T]he proposal of any society governed by Jewish law must convince the vast majority of the Jewish people that what is being proposed is authorized by the power that transcends all human power, whether collective or individual, . . . thus the power of society is limited by individual rights just as the power of any individual is limited by the rights of society. All power and all rights are gifts of God. Neither party can ever claim to have a monopoly on their exercise or distribution.[32]

Novak's overall view is expressed succinctly at the end of Chapter V:

> Based on all of the above, one could say that the commandment of neighbor love should be interpreted as follows: Extend God's love for his people to his people as you yourself want to be loved by that same love—and never leave out anyone who is among God's people, however partially, however temporarily, however involuntarily. And the verse in Leviticus 19:18 ends with the words: "I am the Lord." That is the true ground of the commandment: Because the Lord loves Israel, individual Jews are able to share that love with others in the covenant.[33]

Novak's emphasis on the priority in Jewish social ethics over the individual is not, however, universally conceded. In his essay, "The Structure of Jewish Ethics," Menahem Marc Kellner says just the opposite: "Whatever the reason, however, it is certainly the case that Jewish ethical texts tend to emphasize character development and personal virtues over social ethics. The latter is seen as dependent on the former."[34] In this essay, Kellner argues that for a number of reasons Jewish ethics have tended away from philosophical discourse and toward the individual, whether this be in the shape of specific halachic rulings or in the character formation found in the Musar movement. In this view the autonomy of the individual is important because it is the morality of the individual agent that provides the foundation upon which a just human society is based. S. Daniel Breslauer puts this in slightly different words, but makes essentially the same point in "Modernizing American Jewish Ethics: The Liberal Dilemma": "Jewish ethics assumes human beings to be capable of responsible choosing. The ideal person is the responsible agent."[35] Given this view, Breslaeur draws a conclusion that is the direct opposite of Novak's: "The threefold consequences of the dilemma are first an ambivalence toward God's role in legitimizing a religious ethics, secondly a rejection of the identification of Jewish ethics and American ideals, and finally an affirmation of Jewish particularism and Zionism."[36]

In short, there has been a tendency in late-twentieth-century American Jewish moral thought to place the emphasis more on the individual as a responsible moral agent, a view certainly in accord with American values. This has the advantage of making each human being (Jewish or not) equally moral and thus due the freedom, respect, and dignity of that status. It removes the ethnic exclusivity of Judaic ethics, that is, Jewish ethics applies to all and not just to Jews. At the same time, it raises the question of what makes such an ethic "Jewish" at all. One answer is that even as free moral agents, Jews should try to respond in their decisions to their religious tradition and the covenant with God. But the initiative comes from the individual. This is a point made, for example, by Eugene Borowitz in his essay, "The Jewish Self."[37] A more systematic attempt to work out the logic of this approach is found in the work of Lenn E. Goodman. Unlike Novak, Goodman does not assume God as the starting point of his considerations. In fact, for him, the Judaic notion of human rights is ontological and so are attributed to, rather than derived from, God. His starting point is the observation that Westerners have so overused the term "rights" and have become so worried about intolerance that they have essentially emptied the term into a hollow rhetorical tag. The aim of his book *Judaism, Human Rights, and Human Values* is to reestablish the concept of universal human rights as a concept with a certain real content. To achieve this universality, Goodman take pains to point out that while his book intends to be normative, it is not theological in the sense that it cites God as the authority of its theory of rights. Citing authority, as he points out, is only persuasive to those who already accept the authority of God. Rather, the argument is philosophical and ontological and gives us a theory of rights that can apply to God.[38] And, as his title indicates, this view of rights is deeply embedded in the Jewish tradition.

The foundation on which the argument rests is Goodman's theory of just deserts. Historically, he claims, it has been argued that these come from either God or society, that they adhere either to individuals or to communities. In each case, these are false dichotomies that in the end have only obfuscated the problem. In fact, just deserts are what individuals get as members of communities, and the values of society are derived from an ideal type that has come to be identified as God. So in the end all of these should work together to give us a sense of what are our just deserts. This is precisely what Goodman finds in the Jewish tradition, especially as articulated by the philosophers Maimonides and Saadia Gaon. Rights, for these Jewish thinkers, always reside in the individual. To be sure, Judaism also has a monarchical tradition, one that Maimonides in particular writes about. But the king is never absolute and is also under the law, answerable to the community. In making this point, Goodman stresses again and again that the concept of rights was well-known in the premodern world, and that people who claim that there is no word for rights, and therefore no such concept existed before modernity, are simply wrong. It is deeply embedded in the classical Jewish philosophical tradition. It is the popular notion and trust in ultimate goodness that in the end grounds just rules and thus human rights.

Goodman is willing to make an even stronger claim. Not only did the concept of human rights exist in premodern times in Jewish thought, but "the values of the Judaic tradition and the principles articulated in its canon stand proudly among the ancestors of modern liberal humanism. They offer striking early support to the idea of the consent of the governed . . . for example."[39]

In his chapter, "*On Liberty* Reconsidered," Goodman uses his construction of the Jewish liberal tradition on human rights to analyze and critique John Stuart Mill's famous work, "On Liberty" (1869). In this chapter, Goodman focuses his attention on a number of institutions in our current civil society, from taxation to Little League, and argues that in light of the Judaic/liberal tradition of human rights, a vantage point is afforded for evaluating not only the worth of these institutions, but how best they should be managed and deployed:

Reaching beyond the invidious display of the symbolisms of wealth and power that attach themselves to art and sport and all cultural institutions, we should deliberate together with a view to the enrichment of the human experience, pronouncing to ourselves, through our institutions in all their diversity, who it is that we think we are.[40]

Emanuel Rackman, a leading Orthodox thinker, made a very similar point in his essay, "Judaism and Equality":

Since God had created all men equal, their natural inequality can only be justified with reference to His service, which means the fulfillment of the very equality God had willed. Freedom does not serve primarily the purpose of mans's self-fulfillment, as in the writings of John Stuart Mill, but rather God's purpose—that justice and righteousness shall reign on earth. In Judaic thought, therefore, freedom is more the means and equality more the end.[41]

At the end of the twentieth century, the North American Jewish community, while slowly returning to its religious and ethnic roots, is doing so with one foot still firmly planted in the soil of North American democratic liberalism. Although there is a noticeable rightward trend in the Jewish vote, the official voice of the American Jewish community is still decidedly liberal in orientation. There are even strong trends bringing this American liberalism to Israel. In some sense, the American Jewish community sees itself as one of the two great axes of modern Judaism, Israel being the other, and as such having the right to establish the Jewish agenda for the future. This agenda will be a sort of religious Americanism, promoting democracy, civil rights, and liberal individualism to Israel and the rest of the world. This is what being American and being Jewish demand. This is the messianic mission of this historically new amalgam of American Judaism. How this is being received in Israel is the subject of chapter 9.

9

HUMAN RIGHTS IN PRACTICE IN ISRAEL

THE DISCUSSION OF HUMAN RIGHTS in Israel is complicated by the fact that it occurs at the intersection of four historical trends, all of which are to this day very much in a state of flux. The first of these is the transition from Zionism to what has been called Israeli statism, the second is the transition of the state from one based on socialism to one based on liberal Western democratic capitalism, the third is the difficult security situation in the Middle East in general and with the Palestinians in particular, and the fourth has to do with the question about the nature and role of Judaism in the modern state. Each of these four trends individually and in combination has had a role in shaping the human rights debate in Israel. Before proceeding, these need to be spelled out more fully.

First, it should be noted that Zionism in some sense ended in 1948 when the state of Israel was proclaimed. From that point on, public affairs in the Jewish community in Western Palestine were no longer a matter of Zionist thinking, ideologies, and organizations, but of the Israeli government and its political bureaucracy. Thus, even though the World Zionist Organization continued to exist and even though Zionism was and still is a living ideology among many Jews inside and outside of Israel, there is now an Israeli national government that rules a state with its own interests and concerns. Part of the difficulty lies in the fact that while Zionism encompassed all Jews (and only Jews), the state of Israel by the very nature of things owes its first obligation to its various citizens, whatever their ethnicity. Thus, it is Israelis (Jewish or not) who have Israeli citizenship, Israelis (Jewish or not) who vote, and Israelis (Jewish or not) who pay taxes, while Jews outside of Israel have no such connection to the state. At the same time, Israel, on the basis of its Zionist roots, sees itself as the homeland of all Jews (Israeli or not). This built-in contradiction has created some bizarre realities on the ground. Public or state land, for example, is land available by law for the use of all citizens of the state. But much of this land in Israel is actually owned, according to law, by the pre-state Jewish National Fund, which holds the land in the name of the Jewish people. So public land in Israel is, in effect, often available only to the Jewish public. For Zionists (inside or outside the state) this is a perfectly logical legal reality connected with the purpose of the state. To non-Zionists in Israel (Jewish or not), this is a bizarre and quirky relic of nineteenth-century nationalism and a source of grave human rights violations for tax-paying but non-Jewish Israelis.

The second factor is the transition from a centralized social democratic state to a Western liberal and capitalistic society. The early state, led in its first years by the Labor Zionists, considered itself part of the socialist world and saw the communal organization of the kibbutz as one of its crowning social achievements. In socialism, by definition, the welfare of the group takes precedence over the rights of any single individual. Although the government was a parliamentary type whose members were elected, it was also a government of the workers who owned a significant portion (90 percent or so) of the business sector of the economy. In fact, the dominant party, Labor, originated organizationally as an arm of the General Labor Federation (the Histadrut), which in turn owned the factories and other major enterprises in which its members (and so the basic constituency of the Labor party) were employed. Given this interlocking economic socialist structure, individual human rights as understood in the West, as opposed to the subordination of the individual to the community, did not emerge as a topic of great concern. Israel did enjoy the rule of law, but the law always placed the communal over the individual. This structure began to unravel only in the 1970s and 1980s, so that by the 1990s Israel was well on its way to leaving the socialist world behind and entering the community of liberal Western capitalist societies. While this had the effect of giving the state a modern, even hi-tech and globally competitive economy, it also created unprecedented (for Israel) levels of unemployment and differences in wealth and opportunity, developments that cast some doubt on the wisdom of giving up the old socialist values that characterized the much more egalitarian early state. In light of these new economic and political structures, human rights entered public discourse for the first time as a central topic in the creation of the new Israel. The need for capital formation and entrepreneurship meant that individual private rights in many spheres of public life had to take precedence over the communal. At present, the state is still somewhere in the middle of the transition from one model to the other. So the debate between socialist communal, egalitarian principles, and Western individual human rights (to oversimplify a very complex matter) is still in full swing.

Third, the security situation with the Palestinians has shaped a good deal of public attitude and policy toward human rights. Violence against Israel and Israelis—whether in the form of open warfare, terrorist homicide bombings, military ambushes or drive-by shootings of settlers—has been an unceasing fact of life since the proclamation of the state, and in fact stretches back, as stated earlier, into the 1930s and even to the 1920s. During the first generation or two of the state, the combination of a Socialist ideology and severe security needs created a strong communal ethic that regarded human and civil rights for all Israelis as a luxury that could hardly be afforded. With the changes to Western capitalism and liberalism over the last few decades and the modernization of the Israeli army and other security forces to a level significantly beyond anything available to its Arab neighbors individually or combined, the pressures of the security situation have diminished to some extent but still remain a powerful factor.

In very rough terms, it can be said with some degree of accuracy that with respect to the Israeli-Palestinian axis, the current situation of human rights in Israel breaks down into three categories. At one extreme, civil liberties and individual human rights are gradually being granted and/or extended to Israeli Jewish citizens. They approach (as far as the security situation allows) what one would find in Western Europe. At the other extreme are the Palestinians under Israeli military control. These people are not Israeli citizens and therefore have none of the rights and protections such citizenship bestows. For the occupied population, there are certain rights indirectly extended to them by Israeli law insofar as this law regulates the activities of the government and the military, but security concerns are consistently understood to take precedence. Thus while the military or the border police are prohibited from wanton violation of human rights in the Occupied Territories, the West Bank and the Gaza areas are considered to be a sort of military zone of operation in which harm to civilians, whether wounding by hostile fire, victims of collateral damage, or imprisonment for security concerns, is regarded as an unfortunate but inevitable part of the nature of things.

Caught in the middle are Israeli Arabs, that is, those Arabs (Muslim, Christian, Druze, and so forth) who live in Israel and hold Israeli citizenship. On the one hand they are Israelis and so share the same legal rights (in theory) as all other (that is, Jewish) Israelis. On the other hand, they are Arabs and non-Jews and so in fact they face systematic discrimination. Many of the social services in the country are delivered by Zionist or Jewish welfare organizations, for example, so that Israeli Arabs are often ineligible to avail themselves of these services (as in the use of public land, as noted above). Thus, Israeli Arabs find themselves in the curious position of having more rights and greater freedoms than any other Arabs in the Middle East because they are Israeli, but having fewer rights and freedoms than other Israelis because they are Arab.

Finally, a word has to be said about the fourth theme, the role of Judaism itself in the state. As should be clear from chapter 7, Zionist thinkers conceived of the creation of a Jewish homeland in secular, nationalistic terms rather than in religious terms. There were, to be sure, groups of religious Zionists that were formed (such as Mizrachi), but these were minority voices in the Zionist universe and remain so in the contemporary state of Israel. The result was that Israel was conceived of, and finally established as, a purely secular socialist state, albeit one with strong roots in Jewish culture and tradition. But what was this Jewishness and how was it to play itself out in a secular state?

The Declaration of the Establishment of the State of Israel in 1948 is marvelous testimony to the fact that this ambiguous duality already existed in the minds of the state's founders. The proclamation, for example, announces that the new state "will be open for Jewish immigration and for the Ingathering of the Exiles; it will foster the development of the country for the benefit of all its inhabitants; it will be based on freedom, justice and peace as envisaged by the prophets of Israel; it will ensure complete equality of social and political rights to all its inhabitants irrespective of religion, race or sex." A careful reading of even this one small section reveals the schizophrenic nature of the state. It is open to "Jewish immigration" and the "Ingathering of the Exiles" (the latter being a traditional Jewish theological concept) and yet guarantees rights to "all its inhabitants." It is to be based on the secular Enlightenment values of "freedom, justice and peace," including equality "irrespective of religion, race or sex," but then does so "as envisaged by the prophets of Israel." In short, from the very start, Israel was to serve, as it were, two masters: democracy and Judaism.

This intermixture of secular nationalism with the concept of a Jewish state is especially confounding when one bears in mind that nearly one out of every five Israelis is not Jewish, and that a considerable bulk of those who are Jewish are Jewish in a secular or ethnic sense and not a religious sense. Consequently, when studying the laws and policies of the state of Israel, it is important to keep in mind that what is being examined in the first instance is a secular state that happens to have a large Jewish majority, and that this Jewish majority is itself made up largely of that particularly modern invention, the secular Jew, rather than of Jews who practice the rabbinic religion in some classical sense of the term. This has led to an increasingly fierce debate about whether the state, as it evolves into a Western democracy, is to be regarded as primarily Israeli or primarily Jewish, and if Jewish, whether it is to be primarily secular or primarily religious, that is, whether it is to be governed according to Jewish law or secular law.

Part of the problem is that Orthodox Jewish religious parties have been part of the government since 1948 and control matters of religion and personal status in the state. Thus, for example, there is no civil marriage and all Jews have to go through Orthodox Jewish channels to be married. For a variety of reasons this has led thousands of Jewish Israelis each year to go to Cyprus or Amman, Jordan, to get married, since Israel does recognize civil marriages carried out elsewhere. Another good example is the question of whether the state can impose Jewish values (like forcing businesses to close on the Sabbath or disallowing the selling of pork) even on its non-Jewish population.[1] The result is that public opinion ranges from those who find the heavy hand of Judaism to be so pervasive as to be stifling, to those who find the state so militantly secular as to regard it as an enemy of true Judaism, and of course every conceivable view in between.

These debates about the very character of the state, and therefore its attitude toward human rights for its Jewish and non-Jewish citizens, are still taking place with such heat because the state is still, even after nearly sixty years, very much a work in progress. Its final character has not been set and is still open to all possibilities. This is so because in the years of its existence—two generations or so—the population has grown from slightly under 1 million to slightly over 6 million (the impact of this growth leads to the startling statistic that as late as the year 2000, approximately one out of every six Israelis had been in the country less than ten years). This growth is due primarily to immigration, which has brought together in a tiny country people from an unbelievable variety of backgrounds: Western European middle-class Ashkenazic Jews; Jews from the former Soviet Union; Holocaust survivors; Jews from Muslim countries like Morocco, Yemen, Syria, Iraq, and Iran; North Americans, Latin Americans, Ethiopians, and South Africans, all with different traditions and notions of human rights. At the same time, Israel has developed economically from a decidedly agricultural, third-world backwater to a high-tech, industrialized modern economy supporting a large middle class at a European standard of living. These massive changes in the span of a lifetime have created wrenching changes in the social conditions of the population, similar to what is still going on in the former Soviet Union.

At the same time, Israel has undergone five wars (six, if one counts the Iraqi SCUD missile attacks during the Gulf War in 1991) and a continuing security threat of war and terrorism. If this were all not confusing enough, for most of this period, and especially the last thirty years, it has gone through all this with a series of coalition governments that have included members from opposing parties with sometimes diametrically opposing points of view and policy objectives.

In short, it is extremely difficult to talk about any real Israeli policy or consensus on almost anything, especially something as amorphous as human rights. It is for this reason that Israel is only just now in the process of attempting to write a constitution (called the Basic Law) through which it might define for itself a basic position on a variety of fronts, including human rights. This chapter will try to make some sense out of this morass of policy formation and of the complex relations between the state and its own citizens, Jews and Arabs, and between the state of Israel and the Palestinians.

The best way to make sense of the situation in Israel is to follow its historical evolution over the last fifty or so years. Such a survey will show that as the ecology of Israeli society and law have evolved, so has recognition of human rights.

THE STATE OF ISRAEL

WHEN DAVID BEN Gurion, soon to become Israel's first prime minister, announced the creation of the state of Israel in May 1948, he faced at least four mutually exclusive streams of Zionism that had to be melded into a single state. There was, of course, his own group, the Labor or Practical Zionists who conceived of a secular, socialist nation-state that would take its place among all the other states of the Western World. A second, and rather significant minority group, the Revisionists, led by Vladimir (Zeev) Jabotinsky and then Menahem Begin, opposed (in the wake of the Holocaust) any collaboration with the British or anyone else who tried to place limitations on Jewish self-autonomy. It was this group that spawned Jewish terrorist groups like the Stern Gang and Etzel. Disagreements with ben Gurion's accommodationist views became so heated that during the Israeli War of Independence the Revisionists actually took up arms against ben Gurion and eventually had to be quashed by the newly created Israel Defense Forces in a mini civil war in 1947–1948. The third group was the religious Zionists, who supported the effort to create a Jewish state, but felt that to be legitimate such a state had to institutionalize Jewish law and thus were dead-set against Israel being a secular democracy ruled by secular parliamentary law. Ben Gurion was able to some extent to co-opt this group by bringing it into the new government and giving it control of Jewish civil status, such as marriage and divorce, thus giving the Orthodox Jewish parties the control over personal status that they have to this day. Needless to say, this accommodation (the status quo) has left non-Jews in the state in a rather awkward position. Finally, there were ultrareligious groups who not only opposed the secular, socialist state of ben Gurion, but bitterly attacked those elements of the Orthodox community who collaborated with the new government, seeing the whole Zionist enterprise as a form of Western nationalistic idolatry. Many religious Jews in this last category have remained outside the government altogether (even refusing to speak modern Hebrew) and have even worked with groups like the PLO who have sought the destruction of the state. After the Declaration of the Establishment of the State of Israel each of these strands (with the exception of the anti-Zionist Jews), often with their own sub-groups, coalesced into a rainbow of political parties in order to continue the struggle to achieve their particular agendas.

In addition, at least two new ideologies have emerged and given rise to political movements. One represents the interests of the indigenous Arab population (i.e., those who are Israeli but not Jewish, and certainly not Zionists), and the other represents right-wing nationalist Zionists (secular and religious), who see accommodation with the Arabs in general and the Palestinians in particular as a betrayal of either Zionism (the view of the secular nationalist) or of God (the view of the religious nationalists) by giving up land (especially in the West Bank and Jerusalem, but also in Gaza) that belongs by right to the Jewish people. Needless to say, each party understands the concept of human rights through the prism of its own ideology.

It is in this context that the contradictory wording of the Declaration has to be understood. The Declaration was not intended to be, and has not been taken by the Israeli judicial system to be, a legal document enforceable in the courts.[2] Rather, it was a piece of crafted rhetoric that allowed as many factions of Jews as possible to support the new state and to do so in terms amenable to the United Nations. For these reasons, it is clear why from the very beginning human rights in the Western democratic and secular sense were not going to be given any clear-cut public articulation. What did prevail, mostly by default, in the early socialist state, was a communal and cooperative mentality as developed by the kibbutz members. On the kibbutzim all authority rested in the membership, who could decide where members lived (who got the new housing for example, and who had to stay in the original barracks) and where members worked. Even the family was dissolved, and children were raised communally. Goods and services were parceled out by need as determined by the membership (usually through one of its committees). While this kind of communal living was not as possible in the towns and cities, the ethics of the collective pervaded the body politic. This was reinforced by the critical security situation. Virtually everything was subordinated to homeland security. All of this was located within the larger frame of the assumption that this was to be a state of, by, and for Jews (in some definition of this term or another).

In this system, the indigenous Arab population was not so much persecuted as ignored. On paper they were granted equal citizenship under the law, but in actual government policies they were systematically marginalized if not disregarded. Funding for sewage, schools, and other public works flowed first to address the needs of newly arriving Jewish immigrants, second to the existing veteran Jewish population, and third, as a sort of afterthought if anything was left, to the indigenous Arab villages. From a certain perspective this unequal treatment made sense at first since much of the funding for the new Israeli government came from diaspora Jewish philanthropy and was aimed at helping Jews, while the remaining Arab population was largely living in its own communities, farming its own land, and governing itself in its customary manner.

Socially, Israeli Arabs were distinguished in Israeli society by being exempted from military service for the very logical reason that they would otherwise be put in the impossible position of being ordered to fight against their former fellow villagers, and even family or clan members. But this had the (unintended?) side effect of making Arabs citizens of the state ineligible for all of the benefits earned as part of military service such as educational stipends, low home-mortgage rates, contracts in government and business, and so forth.

Over time, these distinctions, however logical in the beginning, became embedded in Israeli society such that the view of Israeli Arabs as second-class, non-participatory citizens became accepted by the Jewish majority as a matter of course. As the Israeli economy grew and the national standard of living was raised, the relative neglect of the indigenous Arabs was often justified by arguing that even though they were being left behind by Jewish Israelis, they were nonetheless participating in the overall improvement of the national economy (and, some added, without the burden of having to serve in the military). While it is indeed true that Israeli Arabs are by virtually all standards better off today than they once were, and enjoy more rights and a higher standard of living than virtually any of the their fellow Arabs in the surrounding countries of the Middle East, the discrimination is nonetheless real and the neglect of the Arab sector has continued to grow, fueling an ever deeper sense of injustice, resentment, and alienation by Arab Israelis. Only recently has this gap been taken seriously.

In fact, however, the worst allegations of human rights abuses during these early years came not from the Arab communities, who were largely left alone, but from the "Oriental" (Middle Eastern) Jews. These Jews migrated to Israel in the early years of statehood from the Arab world, from countries such as Morocco, Yemen, and Syria. In most cases they were little more than medieval peasants, barely literate and with virtually no useful skills. They settled in their own slum neighborhoods in the cities or were sent by the government to remote development towns, often along the dangerous borders. Many have come forward in recent years to allege that in the confusion of those early years, thousands of their children were taken by government social workers out of hospitals, day carecenters, even their homes, and put up for adoption with wealthier Ashkenazic families. The parents were subsequently told that their children had died but in virtually no case were death certificates or other information ever forthcoming. What exactly happened remains unclear.

In the late 1960s the Bahaloul-Minkovsky Commission was set up to investigate allegations that the government had kidnapped and sold babies and young children. Although the commission could not account for many of the missing children, it also could find no evidence of actual criminal activity. This was hardly satisfactory to the plantiffs. Their continued agitation led to the creation of a second inquiry, conducted by the Shalgi Commission, which was in session from 1988 to 1994 and did an extensive investigation. Like its predecessor, it could not explain the disappearance of the children, but it also could not find any evidence of illegal adoptions or other criminal acts. The Yemenite community remained unconvinced, and a third commission (the Cohen Commission) was established in 1997. That year also saw a major court case on the question of the "lost" children. The government finally conceded that some children were taken from Yemenite (and other Middle Eastern immigrant) parents in the early years of the state, but this was either for the child's own welfare, or because record keeping was so haphazard that children who were in hospitals or other institutions were not returned simply because the parents could not be identified or located. What really happened fifty years ago may never be fully known, but this remains one of the most emotional allegations of human rights abuses emerging from the early years of the state.

THE POST-1967 YEARS

THE HUMAN RIGHTS situation began to move much closer to the Western norm on a number of fronts in the decades after the 1967 Six-Day War. There are a number of factors that may have played a role in this development. The obvious and most immediate change was a marked amelioration of the security situation. For the first time, Israelis began seriously to think about living a normal life as opposed to living in a sort of Sparta. It was in the wake of this war, for example, that the first moves toward a consumer economy were made: the opening of department stores, boutiques, and fancy restaurants, a concern with fashion, and the like. Another more subtle reason was the maturation of Israeli society, which had been slowly becoming less of an immigrant community and more of a native-born community, meaning, among other things, that there was a new sense of citizenship and therefore of citizenship rights. At the same time, the government itself had become more organized and professionalized, although Israel was still socialist and far from displaying the kind of governmental transparency that was common in the West. Nonetheless, the norms of Western liberal democracy and the rule of law in the Western sense were beginning to emerge. Another factor was that the Israeli economy became increasingly industry based, along with the corresponding drift away from socialism to Western captialism. This not only lessened the cultural influence of the communal kibbutz movement but strengthened the influence of the urban, Westernized, more capitalistic middle class. In short, Israelis slowly started to think of themselves as normal people living a normal life in what they wanted to see as a normal Western country. Among other things, this meant that for the new generation, issues other than national defense began to take some priority—issues like ecology, international trade, and human rights. It is surely no coincidence that the first investigations into the missing babies allegations occurred at this time.

By the late 1970s, this trend was reflected in decisions of the Israeli Supreme Court. One case that serves as a good example is *Katlan v. the Prisons Service* (1980). This case addressed the prison service's policy of forcibly giving enemas to prisoners who had been let out on furlough and who were then, on their return, suspected of having swallowed drugs in order to smuggle them into the prison. Forcing them to accept enemas was, the prisoners claimed, a violation of their rights and their human dignity. The case rose all the way through the court system to the Supreme Court, indicating how seriously the issue of human rights was now being taken. The prevailing position (the case was heard by three justices) was written by Justice Aharon Barak and addressed the issue of human rights explicitly. He wrote:

Every person in Israel has the basic right to preserve his bodily integrity and human dignity. These rights are included in the "scroll of judicial rights" . . . recognized by this court. Even prisoners have the right to bodily integrity and human dignity. The walls of the prison do not place a barrier between the prisoner and human dignity.

The opinion concludes that if such an invasion of privacy (e.g., forced enemas) is deemed essential to running the prison, then the Knesset should pass an explicit law to the effect that this will be "the informed determination of the chosen representatives of the public."[3] The deputy president dissented, but the president (the third of the three Justices hearing the case) agreed and so this became the majority opinion. It is worth noting here that the right to human dignity was upheld by Justice Barak as a matter of positive law, that is, there was no specific law allowing this violation of human dignity, but if the Knesset should pass a law allowing such enemas, then it would be acceptable. No mention is made of a natural law right in this regard. Human rights in Israel were still seen as positive rights but not yet as natural rights.

Contrast this with the 1992 case of *The State of Israel v. Guetta*. By this time, the Knesset had passed (in March 1992) the Basic Law: Human Dignity and Liberty, which stated as its first stipulation that "The purpose of this Basic Law is to protect human dignity and freedom, in order to enrich the values of the State of Israel as a Jewish and democratic state in a Basic Law." Of particular interest to us here is paragraph 4, in which the Basic Law states that "Every person has the right to protection of his life, his person and his dignity."[4] That is, according to the Basic Law, a right to human dignity is grounded in the very character of the state as democratic and Jewish. Human rights are recognized by the state as transcending the power of the Knesset to confer or deny them at will. In short, unlike in the case of *Katlan v. the Prisons Service*, there was now a legal and judicial foundation for human rights that was enforceable by the courts. It should be noted that the Basic Law does not in the end raise the right of human dignity and freedom to the level of an inalienable natural law under all circumstances; some exceptions are explicitly allowed. In particular, the Basic Law stipulates that human dignity and freedom are to be protected only insofar as they reflect the values of the state of Israel as a Jewish and democratic state, and violations of these rights are permissible if they serve an appropriate objective and if they infringe individual rights only to an appropriate extent.

With this legal background in mind, it is possible to understand the changing attitudes reflected in *The State of Israel v. Guetta*. The case in question was one of the first brought to the Supreme Court in which the new Basic Law provision was invoked. The case involved a suspected drug dealer who was under surveillance and was seen engaged in what appeared to be the selling of drugs. He was pulled into an alley by a policeman and told to strip. During the ensuing search, a packet of heroin was indeed found on his person. He was arrested and imprisoned. The defendant argued that the search was illegal in that his right to bodily integrity was violated. His argument was upheld by a lower court on the basis of the Basic Law: Human Dignity and Liberty. The court pointed specifically to paragraph 2, which stipulates that "No one may infringe the inherent right of every human being to life, bodily integrity and dignity." Even more to the point, the court noted in paragraph 7 (c) that "No one may conduct a search of a person's private domain, or a search on or inside his body, or of his personal belongings."[5] The lower court's ruling was appealed and ended up in the Supreme Court. In the end, the Supreme Court threw out the lower court's ruling, basing its argument precisely on the exemptions written into the Basic Law cited above. In particular, the Supreme Court argued that (a) the Basic Law allowed infringement of one's human dignity in the case of specific legislation that allows such a violation in order to uphold the values of the state of Israel, (b) that such a law existed as regards drug trafficking, (c) that there was reasonable cause for the search since the defendant was a known drug dealer already under surveillance, and (d) that in fact heroin was found on the suspect.[6] Although in the end the defendant lost the case, it is important to note that the Basic Law did force the Supreme Court to confront the issue and that it does represent a recognition in Israeli law of the need to protect human rights and dignity except for specifically spelled-out exceptions.[7]

THE PALESTINIANS

THE 1967 WAR (or Six-Day War) and its aftermath had another side effect. While Israeli society from within began its slow, but inexorable development toward Westernization, capitalism, and the rule of law, it also began a period of military occupation of the heavily Arab areas of the West Bank and Gaza. At first, the Israeli government assumed that its rule of these territories and the inhabitants therein would be of limited duration. But as the hoped-for offer of a land-for-peace deal never materialized, the Israelis gradually came to regard their occupation as more or less a permanent fact of life. This opened the possibility among some that the victory was really the final phase of the War of Independence and that the new territories were now open for Jewish migration and settlement. The municipal boundaries of Jerusalem were extended to cover East (Arab) Jerusalem, and new Jewish suburban neighborhoods in north, south, and east Jerusalem began to appear. By the mid-1970s the process of settlement had set in on the West Bank and in Gaza as well. Israeli developers built housing areas across the "green line" (separating Israel proper from the West Bank and the Gaza Strip) ranging from small suburbs to whole towns (such as Ariel in the middle of the northern West Bank, with 16,000 inhabitants and Maale Adumim outside of Jerusalem with some 25,000 inhabitants). Over the next several decades, roughly 150 Israeli settlements were constructed in the West Bank and Gaza, today housing some 200,000 residents.[8] By the turn of the twenty-first century, a whole generation of Israelis who had come of age and were serving in the military had never known a time when the West Bank was not "Israeli."

The word "Israeli" is in quotation marks because the status of the land and its inhabitants are profoundly ambiguous. The West Bank and Gaza never became fully a part of Israel per se and the Arabs living there in their villages and refugee camps remain stateless. Only East Jerusalem was ever formally annexed, although the legality of that move is still a matter of some debate, even inside Israel.[9] In all events, the local Arab inhabitants, indigenous as well as those in refugee camps, were not given Israeli citizenship and so lived with ill-defined status under a strange amalgam of civil and military rule. They remain largely ignored by the Israel government. It is common today in these areas to see Israeli suburbs and towns, with all the modern conveniences and amenities one would expect in an American suburb, located within kilometers of refugee camps or indigenous villages that more often than not lack even such basics as paved roads and sewage systems.

This whole process accelerated after 1977, when the Labor Party lost its majority and the right-wing Likud Party (based in part on the old Revisionists) made the abandonment of socialism and the adoption of Western capitalism official policy. The new right-wing government also actively encouraged investment in and the settlement of the West Bank and the Gaza Strip so as to make them an integral part of "Greater Israel", meaning a Jewish State filling the entire area between the Jordan River and the Sanai Peninsula, including what is now the West Bank and the Gaza Strip. This was in some sense a natural enough development for a booming economy that was running out of land. In some cases such development was part of normal growth—the suburbs of Tel Aviv spread out across the old green line, for example. But in most cases, settlements were established in the service of right-wing nationalism, part of the Likud's program to complete the conquest of what they regarded as the biblical inheritance of the Jewish people. But whatever the motivation, such development almost invariably had an acutely negative impact on the local Arab population. Arab private land was confiscated; olive trees and orchards were bulldozed to create roads, housing, and commercial areas; highways cut off Arab villages from each other; grazing land was hemmed in by new construction; and Arab communities lost room for further growth. In a few cases, Israeli human rights groups took the government to court for illegally confiscating land and occasionally managed to eke out a court victory (including a Supreme Court judgment), but these victories led only to changes in government tactics, not any real changes on the ground.

To be sure, many of these new Jewish communities tried to maintain good relations with neighboring Arab villages, but in most cases, the local Arabs simply became a massive pool of day laborers, hired to work as gardeners, garbagemen, ditchdiggers, or at other menial jobs that no Israeli would now deign to take. Wages were minimal and there was no such thing as fringe benefits. By the mid-1980s, the majority of Gaza and West Bank Arabs were employed by Israelis (whether in Israel proper or in the Territories), so in an ironic twist, the vast expansion of the Israeli infrastructure during the 1970s and 1980s was built "by Jewish heads and Arab hands." Given that such jobs were highly prized by the Arabs, in that few alternatives existed for feeding one's family, and that the Gaza and West Bank Arabs were politically unorganized and in any case under military occupation, it comes as no surprise that there were few overt complaints. The inevitable result was that human rights abuses of the Arab workers abounded but were not even on the radar screen for most Israelis. In fact, most Israelis regarded the Arabs as quintessential, even irredeemable, third-world masses. On the extreme right, there were even voices calling for the mass evacuation of the Arab population to neighboring Arab states such as Jordan where they could "live among their own kind."

This attitude has had its effect on Israeli Arabs as well. While they had become more Israeli since the 1948 War of Independence, they were still regarded as Arabs and not real Israelis by the majority of the Jewish population. Thus, Israeli Arabs were becoming more educated and affluent while still being treated individually and collectively as second-class citizens. As the Israeli Arab community became more Israeli, they began to regard themselves as Israelis and felt they were owed the same rights as other Israelis. The younger generation in particular was learning how to play the system and make their demands for equal rights felt on the political level. By the early 1980s, as human rights abuses were increasing in the Territories, Israeli politicians found that they had to take more and more notice of the Israeli Arab sector. Politicians up for election, especially from the leftist parties, routinely promised to direct more resources to the amelioration of the Arab Israeli's lot, although once in power, these politicians usually made only symbolic gestures. In reaction, the Arab Association for Human Rights (HRA) was founded in 1988 by lawyers and community activists as an independent, grassroots, non-governmental organization (NGO) to press Arab claims for increased rights for non-Jews both in Israel and in the Territories. In their efforts to win the rights promised them under Israeli law, groups like the HRA were aided by a small but growing number of grassroots Israeli civil and human rights advocacy groups. Although these efforts made the Israeli public more aware of the problems in the Arab sector, and while important court cases were won, little actual change occurred. But at least Arab demands were being heard and real changes in attitude seemed to be in the works. There was growing awareness of discrimination not only of Israeli Arabs, but of at least some of the injustices being visited on the occupied Arabs in the Territories.

This whole situation changed radically in late 1987, when an automobile accident set off rioting in Gaza City. Rather than dying out, the riot gained in force and breadth until the entire Gaza Strip, and then all of the West Bank, were engulfed in open rebellion against the Israeli occupation. The first Intifada had begun. The response on the part of the Israeli government was at first shocked disbelief. They simply could not imagine that the uprising was serious or that the Arabs were capable of sustaining any organized opposition. The initial strategy was simply to literally crack heads and break bones until the Arabs had been made to suffer so much pain that they would came to their senses, settle down, and go back to work. Only gradually did it dawn on Israelis, from the government on down, that this was not going to happen. Two diametrically opposed Israeli positions emerged in response to the first Intifada. The first was to regard any peace with the Arabs as a hopeless dream, the second pointed to Israeli human rights violations in the Territories as the root cause of the problem, arguing that if the humiliation of the Arabs could be stopped then the two peoples could find a way to coexist in peace. Developments in the Israel-Palestinian conflict in the subsequent years have provided ample evidence for both sides. The ideological battle for the minds and hearts of Israelis between these two poles continues to this day.

It is much too complicated to try to unravel and explain the various movements as they have taken shape up to today. Instead, the focus will turn briefly to a few movements that represent the general contours of the debate. Most Israelis, it must be said, are confused and bewildered by the situation and find themselves somewhere in the middle, shifting back and forth as the situation on the ground changes. Poll after poll indicates that the Israeli population approves granting greater rights to Palestinians in the Territories, even granting them independent statehood. At the same time, the vast majority of Israelis approve of military action in the Territories to control and even eliminate terrorist organizations. That these two positions are to some extent mutually exclusive is part of the reason no coherent policy has been implemented one way or the other.

At one extreme, as already noted, are those who have come to the conclusion that Israel and the Palestinians will never be able to live in peace. Many who subscribe to this view see the Arabs as quintessential Jew-haters, the modern-day equivalent of Amalek (the biblical archenemy of the Hebrews) and the Nazis. In this view, the Palestinians want only to finish what Hitler started. The only rational solution was to beat the riot to death, increase settlement in the Territories for security reasons (while in the process squeezing the Arabs off the land and across the border into Jordan, Lebanon, or Syria), and to make sure the Arabs were never allowed to forget for a moment that they would have to pay a bitter price for attacking any Jew. This became the official position of the political movement Kach—an acronym for Kahane Chai, which means Kahane lives—founded by the American-born rabbi Meir Kahane. Kahane had founded the Jewish Defense League in New York, adopting as its symbol a raised (Jewish) fist grasping a combat rifle. In Israel he openly advocated the complete expulsion of Arabs from the entirety of the Jewish homeland between the Mediterranean and the Jordan River. So violent had his anti-Arab rhetoric become that the party was officially banned in Israel in 1985. In response, it simply went underground and transmogrified into a Jewish terrorist organization. Although Rabbi Kahane was assassinated in New York in 1990, the group continues to exist. It is remembered most notoriously, perhaps, for the shooting in 1994 of twenty-nine Muslim worshippers at the mosque of the Tomb of the Patriarchs in Hebron by Kach member Dr. Baruch Goldstein.

At the other extreme, a number of groups emerged that called for an end to the Israeli "colonialist" occupation of the Territories and for equal treatment of Arabs—Israeli and Palestinian alike—as the only way to achieve a just and lasting peace. For those subscribing to this view, the riots were not due so much to inherent anti-Semitism or Judeophobia as to the humiliation and human rights abuses that had become the stuff of everyday life in the Palestinian areas. One of the first organized groups that argued this position, Peace Now, was founded as early as 1978 by a group of Israel army reserve officers and soldiers who refused to serve in the West Bank and Gaza. It understood the Intifada to be the logical outcome of systematic Israeli mistreatment of the Arab population of the Territories and demanded that the government negotiate a settlement rather than try to beat one out of the population by force.

Most Israelis stood, and still stand, somewhere in the middle. But throughout the 1980s and 1990s, the position of groups like Peace Now slowly gained a measure of grudging support, while the Kahanists of groups like Kach drifted into a kind of radical extremism that put them on the very fringes of Israeli politics and all but excluded them from serious public discourse. As one example of this trend, a group of rabbis from across the religious spectrum joined to form Rabbis for Human Rights (RHR) in 1988. It was formed in response to the severely brutal measures adopted by the Israeli government to repress the Intifada. Since its founding, the organization has engaged in a number of human rights projects involving Palestinians, Israeli Arabs, foreign workers in Israel and the Bedouins, as well as issues like women's status and health care. More recently, it has organized interfaith dialogue groups, engaged in educational activities, and become involved in law and court cases. For its wide-ranging work, the organization received the Speaker of the Knesset's Award for the Quality of Life in the Field of Enhancing the Rule of Law and Democratic Values, Protecting Human Rights, and Encouraging Tolerance and Mutual Respect.[10] In many ways the group represents the schizophrenic attitude in Israel about the Palestinians. For example, when the Israeli government issues a demolition order to destroy the house of an Arab family of a suicide bomber, RHR members often take it upon themselves to appeal the order, try to find housing for the now homeless family, and even at times join with neighboring Arabs to rebuild destroyed houses.

A third important faction that emerged at this time (1989) was organized by a group of academics, attorneys, journalists, and Knesset members. The ideas was to create a professional human rights organization that could investigate and create reliable documentation of human rights abuses, especially in the West Bank and Gaza. What resulted was The Israeli Center for Human Rights in the Occupied Territories, also known as B'tselem, in reference to the biblical story of humankind being made "in the image"—b'tselem—of God. This group complemented the others by concentrating not so much on street protests (as did Peace Now), or on education and dialogue (like RHR), but on monitoring, data collection, and the publication of reports documenting Israeli human rights abuses in the Territories. Its target audience was not so much the government but the Israeli population and the worldwide human rights community. It has published studies on human rights abuses in the army, violations of human and community rights in the Territories, and discriminatory practices against both Israeli Arabs and Palestinians.

As the Intifada dragged on into its fourth year and popular protests mounted, the Israeli government realized that the uprising could not be put down by force. Peace of a sort was finally achieved by the signing of the Oslo Accords in 1993, which itself was the result of a series of secret talks between Israeli and Palestine Liberation Organization (PLO) officials. The basic concept was that the PLO, under the leadership of Yasser Arafat, would be allowed to "return" to Palestine from its exile in Tunisia and would be given civil control over Gaza and the West Bank. A quid pro quo was arranged that called for the PLO to reign in the Intifada and its terrorist attacks on Israel and, in turn, for Israel to evacuate Palestinian territory (or at least major chunks of it) and turn it over to PLO control, with the eventual goal of establishing a Palestinian state. During this transitional phase, the PLO would rule through a semigovernmental entity called the Palestinian National Authority (PNA), which would have civil control over the lives of the West Bank and Gaza Arabs but no military force. As the rule of law was established in PNA-controlled areas, more territory would pass under its control. The implication was that by the end of the process, at least some of the Jewish settlements in the West Bank and Gaza would be dismantled and military control of the region would be ceded in most cases to the Palestinian police. There were also to be some arrangements to deal with the Palestinian refugees, and the question of sovereignty over Jerusalem was also eventually to be addressed and resolved. At the end of the process, two states, one Jewish and one Arab, would live side by side in peace and cooperation.

This agreement was greeted with great emotion on both sides of the Israeli political spectrum. The right wing, especially the religious ultranationalists, saw the Olso Accords as an illegitimate giving away of the land of Israel to non-Jews. Others saw the establishment of a PLO state on the very borders of Israel as a recipe for disaster, offering Arafat a launching pad for terrorists strikes. In 1995, the Israeli prime minister who signed the Oslo Accords, Yitzhak Rabin, was assassinated by a right-wing Israeli student, Yigal Amir, who had contacts with, but was not a member of

Kach. The assassination followed in the wake of curses called down upon Rabin by some ultra-Orthodox authorities. Most Israelis reacted in horror to the assassination of their prime minister, and this helped isolate Kach and the extreme Right even more.

In the left wing, on the other hand, there was great hope that the colonial mentality generated by the occupation was finally at an end and that peace and justice now had a real chance to take root in Israel and the Territories. In fact, the entire region seemed to breathe a sigh of relief. Shortly after the Oslo Accords went into effect, a peace treaty was signed between Israel and Jordan and the Arab boycott, which had been imposed in 1948 on Israel and on all companies dealing with Israel (and on all companies dealing with those companies), simply fell away. Other Arab countries, especially in the Gulf region, began to send out feelers about future trade and even eventual diplomatic relations. As the accords took hold, the star of the left seemed ascendant, while the right undertook a period of reflection and self-examination in the wake of the Rabin assassination. Human rights in Israel and in the Palestinian territories seemed to be improving as the security situation came under control and prospects of peace came into view.

But as time went on it became clear that the peace process, if not entirely stillborn, was nonetheless severely crippled. The violence of the Intifada did in fact fade, but acts of terrorism (such as bus bombings) continued to occur, reaching such a degree in 1996 that the Oslo Accords were essentially renegotiated. In light of the failure of the Palestine National Authority to end violence, the transfer of territories to its control ground to a halt. Further disillusionment grew out of the ever more apparent incompetence and outright corruption of the PNA. By 1999, the mutual process envisioned by the accords seemed to have run its course. The Israeli elections in that year were in effect a kind of referendum on peace with the Palestinians. Ehud Barak, of the Labor Party, pledged to carry on Rabin's legacy. He promised to withdraw Israeli troops from its security zone in Lebanon, to negotiate a final settlement with the PNA, and to open talks with Syria to return the Golan Heights in return for a peace accord. Barak won handily and began to fulfill his promises. Talks with Syria moved to the edge of agreement, only to finally collapse in early 2000. In the meantime, Barak had set in motion a unilateral troop withdrawal from Lebanon, which was concluded at the end of May 2000. Talks with the PNA were initiated and led eventually to a long meeting at Camp David under the auspices of U.S. president Bill Clinton. After weeks of negotiation, no agreement was reached and Barak and Arafat returned home in August empty-handed. At the end of September, Ariel Sharon made a visit to the holy site of the Temple Mount (*Haram ash-Sharif*), setting off (or giving the pretext for) the Second (or Al-Aqsa) Intifada. In an attempt to restore peace, Barak agreed to a conference with Arafat at Sharm al-Sheik in mid-October 2000. At roughly this same time, a group of Israeli Arabs demonstrated in support of the Palestinians. In dealing with the unrest, Israeli police killed over a dozen rioters and wounded hundreds of others. In the end, nothing came of the summit and the al-Aqsa Intifada continued, leading to at least two and a half years of some of the most sustained and vicious acts of terrorism and counterterrorist repression that the region has ever seen. On the second anniversary of the Intifada, September 30, 2002, the British newspaper *Guardian Unlimited* reported:

> More than 625 Israelis have been killed in a total of 14,280 attacks in the past two years. Some 1,372 Palestinians have been killed by Israeli military forces. A total of 4,500 Israelis have been injured in terrorist attacks, and among the Palestinians, the numbers are much higher—the Palestinian Red Crescent organization reported two weeks ago a total of 19,684 wounded.[11]

In the wake of this failure, and the mounting death toll of terrorists attacks in Israel, Barak lost the election and on February 6, 2001, Ariel Sharon became prime minister. Over the ensuing months, Israeli reaction to the Intifada became more and more violent, including air and missile attacks within civilian areas. In spring 2002, Sharon ordered Israel troops to began a process of reoccupation of the West Bank and Gaza, including the destruction of most of the institutions of the PNA. By the end of 2002, the PNA existed in little more than name, and Israel, through a series of targeted assassinations, had largely eliminated the political leaders and technical experts of the most violent of the Arab terrorist groups, Hamas and Islamic Jihad. Arafat remained in the West Bank as a virtual prisoner in his ruined office in Ramallah. Violent attacks against Israelis virtually ceased, but the West Bank and Gaza were left in ruins, and the population was faced with rising poverty from lack of jobs, rising malnutrition, and severe travel restrictions. Israeli military raids against suspected terrorists continued on a regular basis with a steadily rising toll of civilian casualties.

THE PRESENT SITUATION

WHAT HAS ALL this meant for human rights? As noted earlier, the answer can be broken down into three parts: human rights for Jewish Israelis, human rights for non-Jewish (basically Arab) Israelis, and human rights for Palestinians in the Occupied Territories. Below is a summary of the situation of each population as it exists today as regards human rights.

For Israelis, the need for security has dominated public life for most of the state's existence and so the outbreak of the recent Intifada only returned to the situation as it was before. Israeli citizens have accepted searches and other intrusions of their personal space as a necessary means to stop terrorist attacks. But the legal advances made to ensure civil liberties have not been reversed. The passage of the Basic Law: Human Dignity and Liberty marked an important milestone and has continued to influence the development of human rights legislation and common law court decisions in Israel. Other repressed groups like gays and lesbians, for example, have begun to feel empowered to speak out for their own rights. It is significant, in this regard, that the role of women in Israeli institutions is also growing. The elections in early 2003 showed a significant number of women rising to positions of power in the once nearly all-male Israeli political establishment.

For the Palestinians, the situation has regressed almost entirely. Between Israel military actions, and Palestinian attacks and death sentences carried out against collaborators, the Palestinian population has lost virtually all protection against abuses by both sides. Although violence dramatically decreased by the end of 2002, the economic collapse, travel restrictions, harsh curfews, and other actions barely abated. The Israeli reoccupation of the West Bank and Gaza Strip has halted any progress as regards human rights for Palestinians. They are, in effect, an occupied people with no legal recourse. Israeli human rights groups (like Rabbis for Human Rights and B'tselem) have been doing yeoman advocacy work for Palestinians in Israeli courts, but the victories, though important, are only a drop in the bucket.

The Israeli Arabs find themselves once again caught in the middle. On the one hand, the pro-Palestinian riots (which were also protests against their own second-class treatment) of October 2000 placed them under suspicion in the Jewish public mind. On the other hand, the HRA (the Israeli-based Arab Association for Human Rights) report on the killing and wounding of Israeli Arab citizens exercising their presumed right to demonstrate publicly and openly in a democracy indicated that many of the actions of the Israeli police against Israeli Arabs ran counter to the Israeli police's own regulations. This has brought the issue of Israeli democracy and the need to treat Arab Israelis as equal citizens back into public discourse. The current government has promised to make significant moves in this direction and has begun to do so although its attention has been drawn largely to the situation in the Territories. In the period following this initial violence, relations between Israeli police and Israeli Arabs have been more relaxed, but Israeli Arabs still live under a cloud of suspicion and feel they are bearing more than their share of Israeli security precautions. A growing movement of sympathy with Islamic fundamentalism within the Israeli Arab community is both a reaction to this and a cause for increasing police scrutiny. On the other hand, it seems clear that the situation of the Arab Israelis is now firmly on the Israeli public agenda.

In the end, then, the establishment of a Western human rights tradition in Israel has been, like the state itself, very much a work in progress. Considerable movement in this direction has taken place over the last thirty years or so, but much still needs to be done, especially for minority groups in Israel itself (Arabs, Druze, and so forth). Counter to this is the violent security situation and the brutal (but effective?) military suppression of the Intifada and the groups behind it (Hamas, Islamic Jihad, Hezbollah, Al-Aqsa Brigade, and so forth). A good sign of hope is that there has been a consistent and strong feeling among the Israeli public, expressed in poll after poll, that the current situation is untenable, that for true democracy to be established in the state the local Arab population has to be treated equally in all respects, and that the Palestinians must eventually have self-rule, even their own state (albeit under responsible leadership). It is this underlying and tenacious grassroots support among the Israel Jewish public for the extension of basic human rights that offers the real hope for improvements in the entire region in the future.

Part II
Human Rights
Resources in the Jewish
Tradition

10

SOURCES ILLUSTRATIVE OF HUMAN RIGHTS IN THE JEWISH TRADITION

RESPECT FOR HUMANS IN THE BIBLE

THE HEBREW SCRIPTURES MAKE several references to the sacredness of all human life. This goes back to the very beginning of the Torah where we are told that humans were created in the divine image (see citation 1 below). This was taken to mean by the Bible and all subsequent Jewish thinkers that the abuse of human life is tantamount to abuse of the Creator. Thus, although the Bible does tolerate war and capital punishment in certain cases, it regards the taking of an innocent human life as one of the most heinous crimes one can commit (see citations 2–4). In addition to the preservation of life, the Torah also makes it clear that the sacredness of human life means that each person, as a creature made in God's image, is due respect, justice, and fair treatment (citations 5–12).

THE SACREDNESS OF HUMAN LIFE

1. And God created man in his image, in the image of God He created him; male and female He created them. (Gen. 1:27)
2. Am I my brother's keeper? (Gen. 4:9)
3. Whoever sheds the blood of man, / By man shall his blood be shed; / For in His image / Did God make man. (Gen. 9:6)
4. The men went on from there to Sodom, while Abraham remained

standing before the LORD. Abraham came forward and said, "Will You sweep away the innocent along with the guilty? What if there should be fifty innocent with the city; will You then wipe out the place and not forgive it for the sake of the innocent fifty who are in it? Far be it from You to so such a thing, to bring death upon the innocent as well as the guilty, so that the innocent and guilty fare alike. Far be it from YOU! Shall not the Judge of all the earth deal justly?" (Gen. 18:22–25)

SOCIAL JUSTICE

5. You shall rise before the aged and show deference to the old; you shall fear your God: I the LORD am your God. When a stranger resides with you in your land, you shall not wrong him. The stranger who resides with you shall be to you as one of your citizens; you shall love him as yourself, for you were strangers in the land of Egypt: I the LORD am your God. (Lev. 19:32–34)

6. You shall have one standard for stranger and citizen alike: For I the LORD am your God. (Lev. 24:22)

7. When you reap the harvest of your land, you shall not reap all the way to the edges of your field, or gather the gleanings of your harvest. You shall not pick your vineyard bare, or gather the fallen fruit of your vineyard; you shall leave them for the poor and the stranger: I am the LORD your God. You shall not steal; you shall not deal deceitfully or falsely with one another. You shall not swear falsely by My name, profaning the name of your God: I am the LORD. You shall not defraud your fellow. You shall not commit robbery. The wages of a laborer shall not remain with you until morning. You shall not insult the deaf, or place a stumbling block before the blind. You shall fear your God: I am the LORD. You shall not render an unfair decision: do not favor the poor or show deference to the rich; judge your kinsman fairly. Do not deal basely with your countrymen. Do not profit by the blood of your fellow: I am the LORD. (Lev. 19:9–16)

8. When you make a loan of any sort to your countryman, you must not enter his house to seize his pledge. You must remain outside, while the man to whom you made the loan brings the pledge out to you. If he is a needy man, you shall not go to sleep in his pledge; you must return the pledge to him at sundown, that he may sleep in

his clothes and bless you, and it will be to your merit before the LORD your God. (Deut. 24:10–13)

9. To Me, O Israelites, you are / Just like the Ethiopians. (Amos 9:7)

10. He has told you, O man, what is good, / And what the LORD requires of you: / Only to do justice / And to love goodness, / And to walk modestly with your God. (Mic. 6:8)

11. Have we not all one Father? Did not one God create us? Why do we break faith with one another. (Mal. 2:10)

12. Lord, who may sojourn in Your tent, who may dwell on Your holy mountain?

He who lives without blame, who does what is right, and in his heart acknowledges the truth;

Whose tongue is not given to evil; who has never done harm to his fellow, or borne reproach for [his acts toward] his neighbor;

for whom a contemptible man is abhorrent, but who honors those who fear the LORD; who stands by his oath even to his hurt;

who has never accepted a bribe against the innocent.

The man who acts thus shall never be shaken. (Ps. 15)

SOURCE: *Tanakh: The Holy Scriptures* (Philadelphia and New York: The Jewish Publication Society of America, 1988).

❖

RESPECT FOR HUMAN LIFE IN THE MISHNAH

THE MISHNAH IS the earliest document we have of early rabbinic Judaism. Compiled around the middle of the third century C.E., the Mishnah laid the intellectual and legal foundations on which rabbinic Judaism was built. While rarely entering into overt theoretical discussions, it does so in tractate Sanhedrin, which deals with the makeup and operation of the ideal rabbinic court system. This is so because a court can have the power to impose capital punishment. Chapter 4 of the Mishnah wants to ensure that the members of the court and the witnesses realize the gravity of this power and so explicates in detail the specialness of all human life.

Why did God create Adam alone? He did so in order to teach us that Scripture regards whoever destroys a single life in Israel as though he had destroyed the whole world; and whoever saves one life, as though he had saved the entire world. And in order to keep peace among mankind so that no one will say to his fellow, "My lineage is better than your lineage." And also so that heretics (or polytheists) cannot say, "There are several powers in the heaven (each creating or governing a different race). And also to proclaim the greatness of the Holy One Blessed Be He. For when a man uses a die to stamp coins, they all come out the same; but when the King of Kings, the Holy One Blessed Be He, stamped all men with the die of Adam, no two of them look alike. For this reason each person has the right to say, "On my account was the world created."

SOURCE: Mishnah Sanhedrin 4:5. (Translation by Peter J. Haas.)

❋

RESPECT FOR HUMAN LIFE IN THE TALMUD

THE TALMUD is an eclectic compilation of rabbinic sayings, judgments, court cases, stories, and customs structured as a commentary on the Mishnah. It represents the development of early Mishnaic Judaism into the fully developed religious system of the rabbis. There are, in fact, two Talmuds, an earlier Jerusalem Talmud completed probably in the fourth century in the Land of Israel and a Babylonian Talmud that was redacted in more or less its present form around the early seventh century C.E. It is the latter that has become the foundational document of rabbinic Judaism. Because of its rambling and free-association style of discourse, the Talmud rarely has a sustained discussion of any one issue or principle. Rather, principles and underlying values are brought into play obliquely only as they become relevant to the discussion at hand. Below are a number of excerpts that illustrate the general view of the document as a whole. (Translation by Peter J. Haas.)

1. "Love your neighbor as yourself" (Lev. 19:18) is the major principle of the Torah. (Jerusalem Talmud, Nedarim 9:4)
2. Anyone who is able to protest against the transgressions of one's household and does not do so is punished for the actions of the members of the household. Anyone who is able to protest against the transgressions of one's townspeople and does not do so is punished for

the transgressions of the townspeople. Anyone who is able to protest against the transgressions of the entire world and does not do so is punished for the transgressions of the entire world. (Babylonian Talmud, Shabbat 54b)

3. One should never embarrass a neighbor in public. (Babylonian Talmud, Baba Metzia 59a)

4. Rabbi Joshua ben Levi found Elijah sitting at the opening of the burial cave of Rabbi Simeon ben Yohai. . . . He said to him, "When will the messiah be coming?" He said to him, "Go ask him." He said, "Where is he sitting?" He said, "At the city gate." "And what is his sign?" He is sitting among the poor who are sick and he is taking off their bandages and redressing their wounds all at one time." (Babylonian Talmud, Sanhedrin 98a)

5. Rabbi Ishmael ben Elisha said, "Once I entered the inner sanctum of the Temple and I saw God Himself sitting on a high and exalted throne, and He said to me, 'Ishmael, My son, bless Me.' So I said to Him, 'May it be Your will that your compassion overpower Your anger and your mercy overwhelm your rectitude and that You conduct Yourself toward Your children with compassion and beyond the letter of the law.' And He nodded His head [in assent]." (Babylonian Talmud Berachat 7a)

6. The Holy One Blessed Be He has no pleasure in the downfall of the wicked. Said Rabbi Yohanan, "Why is it written [in Exod. 14:20], 'and the pillar of cloud . . . came between the army of the Egyptians and the army of Israel [at the crossing of the Sea of Reeds]. Thus there was the cloud with the darkness, and it cast a spell upon the night, so the one could not come near the other all through the night?' The serving angels want to sing a song [of joy over the impending destruction of the Egyptians] but the Holy One Blessed Be He said, 'the works of my hand are drowning in the sea and you want to sing?" (Babylonian Talmud Megillah 10b)

7. Our rabbi taught, "The charity fund is collected by two people and distributed by three. It is collected by two people because you do not make demands on the public with less than two, and it is distributed by three according to the laws of finance. But as regards the soup kitchen, donations are collected by three and distributed by three showing that (for feeding the hungry) collecting and distributing are of equal value. (Babylonian Talmud Baba Batra 8b)

CARE FOR THE OTHER IN THE MIDRASH

MIDRASH REPRESENTS A vast genre of rabbinic writings from the post-Talmudic period forward. By and large the midrashic literature is homiletical and moralistic in nature, often drawing lessons out of biblical texts. Some texts, like Avot d'Rabbi Nathan (excerpts 1 and 2) are little more than a collection of apothegms and short sayings. Others, like Tanhuma (excerpts 4 and 5), are long, sermonlike discussions of bibilical passages. In both types, a variety of statements can be found about human rights, interpersonal relationships, and care for the less fortunate. (Translation by Peter J. Haas.)

1. "Let your fellow's honor be as dear to you as your own" (Pirqe Avot 2:15). Is this even possible? Rather this teaches that just as one looks out for one's own honor, just so should one look out for the honor of one's fellow. Just as you desire that there should be no blemish on your name, so should you be careful not to blemish the reputation of your fellow. (Avot d'Rabbi Nathan 15:1)
2. Who is mighty? One who transforms one's enemy into one's friend. (Avot d'Rabbi Nathan 23)
3. From where do we learn that if you are in a position to offer testimony on someone's behalf, you are not permitted to remain silent? From the verse, "Do not stand idly by the blood of your fellow." (Sifra on Lev. 19:16)
4. Said Rabbi Eleazar, "Take care to give allocations to the poor even on the Sabbath," and Rabbi Jacob bar Idi said that Rabbi Yohanan said, "They go to synagogues and to schools (even) on the Sabbath to look after the needs of the public," and Rabbi Yohanan said, "They take care to save lives [pikuach nefesh] on the Sabbath," and said Rabbi Simeon bar R. Yohanan, "They go to the public thoroughfares [istratayot] and public buildings [qirqesayot, "circuses"?] to watch out for the needs of the public." (Tanhuma, Bereshit 2)
5. When Rabbi Assi's hour came to die, he wept bitterly. His nephew asked, "Why are you weeping so? Is there any passage of Torah that you have not learned and taught? Is there any kindness that you have not done? You never accepted public office nor sat in judgment over others." The rabbi replied, "This is why I weep. I was given the ability to extend justice, but I never carried it out." (Tanhuma, Mishpatim 2)

Care for the Other in Classical Jewish Law

Jewish communities whether in Christendom or the lands of Islam usually were organized as semi-independent corporations. As such they handled many of their own internal affairs, including providing social services for the poor, care for the sick, and aid for travelers. While there is no overall discussion of concepts such as human rights in medieval Jewish law, there is a good deal of attention paid to the obligation to help one's fellow. Two codes of law emerge from the medieval period. The first was compiled by Moses ben Maimon (Maimonides) and is dated 1178 . The most comprehensive and authoritative code of Jewish law from this period is the *Shulkhan Arukh*, which was first published in 1565. The *Shulkhan Arukh* in original form reflects Jewish laws and customs of the Muslim world. In around 1570, a series of glosses were added by Moses Issereles to address the laws and customs of Europe's Jews. Where relevant, I have added these glosses in square brackets.

In the excerpts below, I have chosen just a few sections to illustrate the concern given to taking care of the needy and of preserving life. In the first citations I have retained the Hebrew word *tzedakah* rather than use the normal translation, "charity," because the Jewish concept of *tzedakah* carries a different connotation. Charity is to be given out of concern and care (Latin, *caritas*). *Tzedakah*, on the other hand, is regarded as a social responsibility from which no member of the community (including the poor themselves) are exempt. It is thus a mitzvah, which means both a "good deed" and "a divine commandment." (Translations by Peter J. Haas.)

Moses Maimonides, *Mishneh Torah*

"Laws of Gifts to the Poor" Chapter 10

1. We are obligated to take care in fulfilling the mitzvah of tzedakah more than any other positive command. For tzedakah is the sign of a righteous person, seed of Abraham our father as it is said, "For I have singled him out, that he may instruct his sons . . . to do tzedakah" (Gen. 18:19). And the throne of Israel is not firmly established and the true faith stands only because of tzedakah as it is said, "You shall be established through righteousness" (Isa. 54:14). And Israel does not get redeemed except through tzedakah as it is said, "Zion shall be saved in the judgment; her repentant ones in tzedakah." (Isa. 1:27)

2. A person will never become poor by giving tzedakah and nothing bad or damaging will come about because of giving tzedakah and it is said, "For the work of righteousness will be peace" (Isa. 32:17). Whoever shows mercy, mercy will be shown to him as it is said, . . . in order that the LORD . . . show you compassion and in His compassion increase you as He promised. (Deut. 13:18)

3. Anyone who avoids giving tzedakah lo this one is called lawless just as the idolators are called lawless. . . . And the LORD is close to the cry of the poor as it is said, "You hear the cry of the needy" (not found in scripture, but probably refers to Job 34:28). For this reason one must be careful about their outcry for behold a covenant has been made with them as it says, "Therefore, if he cries out to Me, I will pay heed, for I am compassionate." (Exod. 22:26)

4. Whoever gives tzedakah to the poor with a sour expression and in a surly manner, even if he gives a thousand gold pieces, loses his merit. But he should give cheerfully and joyfully, and with empathy with him in his sorrow as it is said, "Did I not cry for him whose day is difficult? Did my soul not grieve for the poor?" (Job 30:25) Speak to him with compassion and comfort as it is said, "And I gladden the heart of the widow." (Job 29:13).

5. If the poor asks of you but you have nothing in hand to give him, comfort him with words. It is forbidden to scold the poor or to raise your voice to him because his heart is already broken and defeated and lo it says, "God, You will not despise a contrite and crushed heart" (Ps. 51:19) and it says, "reviving the spirit of the lowly, reviving the hearts of the contrite" (Isa. 57:15). Woe to him who embarrasses the poor—woe to him.

7. There are eight levels of tzedakah one above the other. The highest level of which there is no higher is the one that strengthens the Divine name among Israel by giving him (the poor) a gift or a loan or creates a partnership with him or finds for him a craft in order to empower him so that he no longer needs to rely on others. About this (level of tzedakah) it is said, "If your kinsman, being in straits, comes under your authority, and you hold him as though a resident alien, let him live by your side" (Lev. 25:35). That is to say, hold him up until he will not fall and need help.

8. Lower than this is giving tzedakah to the poor without knowing to whom he gave and the poor does not know from whom he took. Lo this is a good deed for its own sake. . . . Close to this is giving to a

tzedakah fund—and one should not contribute to a tzedakah fund unless he knows that the one in charge of it is trustworthy and wise and knows how to act properly.

9. Lower than this is when the donor knows to whom he is giving but the poor does not know from whom he took. This is like the great among the wise who would go in secret and toss money at the doors of the poor. This is proper to do and of a higher order if those appointed over the charity fund do not act properly.

10. Lower than this is when the poor knows from whom he received but the donor does not know. This is like the great among the wise who would bundle up the coins in their cloaks and scatter the coins behind them such that the poor could come and gather up without embarrassment.

11. Lower than this is when the donor gives the money directly to the poor before being asked.

12. Lower than this is when the donor gives after being asked.

13. Lower than this is when he gives him less than is suitable, but with a pleasant face.

14. Lower than this is when he gives with irritation.

"Laws of Hiring" Chapter 11

1. It is a positive commandment to give a hired worker his wage at its appropriate time, as it is said, "You shall pay him his wage on the same day" (Deut. 24:15). And if you delay it beyond its time, you transgress a negative commandment as it is said, "and not let the sun set upon it." (Deut. 24:15).

2. Whoever withholds the wage of a hired worker is as if he took his life, for it is said, "for he is needy and urgently depends on it." (Deut. 24:15) In so doing he transgresses four negative commandments, namely, (a) not to oppress, (b) not to steal, (c) not to keep the wages of a hired person overnight, and (d) not to let the sun set on it.

"Laws of Hiring" Chapter 12

1. As for workers who are working with whatever grows from the ground but the complete processing of which is not yet complete, whether or not yet harvested from the ground, and it is the workers' job to complete the processing, lo it is a mitzvah for the landowner to allow them to eat of that with which they are working.

Shulkhan Arukh

Yoreh De'ah 247—The Greatness of Tzedakah and Whether One Can Be Forced to Give

1. It is a positive mitzvah to give tzedakah according to one's ability. We have been commanded about this as a positive mitzvah many times, but there is a negative mitzvah in that one should not close one's eyes to this as it is said, "do not harden your heart and shut your hand against your needy kinsman" (Deut. 15:7). And whoever hides his eyes to this is called lawless and is like an idolater and one must be very careful in this for (failure to give) could lead to the shedding of blood, for the poor person may die if he does not respond immediately.

2. Never will a person become poor because of giving tzedakah and no evil thing or damage will come on its account as it is said, "For the work of righteousness will be peace" (Isa. 32:17).

3. Everyone who has mercy on the poor, the Holy One Blessed Be He will have mercy on him. [for one should bear in mind that he wants the Holy One at every hour to provide him with a living and just as he wants the Holy One to hear his plea, so should he hear the plea of the poor. He should also bear in mind that what goes around comes around and that the end of the matter is that he or his descendants will come to this situation. Whoever has mercy on others will get mercy from them.]

Yoreh De'ah 248—Who Is Obligated and Who Is Fit to Receive?

1. Every person is obligated to give tzedakah. Even if he is poor and is supported by tzedakah he is obligated to give from what was given to him and whoever gives less than what is suitable for him, the court compels him and punishes him until he gives what they reckon for him.

3. They do not require tzedakah from orphans, even for the redemption of prisoners and even if they have a lot of money, except if they collect from them for their own honor so that they shall have a good reputation.

Yoreh De'ah 249—How Much Should One Give and How Does He Give It?

1. The amount of giving: if he has the ability, one gives according to the needs of the poor. And if he is not able to do so much—giving

up to a fifth of his property is a good deed of the best sort and one tenth is middling, and less than this is greedy.

2. Never should one allow himself to give less than a third of a shekel per year. If he gives less than this, he has not fulfilled the mitzvah of tzedakah.

3. One must give with pleasantness and with joy and good heartedness and with compassion with the poor for his pain and with words of comfort. If he gives angrily and malevolently, he loses any merit (he might have for giving tzedakah).

4. If the pauper asked and he has nothing to give him, he should not scold or raise his voice at him but rather should soothe him with words and show him that his heart is good and his wish is to give but he does not have it. [And it is not permitted to let the pauper who asks go away empty-handed even if he gives him only a single grain.]

Yoreh De'ah 250—How Much Is It Suitable to Give to Each One?

1. How much is he to give a pauper? Enough to make up what he lacks. How so? If he is hungry, feed him; if he needs clothing, clothe him; if he has no utensils, buy him utensils; even if his custom was to ride a horse with a servant running before him when he was wealthy and now he has fallen into poverty, buy him a horse and a servant. Thus it is for each according to his need. If it is fitting to give him bread, give bread; if dough, then dough; a bed, then give him a bed. If it is fitting to give him warm bread, give warm; if cold, cold; to hand feed him, then hand feed him. [It seems to me that all this applies to the tzedakah administrator or to the public at large. But no individual has to make up whatever the pauper needs. Rather, he should report the condition to the community. If there is no community, the individual may give the pauper what he needs if he is able.]

5. If the poor of the city are many and the rich say, "Let them go begging door to door" and the average people say, "They should not go door to door but their support should fall on the community"—the law is with the average people.

Yoreh De'ah 256—How Do They Collect and Disperse Welfare Funds and Food?

1. Every city with Jews in it is obligated to set up a tzedakah official from reputable and trustworthy men who will go around and take

collections from everyone according to his ability to give and the amount set for him. They disburse the funds from Friday night to Friday night and give each pauper what he needs for the week. This is what is called the Welfare Fund. And they also are to appoint officials who will collect bread and other edibles or fruit or coins everyday from each courtyard from those who offer to give according to the situation and they distribute the collected items among the paupers each evening, giving from it to each pauper enough for the following day. This is called the Food Bank. We have never seen or heard of a Jewish community that did not have a Welfare Fund although there are places that have not had a Food Bank.

5. They require anyone who has lived in the city for thirty days to give to the Welfare Fund along with the citizens. If he has lived there three months, they require him to contribute to the Food Bank.

Orekh Hayyim 329—For Whom Do They Violate the Sabbath?

1. Any act that would save a life [pikuach nefesh] sets aside the laws of the Sabbath; and being diligent about this is praiseworthy. Even if a fire broke out in one courtyard and a person sees that it will travel to a second courtyard and create a danger, this one puts out the fire so that it will not spread.

3. For one on whom a building collapsed, if there is some doubt as to whether he is alive or dead, or a doubt if he were there or not, . . . they go out to save his life, no matter how many doubts.

4. Even if they found him so battered that he cannot live much longer, they go out to save him and search until they find his nostrils. If they find no life in his nostrils he is certainly dead, whether he was hit in the head first or the feet first.

5. If they find the upper part dead (i.e., no breath in the nostrils) they are not allowed to say that surely the bottom (i.e., the heart) is also dead, rather they go after the lower parts lest they be found alive.

ETHICAL WILLS

THE WRITING AND publishing of ethical wills was a common genre in medieval Judaism. These wills were meant to leave a moral legacy to the writer's descendants. Following is an example taken from Judah Ibn Tibbon's ethical will written in France in the second half of the twelfth century. Judah had hoped that his son would become a Torah scholar, but the son chose instead to study medicine.

> Therefore, my son! Stay not thy hand when I have left thee, but devote thyself to the study of the Torah and the science of medicine. But chiefly occupy thyself with the Torah, for thou hast a wise and understanding heart, and all that is needful of thy part is ambition and application. I know that thou wilt repent of the past, as many have repented before thee of their youthful indolence. . . .
>
> Let thy countenance shine upon the sons of men; tend their sick, and may thine advice cure them. Though thou takest fees from the rich, heal the poor gratuitously; the Lord will requite thee. Thereby shalt thou find favor and good understanding in the sight of God and man. Thus wilt thou win the respect of high and low among Jews and non-Jews, and thy good name will go forth far and wide. Thou wilt rejoice thy friends and make thy foes envious. For remember what is written in the Choice of Pearls (53:617, of Ibn Gabirol): "How shall one take vengeance on an enemy? By increasing one's own good qualities."

SOURCE: Jacob Marcus, *The Jew in the Medieval World: A Source Book: 315–1791* (New York: Atheneum, 1972), 312.

※

"THE LOVE OF KINDNESS" BY RABBI ISRAEL MEIR KAGAN

RABBI ISRAEL MEIR HaCohen Kagan (1838–1933) has become one of the best known writers on moral virtues in modern traditionalist Judaism. A leading scholar in the nineteenth-century Polish Jewish community, Kagan wrote some twenty-one books, the first of which, *Sefer Chafetz Chaim (The Book of Desiring Life)*, was about the evils of slander and gossip. Because of the fame of this book, Kagan came to be universally referred to as "the Chafetz Chaim." The excerpt below is from a later book, *Ahavas Chesed (Love of Kindness)*, that deals with the need to cultivate the virtue of kindness toward others.

In the selection from chapter 2, Kagan asks what it means to be created in the divine image. The meaning is not that we physically resemble God, but that we share the *middot* (virtues) of divinity, one of the most important of which is "chesed," or lovingkindness. In chapter 6, Kagan discusses the far-reaching effects that even one act of charity toward a fellow human can produce.

Chapter 2

In this chapter we shall elucidate the reason why God, blessed be He, so strongly urged man to acquire this virtue, that every section of the Torah is pervaded by it, as was explained in the introduction. The reason why man is obligated to possess a love of this virtue was explained in Chapter 1. Here we shall proceed to elucidate the subject in various ways, with the help of God. Scripture (Gen. 1:27) records that, "God created man in His image." The commentators take the statement to refer to God's attributes. He gave His creatures the power to emulate His middot; to do good and to act with kindness towards their fellow men, as Scripture has it (Ps. 145:9): "God is good to all."

Chapter 6

Come and see how great a reward is given to the one who is kind to his fellow men! Even the indirect consequences of his act are credited to him just as if he had performed them himself. This takes many forms as we shall, to some extent, explain and thereby demonstrate the importance of the subject.

(1) As affects the person himself: Suppose one was kind to some suffering, ailing individual. Through the kind man's financial help the sufferer's health was restored. Then in the assessment of the kind man's reward, not only are the few silver coins he spent taken into account, but he is considered actually to have restored the sufferer's life to him. The evidence for such a conclusion lies in the words of chazal [that is, the ancient sages] (Tanhuma Mishpatim 15): "So began R. Tanhuma: He that is gracious to the poor lends to God, and his good deeds He will repay him (Prov. 19:17). The one who lends to the poor is, as it were, lending money to God, and He will give him his recompense.

SOURCE: Israel Meir Kagan (the Chafetz Chaim), *Ahavath Chesed: The Love of Kindness as Required by God*, trans. Leonard Oschry (Jerusalem and New York: Feldheim Publishers, 1976), 82, 98.

THE TEACHINGS OF HASIDISM

HASIDISM WAS A SPIRITUAL and mystical revival movement that sprang up in Eastern Europe in the middle of the eighteenth century. It grew out of popular frustration with strict and overintellectualized rabbinism and sought to find a more spiritual and joyful way of practicing Judaism. There are endless numbers of aphorisms and sayings that are given in the name of hasidic teachers. Following is just a small sampling of this vast treasury.

1. Before the Eternal One, the highest of men and lowliest of men are equal (Mendel of Vitebsk).

SOURCE: Leo Rosten, *Treasury of Jewish Quotations* (New York: McGraw-Hill, 1972), 204.

2. Honor, respect, dignity and love are due to each and every human being, not because of the greatness of their achievements, but because they are home to a soul that is inherently holy. Nobody created his or her own soul; everyone has been gifted with a rarefied essence. This is a teaching of Rabbi Chaim of Volozhin, a forerunner of the Musar movement, who explains that one should honor all people simply because they are the handiwork of God. (Ruach Chaim on Pirkei Avot)

SOURCE: Alan Morinis, "Paths of the Soul 5," http://www.aish.com/spirituality/growth/The_Path_of_the_Soul_5_Giving_Honor.asp. Retrieved September 15, 2004.

3. God bade Abraham offer his son, and an angel stopped him (Gen. 22:2, 11). Thus the Bible teaches: None but God can command us to destroy a life, but a mere angel suffices to have us save one, even if it contravenes a divine command. (Mendel of Kosov)

SOURCE: Joseph Baron, ed., *A Treasury of Jewish Quotations* (New York: Thomas Yoseloff, 1965), 275.

✵

4. It is true the law teaches that one's own life comes first, but this applies only to things on which life depends. . . . But if it is a question of bread and clothes and wood on one side, and dinners with fish and meat and fruit on the other side, the latter have to be given up as superfluities. (Shneor Zalman, *Tanya*)

SOURCE: Joseph Baron, ed., *A Treasury of Jewish Quotations* (New York: Thomas Yoseloff, 1965), 7.

✵

5. Gauge a country's prosperity by its treatment of the aged. (Nahman of Bratzlav, *Sefer HaMiddot*, p. 66)

SOURCE: Joseph Baron, *A Treasury of Jewish Quotations* (New York: Thomas Yoseloff, 1965), 6.

✵

6. Seek the good in everyone, and reveal it, bring it forth. (Nahman of Bratzlav, *Likkut Moharam*, p. 279)

SOURCE: Joseph Baron, *A Treasury of Jewish Quotations* (New York: Thomas Yoseloff), 160.

✵

AMERICAN LIBERAL JUDAISM

THE NORTH AMERICAN Jewish community, given its European experience, has always been liberal in its politics, even as it has become assimilated and successful in America. The liberal tendency in North American Judaism manifests itself in many ways. The following is a selection illustrating a variety of voices, from Supreme Court Justice Louis Brandeis, to Abraham Joshua Heschel (who marched in Selma, Alabama, with the Rev. Martin Luther King, Jr.), to a series of scholars and rabbis. It should also be noted that many Jewish intellectuals write and promote liberal and human rights causes, for example, Lenn E. Goodman and David Novak, whose works I drew on in preceding chapters, but who are not writing for a specifically Jewish audience.

LETTER TO GEORGE WASHINGTON FROM HEBREW CONGREGATION OF NEWPORT, RHODE ISLAND

Shortly after the creation of the United States and his election as the first federal president, George Washington visited Newport, Rhode Island. On the occasion of his visit, the local Jewish congregation (organized around 1750) sent the following letter, dated August 17, 1790, expressing its vision of the meaning of the new Republic. A facsimile of Washington's response is still on display at the Touro Synagogue in Newport, Rhode Island.

Sir: Permit the children of the stock of Abraham to approach you with the most cordial affection and esteem for your person and merits and to join our fellow-citizens in welcoming you to New Port.

With pleasure we reflect on those days—those days of difficulty and danger—when the God of Israel who delivered David from the peril of the sword shielded your head in the day of battle. And we rejoice to think that the same Spirit, who rested in the bosom of the greatly beloved Daniel, enabling him to preside over the provinces of the Babylonish Empire, rests, and will rest upon you, enabling you to discharge the arduous duties of Chief Magistrate in these states.

Deprived as we have hitherto been of the invaluable rights of free citizens, we now, with a deep sense of gratitude to the Almighty Disposer of all events, behold a government, erected by the majesty of the people, a government which to bigotry gives no sanction, to persecution no assistance, but generously affording to all liberty of conscience and immunities of citizenship, deeming every one, of whatever nation, tongue, or language, equal parts of the great governmental machine. This so ample and extensive federal union whose basis is philanthropy, mutual confidence, and public virtue, we cannot but acknowledge to be the work of the Great God, who ruleth in the armies of heaven and among the inhabitants of the earth, doing whatsoever seemeth him good.

For all the blessings of civil and religious liberty which we enjoy under an equal and benign administration, we desire to send up our thanks to the

Ancient of Days, the great Preserver of Men, beseeching him that the angel who conducted our forefathers through the wilderness into the promised land may graciously conduct you through all the dangers and difficulties of this moral life.

Moses Seixas, Warden

SOURCE: Paul Mendes-Flohr and Jehuda Reinharz, *The Jew in the Modern World*, 2d ed. (New York: Oxford University Press, 1995), 457–458.

※

THE CENTRAL CONFERENCE OF AMERICAN RABBIS

The Central Conference of American Rabbis is the North American professional organization for rabbis affiliated with the Reform movement. The Reform movement is the oldest organized Jewish religious denomination in North America and has the largest number of congregations and members.

1. Conference of Reform Rabbis, 1885

The first national conference of Reform rabbis in North America convened in Pittsburgh, Pennsylvania, in November 1885. The conference produced the first-ever statement of principles of American liberal Judaism, a statement that was officially adopted as the official platform of North American Reform Judaism by the Central Conference of American Rabbis at its inaugural meeting in 1889. The statement consists of eight paragraphs, the first few dealing with Bible, Jewish law, and other internal topics. The following paragraphs deal with the outside world.

> Fifth: We recognize in the modern era of universal culture of heart and intellect, the approaching of the realization of Israel's great Messianic hope for the establishment of the kingdom of truth, justice and peace among all men. We consider ourselves no longer a nation but a religious community, and therefore expect neither a return to Palestine, nor a sacrificial worship under the administration of the sons of Aaron, nor the restoration of any of the laws concerning the Jewish state.
>
> Sixth: We recognize in Judaism a progressive religion, ever striving to be in accord with the postulates of reason. We are convinced of the utmost

necessity of preserving the historical identity with our great past. Christianity and Islam, being daughter-religions of Judaism, we appreciate their mission to aid in the spreading of monotheistic and moral truth. We acknowledge that the spirit of broad humanity of our age is our ally in the fulfillment of our mission, and therefore we extend the hand of fellowship to all who cooperate with us in the establishment of the reign of truth and righteousness among men.

Seventh: We reassert the doctrine of Judaism that the soul of men is immortal, grounding this belief on the divine nature of the human spirit, which forever finds bliss in righteousness and misery in wickedness. We reject as ideas not rooted in Judaism the belief both in bodily resurrection and in Gehenna and Eden (Hell and Paradise) as abodes for everlasting punishment or reward.

Eighth: In full accordance with the spirit of Mosaic legislation which strives to regulate the relation between rich and poor, we deem it our duty to participate in the great task of modern times, to solve on the basis of justice and righteousness the problems presented by the contrasts and evils of the present organization of society.

SOURCE: Paul Mendes-Flohr and Jehuda Reinharz, *The Jew in the Modern World*, 2d ed. (New York: Oxford University Press, 1995), 468–469.

※

2. The Columbus Platform of American Reform Judaism

The following excerpt is from a statement of principles adopted by the Central Conference of American Rabbis in 1937, fifty years after the adoption of the Pittsburgh Platform. The selection below is from part B dealing with ethics.

6. *Ethics and Religion*. In Judaism religion and morality blend into an indissoluble unity. Seeking God means to strive after holiness, righteousness and goodness. The love of God is incomplete without the love of one's fellowmen. Judaism emphasizes the kinship of the human race, the sanctity and worth of human life and personality and the right of the individual to freedom and to the pursuit of his chosen vocation. Justice to all, irrespective of race, sect or class, is the inalienable right and the inescapable obligation of all. The state and organized government exist in order to further these ends.

7. *Social justice.* Judaism seeks the attainment of a just society by the application of its teachings to the economic order, to industry and commerce, and to national and international affairs. It aims at the elimination of man-made misery and suffering, of poverty and degradation, of tyranny and slavery, of social inequality and prejudice, of ill-will and strife. It advocates the promotion of harmonious relations between warring classes on the basis of equity and justice, and the creation of conditions under which human personality may flourish. It pleads for the safeguarding of childhood against exploitation. It champions the cause of all who work and of their right to an adequate standard of living, as prior to the rights of property. Judaism emphasizes the duty of charity, and strives for a social order which will protect men against the material disabilities of old age, sickness and unemployment.

8. *Peace.* Judaism, from the days of the prophets, has proclaimed to mankind the ideal of universal peace. The spiritual and physical disarmament of all nations has been one of its essential teachings. It abhors all violence and relies upon moral education, love and sympathy to secure human progress. It regards justice as the foundation of the well-being of nations and the condition of enduring peace. It urges organized international action for disarmament, collective security and world peace.

SOURCE: http://www.ccarnet.org/platforms/columbus.html. Retrieved September 15, 2004.

3. Prayer

Help us to be among those who are willing to sacrifice that others may not hunger, who dare to be bearers of light in the dark loneliness of stricken lives, who struggle and even bleed for the triumph of righteousness among men.

SOURCE: *Union Prayer Book* Vol. I (Cincinnati, OH: CCAR, 1940) I, 45.

4. Resolution on Human Rights Watch

WHEREAS the Jewish tradition mandates ultimate respect for the human rights of all humankind (God's mercy is for all the Divine Creation);

WHEREAS the Jewish teaching and experience has recognized that fear, frustration, violence, and war can numb the best in the human heart (Yetzer Hatov) and sometimes bring out the worst (Yetzer Hara) WHEREAS a diverse and distinguished group of rabbis in Israel has united in a Rabbinic Human Rights Watch which will promote in a non-political fashion concerns with violations of human rights that go beyond security or political concerns,

THEREFORE BE IT RESOLVED that the Central Conference of American Rabbis supports the formation of a Rabbinic Human Rights Watch (RHRW) in Israel. We consider their work to be a true Kiddush Hashem (sanctification of God's name) and an important contribution to the vitality of Judaism and Zionism. We urge all rabbis to support RHRW and all Jews to lend solidarity and support to its efforts. (Resolution of the CCAR adopted in 1989.)

SOURCE: http://www.ccarnet.org/cgi-bin/resodisp.pl?file=watch&year=1989. Retrieved September 15, 2004.

❈

5. Statement of Principles, 1999

We bring Torah into the world when we strive to fulfill the highest ethical mandates in our relationships with others and with all of God's creation. Partners with God in *tikkun olam*, repairing the world, we are called to help bring nearer the messianic age. We seek dialogue and joint action with people of other faiths in the hope that together we can bring peace, freedom and justice to our world. We are obligated to pursue *tzedek*, justice and righteousness, and to narrow the gap between the affluent and the poor, to act against discrimination and oppression, to pursue peace, to welcome the stranger, to protect the earth's biodiversity and natural resources, and to redeem those in physical, economic and spiritual bondage. In so doing, we reaffirm social action and social justice as a central prophetic focus of traditional Reform Jewish belief and practice. We affirm the *mitzvah* of *tzedakah*, setting aside portions of our earnings and our time to provide for those in need. These acts bring us closer to fulfilling the prophetic call to translate the words of Torah into the works of our hands. (Statement of

Principles for Reform Judaism adopted at the 1999 Pittsburgh Convention of the Central Conference of American Rabbis.)

SOURCE: http://www.ccarnet.org/platforms/principles.html. Retrieved September 15, 2004.

�֍

THE UNITED SYNAGOGUES OF CONSERVATIVE JUDAISM

The USCJ is the central synagogue organization of the Conservative movement within North American Judaism. The Conservative movement is more traditional in practice than is the Reform movement, but is not regarded as completely Orthodox. The following article is from the executive vice president and was published by the United Synagogues of Conservative Judaism in 1995.

Passover provides a virtual treasure chest of moral lessons. Using the *Haggadah* as our sourcebook, we can discuss the obligation to provide hospitality (*Halahma Anya*—Let all who are hungry come and eat); the mandate to educate our children, and to do so in accordance with each child's own level of understanding (as evidenced in the section on the Four Children); concern for those who are afflicted (We understand your plight, since we too were slaves—*Avadim Hayinu*); and the need to show consideration for the stranger (You shall not oppress the stranger, having been strangers yourselves in the land of Egypt).

We might also focus on the importance of striving for freedom and human dignity or tackle the ever-current need to speak up against abuses of power in the face of an oppressive government structure. Whatever moral teaching we choose to address, chances are our discussions will revolve around a common theme: obligation. Interestingly, while the Exodus represents perhaps the greatest miracle in the history of mankind—and it would be natural to assume that any resulting obligations would be to God, in gratitude for our deliverance—in fact, the primary focus of these prescriptions is behavior toward our fellow man.

Concern for the less fortunate is a hallmark of Jewish tradition, and Jewish teachings are replete with specific guidelines in this regard. Equating religious commitment with following the Torah—and following the Torah with following God—our Rabbis teach that to "follow the Lord your God" means to emulate Divine attributes. Thus, as the Lord clothes the naked, we too should clothe the naked; as God visited the sick, we too should visit the sick, and so forth.

SOURCE: "Sewing up the Safety Net: A Religious Mandate" by Rabbi Jerome M. Epstein. http://www.uscj.org/SocJusSafety_Net5323.html. Retrieved September 15, 2004.

�֎

A SAMPLING OF JEWISH VOICES ON HUMAN RIGHTS

1. The next generation must witness a continuing and every increasing contest between those who have and those who have not. The industrial world is in a state of ferment. The ferment is in the main peaceful, . . . but there is felt today very widely the inconsistency in this condition of political democracy and industrial absolutism. The people are beginning to doubt whether in the long run democracy and absolutism can coexist in the same community; beginning to doubt whether there is a justification for the great inequalities in the distribution of wealth, for the rapid creation of fortunes, more mysterious than the deeds of Aladdin's lamp.

SOURCE: Louis Brandeis, *Business—A Profession* (Boston: Small, Maynard and Company, 1914), 326.

�֎

2. The Filenes recognized that the function of retail distribution should be undertaken as a social service, equal in dignity and responsibility to the function of production; and that it should be studied with equal intensity in order that the service may be performed with high efficiency, with great economy, and with nothing more than a fair profit to the retailer. They recognized that to serve their own customers properly the relations of the retailer to the producer must be fairly and scientifically adjusted; and, among other things, that it was the concern of the retailers to know whether the goods which he sold were manufactured under conditions which

were fair to the workers—fair as to wages, hours of work, and sanitary conditions.

SOURCE: Louis Brandeis, *Business—A Profession* (Boston: Small, Maynard and Co., 1914), 10.

※

3. Thus, at the Passover *seder* a drop of wine is to be spilled from the cup at the mention of each of the ten plagues with which the Egyptians were afflicted, the reason being, say the Rabbis, that one's cup of joy cannot be full as long as there is suffering somewhere in the world. . . . Again, at the *seder* the head of the household reads of the drowning of the Egyptian hosts in the Red Sea; and the Rabbis comment on the passage by relating that when the drowning was taking place, angels in heaven commenced to sing the praises of the Lord, but He rebuked them, saying, "My children are drowning, and you would sing!"

SOURCE: Milton R. Konvitz, "Judaism and the Democratic Ideal," in *Judaism and Human Rights*, ed. Milton R. Konvitz (2nd expanded ed., New Brunswick, NJ: Transaction Publishers, 2001), 124–125.

※

4. Judaism founds human right [*sic*] upon the assumption that, ideally, all human beings are of equal merit (i.e., all are, at least at the outset, equal in their moral potential), equal before God and, therefore, equal in desert before the law and their fellow human beings. . . . Locke, following Hobbes, Machiavelli, and, ultimately, the Sophist equation of right with power, founds human equality on the presumed natural equality of power, not to create but to destroy.

SOURCE: Lenn E. Goodman, "Equality and Human Rights: The Lockean and Judaic Views," *Judaism* 25 (summer 1976): 361–362.

※

5. Whatever its political form or organization, society is required by Scripture to uphold the standards of minimum human dignity. These standards include, for example, the right of any Israelite to

satisfy his hunger at his fellow's expense but not to harvest his fellow's labors. Among the provisions for the administration of justice are many examples of social legislation such as those permitting the poor and the alien access to harvest gleanings, unreaped borders, and the forgotten sheaf. Another illustration of these egalitarian standards is the protest against the creation of landed estates.

SOURCE: Herbert Chanan Brichto, "The Hebrew Bible on Human Rights," in *Essays on Human Rights: Contemporary Issues and Jewish Perspectives*, ed. David Sidorsky (Philadelphia: Jewish Publication Society of America, 1979), 225.

※

6. The fundamental presupposition of the rights of the person in Judaism is a belief in the absolute and uncompromisable worth of human life. This belief is grounded in the unique value of the individual in the divine scheme of creation and is variously articulated in both biblical literature and rabbinic tradition.

SOURCE: Michael Fishbane, "The Image of the Human and the Rights of the Individual in Jewish Tradition," in *Human Rights and the World's Religions*, ed. Leroy S. Rouner (Notre Dame, IN: University of Notre Dame Press, 1988), 17.

※

7. A religious man is a person who holds God and man in one thought at one time, at all times, who suffers harm done to others, whose greatest passion is compassion, whose greatest strength is love and defiance of despair.

SOURCE: Abraham Joshua Heschel, *New York Journal-American*, April 5, 1963. Cited in Simpson's Contemporary Quotations at http://www.bartleby.com/63/44/4144.html. Retrieved September 15, 2004.

※

8. In sum, we have seen that Judaism asserts that man, in imitation of G-d, possesses an inviolate core of personality, and that privacy constitutes the protection of this personality core from the inroads of society and the state.

SOURCE: Norman Lamm, "The Right of Privacy," in *Judaism and Human Rights*, ed. Milton R. Konvitz (2nd expanded ed., New Brunswick, NJ: Transaction Publishers, 2001), 233.

※

9. A society can be judged by the way it treats its disadvantaged. The affluent society that tolerates poverty misuses and abuses its wealth.

SOURCE: Richard Hirsch, "There Shall Be No Poor," in *Judaism and Human Rights*, ed. Milton R. Konvitz (2nd expanded ed., New Brunswick, NJ: Transaction Publishers), 234.

※

10. If God is the God of the whole world, then wouldn't God have the same relationship with everybody? The Torah presents that paradox to us—God is the God of the Jewish People, and also the God of all humanity. That dual set of concerns are mediated through the Laws of the B'nai Noah, the Children of Noah, a way that Judaism and halakhah (Jewish law) incorporate God's sovereignty and love for all people with God's unique mission for the Jews.

SOURCE: Rabbi Bradley Shavit Artson, "God of Jews, God of Humanity," cited from http://myjewishlearning.com/texts/weekly_Torah_Commentary/roach_artson 5759.com. Retrieved September 15, 2004.

※

11. If September 11 taught us anything, it is that our world is in desperate need of repair. Divisiveness and violence must urgently be replaced by kindness and compassion. As the threat of terror looms, we need to find ways to make a positive difference in the world—to turn the pain into positive change, and to lead humanity back on the road to peace.

This is not just a global problem. It is highly personal as well. If someone spills ink on the floor, and asks you to clean it up, you might say, "Hey, you made the mess—you clean it up." But when it comes to world problems, nobody will say: "I didn't cause the problem, so why should I do anything about it?" Everyone agrees we should try to help. If you knew how to cure cancer, you'd cancel your vacation. We're all responsible.

SOURCE: Rabbi Noah Weinberg, http://www.judaism.about.com/gi/dynamic/offsite .htm?site=http://www.aish.com/ar.asp%3Fan=3010. Retrieved September 15, 2004.

❈

12. "Practice Random Acts of Kindness" reads the bumper sticker. Sounds so good, so warm and cozy. But is it the right attitude?

Now what kind of Scrooge would find fault with this philosophy? Well, traditional Judaism, for one, would. Not because, as some uninformed critics would have it, the God of the "Old Testament" is a vengeful, wrathful Creator. Nothing could be further from the truth. Love and kindness are cornerstones of Judaism. Our sages teach us that the world stands on three things: on Torah, on service of God, and on acts of loving kindness (Ethics of Our Fathers, 1:2). Judaism is definitely in favor of kindness! The problem lies in the random nature the bumper sticker alludes to.

Why should our acts of compassion and caring be any more random than the other actions in our life? We wouldn't advocate random acts of spending (except perhaps at a Barney's sale!), or bring that quality of whimsy and serendipity to our workplace. So why treat kindness any less seriously? The Torah teaches that kindness should be offered in a thoughtful and appropriate way

SOURCE: Emuna Braverman, http://www.aish.com/spirituality/growth/Random_ Acts_of_Kindness.asp. Retrieved September 15, 2004.

❈

TIKKUN MAGAZINE

Tikkun, edited by Michael Lerner, has been the leading popular Jewish journal on the Left. The magazine title comes from the Hebrew word for "repair" and is derived from the concept, especially stressed by the Hasidic movement, that the world can be redeemed or repaired only through human acts.

We are a community of people from many faiths and traditions, called together by *Tikkun* magazine and its vision of healing and transforming our world. We include in this call both the outer transformation needed to achieve social justice, ecological sanity, and world peace, and the inner healing needed to foster loving relationships, a generous attitude toward the world and toward others unimpeded by the distortions of our egos, a habit of generosity and trust, and the ability to respond to the grandeur of creation with awe, wonder and radical amazement. We are guided in our work by our belief in the principle of solidarity.

For us, this principle has spiritual roots in the Jewish commandment to remember that we were all slaves in Egypt; we believe that we are all harmed by oppression directed at any group or individual.

SOURCE: http://www.tikkun.org/community/index.cfm/action/core_vision.html. Retrieved September 15, 2004.

❋

ISRAEL

The state of Israel was declared in 1948 with the ending of the British mandate in Palestine, a mandate that followed the defeat of the Ottoman Turkish Empire in World War I. The new state was overwhelmed with war (it was attacked the next day by five of its Arab neighbors) and refugees (both displaced persons from the Nazi persecution and Jews expelled from Arab countries). Over the last fifty years, the state has continued the struggle to create a Western liberal democracy, despite repeated wars, terrorist actions, and a massive intake of Jewish refugees (in the year 2000, roughly one of every six Israelis had arrived in the country within the previous ten years from the former Soviet Union). The commitment to liberal Western values, however imperfectly carried out, was enshrined in the Declaration of the Establishment of the State of Israel. At the time of the establishment of the state no constitution was written, but in the last few years a series of components of a Basic Law have been passed. This Basic Law is to serve as a kind of constitution. As the struggle with the Palestine National Authority has entered a violent stage, a number of Israeli human rights organizations have formed. Statements of the three most prominent conclude this section.

The name B'tselem is a Hebrew reference to the biblical claim that humans were created "in the image" of God.

DECLARATION OF THE ESTABLISHMENT OF THE STATE OF ISRAEL

THE STATE OF ISRAEL will be open for Jewish immigration and for the Ingathering of the Exiles; it will foster the development of the country for the benefit of all its inhabitants; it will be based on freedom, justice and peace as envisaged by the prophets of Israel; it will ensure complete equality of social and political rights to all its inhabitants irrespective of religion, race or sex; it will guarantee freedom of religion, conscience, language, education and culture; it will safeguard the Holy Places of all religions; and it will be faithful to the principles of the Charter of the United Nations.

SOURCE: From the Declaration of the Establishment of the State of Israel, May 14, 1948, http://www.jewishvirtuallibrary.org/source/History/Dec_of_Indep.html. Retrieved September 15, 2004.

THE BASIC LAW: HUMAN DIGNITY AND LIBERTY, 1992

1. The purpose of this Basic Law is to protect human dignity and liberty, in order to establish in a Basic Law the values of the State of Israel as a Jewish and democratic state.
2. There shall be no violation of the life, body or dignity of any person as such.
3. There shall be no violation of the property of a person.
4. All persons are entitled to protection of their life, body and dignity.
5. There shall be no deprivation or restriction of the liberty of a person by imprisonment, arrest, extradition or otherwise.
6. (a) All persons are free to leave Israel.
   (b) Every Israel national has the right of entry into Israel from abroad.
7. (a) All persons have the right to privacy and to intimacy.
   (b) There shall be no entry into the private premises of a person who has not consented thereto.
   (c) No search shall be conducted on the private premises of a person, nor in the body or personal effects.
   (d) There shall be no violation of the confidentiality of conversation, or of the writings or records of a person.

8. There shall be no violation of rights under this Basic Law except by a law befitting the values of the State of Israel, enacted for a proper purpose, and to an extent no greater than is required.

9. There shall be no restriction of rights under this Basic Law held by persons serving in the Israel Defence Forces, the Israel Police, the Prisons Service and other security organizations of the State, nor shall such rights be subject to conditions, except by virtue of a law, or by regulation enacted by virtue of a law, and to an extent no greater than is required by the nature and character of the service.

10. This Basic Law shall not affect the validity of any law [din] in force prior to the commencement of the Basic Law.

11. All governmental authorities are bound to respect the rights under this Basic Law.

12. This Basic Law cannot be varied, suspended or made subject to conditions by emergency regulations; notwithstanding, when a state of emergency exists, by virtue of a declaration under section 9 of the Law and Administration Ordinance, 5708-1948, emergency regulations may be enacted by virtue of said section to deny or restrict rights under this Basic Law, provided the denial or restriction shall be for a proper purpose and for a period and extent no greater than is required.

SOURCE: http://www.knesset.gov.il/laws/special/eng/basic3_eng.htm. Retrieved September 15, 2004.

❖

RABBIS FOR HUMAN RIGHTS

1. "Rabbis for Human Rights" reminds and demonstrates to both the religious and the non-religious sectors of the public need to be reminded that Judaism had another face. Human rights abuses are not compatible with the age-old Jewish tradition of humaneness and moral responsibility or the Biblical concern for "The stranger in your midst."—even in the face of the danger to public order and safety which the uprising represented.

SOURCE: Profile of Rabbis for Human Rights; http://www.rhr.israel.net/profile/index.shtml. Retrieved September 15, 2004.

2. Eloheinu v'Elohei Kadmoneinu (Avoteinu v'Emoteinu), our God and God of our ancestors, we are gathered around this seder table as b'nei khorin, free people who still remember the long years of oppression. We have vowed never to become oppressors ourselves. Yet we know that we have hardened our hearts to those who have paid an excessive price for our people's prosperity and security in Israel. On this Feast of Freedom we proclaim our determination to banish Pharaoh from our hearts and we reaffirm our commitment to universal human rights.

Source: Passover supplement by Rabbis for Human Rights—Israel, http://www.rhr.israel.net/pencraft/index.shtml

Physicians for Human Rights—Israel

PHR—Israel was established in 1988 as a nonpartisan, nonprofit organization, dedicated to promoting and protecting the right to health care in Israel and in territories under Israel's effective control. Our operating premise is that the maintenance of human rights as they pertain to health is a necessary condition for social justice, as well as a legal obligation in accordance with international human rights law. The right to health and medical care transcends political, national, religious, gender, socio-economic or any other considerations.

Source: http://www.phr.org.il/phr/Pages/PhrHomepage.asp. Retrieved September 15, 2004.

B'tselem

The Israeli Center for Human Rights in the Occupied Territories was established in 1989 by a group of prominent academics, attorneys, journalists, and Knesset members. . . . *B'tselem* in Hebrew literally means "in the image of," and is also used as a synonym for human dignity. The word is taken from Genesis 1:27, "And God created man in his image. In the image of God did He create him." It is in this spirit that the first article of the Universal Declaration of Human Rights states that "All human beings are born equal in dignity and rights."

SOURCE: "About B'tselem," http://www.btselem.org/. Retrieved September 17, 2004.

Biographical Sketches of Human Rights Leaders in the Jewish Tradition

Akiba Ben Joseph (ca. 50–135 c.e.)

One of the founding thinkers of early rabbinic Judaism. According to legends about his life, he was an unlearned peasant in his youth and was even an opponent of the scholarly class. In his later life, when he became a scholar, he continued to be mindful of the poor and the socially marginal. He seems to have been supportive of the messianic pretender Simeon Bar Kochba, who led a revolt against Rome in ca. 132–135 c.e. For this political acitivism, Akiba was arrested by the Romans and eventually executed. He is often credited with producing one of the earliest codes of early protorabbinic law, laying the foundation for the later Mishnah of Judah HaNasi. He is cited frequently in the rabbinic literature. **Suggested Readings:** Louis Finkelstein, *Akiva, Scholar, Saint and Martyr* (New York, 1936); Judah Nadich, *Rabbi Akiba and His Contemporaries* (Northvale, NJ, 1998).

Al-Fasi, Isaac ben Jacob (1013–1103)

Among the earliest rabbinic authorities in North Africa and Europe. A native of what is now Algeria, he spent a good part of his career in Fez (hence his name, al-Fasi). During his lifetime the last great leader of the Babylonian Talmudic academies died, leaving leadership to local rabbinic scholars, of whom al-Fasi was one of the best known. In addition to writing hundreds of legal rescripts (*responsa*) he also compiled the first post-Talmudic code of Jewish law. Because of his pivotal position and astounding productivity, a whole legal literature developed in the Middle Ages centered on al-Fasi and his halachic decisions. His commentaries can be found at the back of most editions of the Babylonian Talmud. **Works:** *Sefer HaHalakhot* (Constantinople, 1509; reprint Jerusalem, 1962); *Responsa of Isaac ben Jacob Al-Fasi* (Leghorn, 1781). **Suggested Readings:** Shaul Shefer, *Ha-Rif u-Mishnato* (Jerusalem, 1966); Haim Dimitrovsky, *Seride Bavli: Mavo Bibliografi Histori* (New York, 1979).

Alkalai, Yehudah (1798–1878)

Rabbi and one of the earliest thinkers of modern Zionism. He was born in Sarajevo in the Balkans and later moved to Jerusalem. Along with Zvi Hirsch Kalischer, he was influenced by nationalist movements in the Balkans among the various peoples and empires in the region. In his writings from the 1830s and 1840s, he argued that the traditional Jewish notions of repentance and redemption could be achieved at first only by concrete actions of individuals. This led to his call for individual Jews not to continue to wait for a messianic miracle to effect the return of the Jews to their land, but rather for individual Jews to make the move themselves. He saw this as the only way for Jews to guarantee their own national rights and to bring in the long-promised redemption of all people. He was fiercely opposed by other Orthodox leaders, but he had great influence on early Zionist movements, such as Hibbat Zion, which actually began to send Jewish immigrants to Turkish Palestine at the end of the nineteenth century. **Works:** *Minhat Yehudah* (Vienna, 1843); *Goral la-Adonai* (Vienna, 1857). **Suggested Readings:** Arthur Hertzberg, *The Zionist Idea* (New York, 1959); Yitshak Refa'el, *Kitve ha-Rav Yehudah Alkala'i: Betosafot Mevo'ot, He'arot U-ve'urim* (Jerusalem, 1974).

Alshekh, Moshe (1508–1593)

A Turkish rabbi known for his interest in ethical and moral issues. Alshekh studied in Salonika and subsequently moved to the holy city of Safed in the Land of Israel where he became involved in the mystical movement. He also served as a judge and issued a number of legal rescripts (*responsa*) that reflect these interests. **Works:** *Havazzelet HaSharon* (Constantinople, 1563); *Torat Moshe* (Venice, 1600); *Responsa of Moshe*

Alshekh, edited by Yom Tov Porges (Safed, 1975). **Suggested Readings:** Shimon Shalem, *Rabbi Moshe Alshekh: le-Heker Shitato Ha-parshanit Ve-hashkafotav Be-'inyene Mahashavah U-musar* (Jerusalem, 1966); Eliyahu Munk, *Midrash of Rabbi Moshe Alshich on the Torah* (Brooklyn, NY, 2000).

Asher ben Yehiel (Asheri or Rosh) (1250–1327)

A student of one of the greatest rabbis of the time, Meir of Rothenburg, and a vigorous opponent of the study of secular philosophy. Asher spent the early part of his life in a number of different communities in Central Europe, including Troyes, Cologne, Coblenz, and Worms. Because of local persecutions, he left Central Europe in 1303 for Spain and served as chief rabbi of Toledo. In his fight against the study of philosophy, he used his considerable influence to help establish the study of Talmud and its major commentaries such as the Tosefot in southern France and in Spain. He wrote numerous legal rescripts (*responsa*) in which he tried to temper traditional law with critical intellectual analysis, although he did acquiesce to the use of mutilation and capital punishment in Spanish Jewish law, but only reluctantly and only because this was locally accepted practice. **Works:** *Hanagot Harosh* (Venice, 1579); *Hilkhot Harosh* (1745); *She'elot Uteshuvot* (Vilna, 1885). **Suggested Readings:** Moshe Yitzhok Elefant, *Pathways of Eternal Life: A Compendium of Talmudic and Rabbinic Quotations and Commentaries* (Brooklyn, NY, 1977); Abrahan Hayyim Freimann, *Ha-Rosh Rabenu Asher b. R. Yehi'el Ve-tse'etsa'av* (Jerusalem, 1986).

Ben Gurion, David (1886–1973)

First prime minister of the state of Israel. Born in Poland as David Green, ben Gurion was active in Socialist Zionist circles in Poland and then in Turkish, and later British mandatory Palestine. He was one of the founders of the Labor Party, and as its leader became the first prime minister of the state of Israel, serving from 1948 to 1953, and then again from 1955 to 1963. All through his career he strongly fought for the rights of Jewish workers, whether under Turkish rule before World War I or under the British in the 1920s and 1930s. To this end he was instrumental in founding the Jewish labor federation (the Histadrut) in Palestine. His subsequently forged strong ties with the labor movement in the Soviet Union and envisioned the Jewish Settlement in Palestine as laying the foundation for a true socialist workers paradise. As prime minister he was forced to make many political concessions, including to the religious Orthodox parties, but he always believed that Jewish religion would achieve its full promise not in religous orthodoxy but in the social and economic equality preached by the biblical prophets. **Works:** *Rebirth and Destiny of Israel* (New York, 1954); *Israel: The First Decade and the Next* (New York, 1958); *Memoirs*, comp. Thomas R. Bransten (New York, 1970). **Suggested Readings:** Gertrude Samuels, *Ben Gurion, Fighter of Goliaths: The Story of David Ben-Gurion* (New York, 1961); Avraham Avi-hai, *Ben Gurion, State-Builder: Principles and Pragmatism, 1948–1963* (New York, 1974); Michael Bar-Zohar, trans. Peretz Kidron, *Ben-Gurion: A Biography* (New York, 1978).

Benjamin of Tudela (late twelfth century C.E.)

A Spanish Jew famous for his travelogue. During the fourteen years of his travels, Benjamin recorded data about Jewish life, including political, social, and economic status, from Spain across southern Europe and throughout the Middle East as far as Baghdad. He was also interested in Jewish intellectual life, and so his book is an important source for understanding the decline of the Persian (or Bablyonian) Talmudic academies and the rise of Jewish intellectual centers in Europe and North Africa during the Middle Ages. He also gives invaluable information about the Jewish community in Palestine. **Work:** *The Itinerary of Benjamin of Tudela: Critical Text, Translation and Commentary* by Marcus Nathan Adler (New York, 1965). **Suggested Readings:** Yosef Levanon, *The Jewish Travellers in the Twelfth Century* (Lanham, MD, 1980); Sandra Benjamin, ed., *The World of Benjamin of Tudela: A Medieval Mediterranean Travelogue* (London and Cranbury, NJ, 1995).

Borochov, Ber (1881–1917)

A Russian Jewish intellectual who became active in the Socialist Zionist movement. He strongly supported Palestine as the only place for the Jewish national home (thereby rejecting the British proposal for a Jewish homeland in Uganda) and hoped to see the new society there be a model of socialist and communist ideals. He is best known for synthesizing Zionism—a Jewish nationalist movement—with Marxism, which rejected all nationalisms as creations of the captialist class. His hope was that by creating a national home, the Jewish working masses could free themselves from the exploitation of non-Jewish authorities and create their own organic society along Marxist lines, a society in which Jews were free to create a normal economic structure of their own. In this way, he argued, not only would anti-Semitism, which he saw as based on the abnormal economic conditions of the Jews in Russia, come to an end, but the Jewish proletariat would finally be free to flourish unhindered by ancient predjudices. **Works:** *Class Struggle and the Jewish Nation: Selected Essays in Marxist Zionism by Ber Borochov*, edited with an introduction by Mitchell Cohen (New Brunswick, NJ, 1984); Matityahu Mints, ed., *Igrot Ber Borokhov, 1897–1917* (Tel Aviv, 1989). **Suggested Readings:** Arthur Hertzberg, *The Zionist Idea* (New York, 1960); Mosheh Erem, *Mishnato shel Borokhov Be-mivhan Tekufatenu* (Tel Aviv, 1973); Matityahu Mints, *Ber Borokhov: Ha-ma'agal Ha-rishon, 1900-1906* (Tel Aviv, 1976).

Brandeis, Louis B. (1856–1941)

American Zionist and Supreme Court Justice. Brandeis was born in Louisville, Kentucky, and, after a brief period of schooling in Germany, entered Harvard Law School. As a lawyer, he devoted himself to public causes and to giving voice to those sectors of society that he deemed underrepresented in the law. He thus became a leading liberal voice in American jurisprudence and as such became a confidant of presidential candidate Woodrow Wilson. On election, Wilson nominated Brandeis to the U.S. Supreme Court, where Brandeis continued to be an advocate for liberal legislation until his retirement in 1939. On the bench, he defended states' rights against federal encroachment, pushed for the minimum wage, and voted for protections of labor unions. At this time, Brandeis also became involved in Zionist activities in America, seeing the establishment of a Jewish homeland as a way to rescue Jews from the oppressive, anti-Semitic regimes in Europe. He eventually split with the American Zionist movement due to disagreements concerning the financial and economic structures of the movement. **Works:** *The Jewish Problem: How to Solve It* (New York, 1939); *Other People's Money and How the Bankers Use It* (New York, 1967); *Brandeis on Zionism: A Collection of Addresses and Statements, with Foreword by Felix Frankfurter* (Westport, CT, 1942, 1976). **Suggested Readings:** Ezekiel Rabinowitz, *Justice Louis D. Brandeis: The Zionist Chapter of His Life* (New York, 1968); Lewis J. Paper, *Brandeis: An Intimate Biography of One of America's Truly Great Supreme*

Court Justices (Secaucus, NJ, 1983); Philippa Strum, *Louis D. Brandeis, Justice for the People* (Cambridge, MA, 1984); Ben Halpern, *A Clash of Heroes—Brandeis, Weizmann, and American Zionism* (New York, 1987).

Cicero, Marcus Tullius (106 B.C.E.–43 B.C.E.)

A Roman politician and consul. Cicero was a member of a prominent Roman aristocratic family. Trained in philosophy and law, he became active in Roman politics, serving as consul in 63 B.C.E. Although a prolific writer, he is mostly remembered today as an orator. In his defense of Flaccus, a proconsul of Syria accused of stealing money from the Jerusalem Temple, Cicero denounced Judaism as a "barbaric superstition" that should be opposed. In this attitude he stands with a number of Roman intellectuals of the first century who savaged Jews and/or Judaism and so participated in forming a Judeophobic tradition that was subsequently taken up in early Christianity. **Work:** C. D. Yonge, trans., *The Orations of Marcus Tullius Cicero* (London, 1909–1911). **Suggested Readings:** David L. Stockton, *Cicero: A Political Biography* (London, 1971); Anthony Everitt, *Cicero: The Life and Times of Rome's Greatest Politician* (New York, 2003).

Colon, Joseph (1420–1480)

Jewish legal scholar. Although born in France, Joseph Colon made his name in Italy. He is especially noted for his defense of individual rights when these were threatened by majority opinion, which he often saw as arbitrary. He not only tried to base his decisions on individual precedents, but he also tried to articulate the general principles that stood behind his rulings. His various rescripts (*responsa*) have been collected, published, and widely cited. **Work:** E. D. Pines, *Sheelot Uteshuvot Ufiskei Hamaharik Hahadashim* (Jerusalem, 1970). **Suggested Reading:** Abraham Rabinowitz, *Encyclopedia Judaica*, s.v. "Colon, Joseph ben Solomon" (Jerusalem, 1972).

Dohm, Christian Wilhelm von (1751–1820)

A leading thinker of the Enlightenment in northern Germany. Dohm probably became familiar with the oppressed status of Jews in Germany through his friendship with Moses Mendelssohn. On Mendelssohn's urgings, Dohm wrote his famous pamphlet, "Over the Civic Betterment of the Jews," in which he argued that the Jews of Alsace were corrupt and backward in their social and religious practices only because of the oppressive conditions in which they were forced to live and the constant attacks they suffered. The Jews could become productive citizens of society, he asserted, if only they were given the freedom and right to develop as a normal human society. His calls were welcomed by many Enlightenment leaders both inside and outside the Jewish community and his arguments helped lead to the legal and social emancipation of Germany's Jews. **Work:** Helen Lederer, trans., *Concerning the Amelioration of the Civil Status of the Jews* (Cincinnati, OH, 1957). **Suggested Reading:** Franz Reuss, *Christian Wilhelm Dohms Schrift "Ueber die buergerliche Verbesserung der Juden" und deren Einwirkung auf die gebildeten Stuende Deutschlands* (Olms, 1973).

Duran, Simon ben Zemach (1361–1444)

A North African rabbi, Duran was known for his wide-ranging knowledge and stringency in his legal decisions. Born in Majorca, he was educated in Palma, where he studied astronomy, mathematics, logic, and medicine. For many years he earned his living as a physician and surgeon in Palma, but was also already renowned for his rabbinic learning. In 1391, anti-Jewish riots forced him to leave and settle in North Africa. There he was unable to earn a living as a physician and so eked out a livelihood as a rabbinic official, serving under Isaac ben Sheshet Perfet. He also engaged in the philosophical debates of his day; defended the sacredness of the rabbinic tradition against the Karaites, who refused to acknowledge any true source of Jewish practice outside the Bible; and wrote liturgical poetry. **Work:** Excerpts from his *responsa* are available in Isidore Epstein, *The "Responsa" of Rabbi Solomon ben Adreth of Barcelona (1235–1310) as a Source of the History of Spain; Studies in the Communal Life of the Jews in Spain as Reflected in the "Responsa" and the Responsa of Rabbi Simon b. Zemah Duran, as a Source of the History of the Jews in North Africa* (New York, 1968). **Suggested Reading:** Hirsch J. Zimmels, *Encyclopedia Judaica*, s.v. "Duran, Simeon ben Zemah" (Jerusalem, 1972).

Einhorn, David (1809–1879)

Liberal rabbi in Germany and the United States. Einhorn was born in Bavaria and received his rabbinic training in Germany. He soon became embroiled in a number of religious controversies. During these controversies he publically stated his rejection of the divine authority of the Talmud and his support for translating the prayerbook into the vernacular while editing out all references to sacrifices and the Temple. His increasingly radical views finally led him to leave Germany (he was then chief rabbi of the German principality of Mecklenburg-Schwerin) and take up a position in Budapest. After a few months he migrated to the United States, where he became a leading voice in American liberal (Reform) Judaism. He settled at first in Baltimore where his staunchly abolitionist stance led to his removal. He held that historically Judaism had always undergone change and needed to do so again, without restrictions from the medieval past. He thus pushed for a liberal Judaism of social justice and compassion, rejected Zionism as a narrow minded nationalism, and resisted any compromise with more traditional views. **Works:** "The Rev. Dr. M. J. Raphall's *Bible View of Slavery* Reviewed by the Rev. D. Einhorn, D.D.,*" *Sinai* (February 1861); *Bestaendige Leuchte, die Lehre des Judenthums dargestellt fuer Schule und Haus* (Philadelphia, 1866); *Book of Prayers for Jewish Congregations, New Translation after the German Original* (Chicago? 1896, 1913, 1921). **Suggested Reading:** Kaufmann Kohler, ed., *David Einhorn, Memorial Volume: Selected Sermons and Addresses* (New York, 1911).

Eleazar ben Zadok

The name of two early rabbinic authorities of the first and second centuries C.E. The younger Eleazar is thought to have been the grandson of the older. The older Eleazar witnessed the destruction of the Temple and is said to have undergone forty years of self-affliction in order to gain divine mercy and prevent the destruction. The second Eleazar is credited with arguing that no rabbinic ruling should be enacted that places an undue burden on the community. Both are cited in the early rabbinic literature, although it is hard at times to know which of the two is meant.

Eliezer ben Hyrcanus (late first century to early second century C.E.)

A pupil of Yohanan ben Zakkai and so a founder of rabbinic Judaism. Eliezer was a member of the first generation of *Tannaim*, that is, authorities cited in the Mishnah. He was a renowned scholar and teacher and as such, according to legend, was sent to Rome as part of a delegation headed by the patriarch to plead for better conditions for the defeated Judeans. He was staunchly antipagan, to the extent that he argued that any charity shown by pagans was to be taken as motivated by pride and not sincere altruism. He was also a powerful advocate among his peers for maintaining traditional laws and practices and argued against taking intention into account when determining cases of law. Although he was eventually ostracized by his fellow *Tannaim*, he continued to be an important influence in the development of early rabbinic Judaism. **Suggested Readings:** Jacob Neusner, *Eliezer ben Hyrcanus: The Tradition and the Man* (Leiden, 1973); Yitzhak D. Gilat, *R. Eliezer ben Hyrcanus: A Scholar Outcast* (Ramat-Gan, Israel, 1984).

Eliezer ben Isaac (of Worms) (eleventh century)

German Talmudic scholar. Eliezer was one of the earliest legal authorities of German Jewry and even founded a rabbinic school (a yeshiva) in Mainz. He was responsible for training a number of important scholars who went on to become the intellectual formulators of the Ashkenazic (that is, Central European) Jewish legal tradition. He is quoted by many later authorities.

Ginzberg, Louis (1873–1953)

Preeminent North American scholar of Jewish law. Born in Kovno, Lithuania, Ginzberg received a traditional rabbinic education in the yeshivas (traditional rabbinic academies) of Lithuania and a secular education in oriental languages at the universities of Berlin and Strasbourg. In 1899, he immigrated to the United States and joined the editorial staff of the *Jewish Encyclopedia*. In 1903, he accepted a faculty position in Talmud at the Jewish Theological Seminary of America. His scholarly work involved mostly research in the history and evolution of Jewish legal and ethical literature, claiming that one could not understand Jewish society without understanding its law. He also wrote some legal opinions from the perspective of the Conservative movement. He also became known for his work with the Geniza material from Cairo, a trove of ancient manuscripts found in the walls of an eighth-century Egyptian synagogue. His research showed that Jewish law was a human product growing out of particular social and political contexts. **Works:** *On Jewish Law and Lore* (Cleveland, OH, 1955, 1962); David Golinkin, ed., *The Legends of the Jews* (Philadelphia, 1968); *Geonica* (New York, 1968); David Golinkin, ed., *Responsa of Professor Louis Ginzberg* (New York, 1996). **Suggested Reading:** Eli Ginzberg, *Keeper of the Law, Louis Ginzberg* (Philadelphia, 1966).

Gordon, Judah Leb (1831–1892)

Judah (born Leon) was one of the earliest Enlightenment writers and poets who wrote in Hebrew and so is regarded as one of the founders of modern Hebrew. Gordon was an enthusiastic backer of the Enlightenment and was severely critical of the anti-Enlightenment traditionalist rabbis of the time. He urged the Jews of Russia to abandon their old ways, including Yiddish, and to participate in modern Russian life. After the imposition of the repressive May Laws in 1881, Gordon gave up on his idea of a future for Jewish life in Russia and became a Zionist. Despairing of both the Yiddish and Russian languages, he urged that all important literature be translated into Hebrew so that the language would not be lost to the Jewish people. Although he backed the immigration of Jews to Palestine, he always held that true redemption would only occur with the spiritual regeneration of the people. **Works:** *Kitve Yehudah Leb Gordon: Shirah* (Tel Aviv, 1950); *Kitve Yehudah Leb Gordon: Prozah* (Tel Aviv, 1960). **Suggested Readings:** Ya'akov Fikhman, *Alufe Ha-haskalah: Avraham Mapu, Yehudah Leyb Gordon, Perets Smolenskin* (Tel Aviv, 1952); Michael Stanislawski, *For Whom Do I Toil? Judah Leib Gordon and the Crisis of Russian Jewry* (New York, 1988).

Herzl, Theodor (1860–1904)

Founder of the modern Zionist movement. Born in Budapest, Herzl was serving as a foreign correspondent for the Viennese newspaper *Die Neue Freie Presse* when he was sent to Paris to cover the trial of Alfred Dreyfus. Herzl came away convinced that the only solution to the Jewish Question was to create a national home for the Jews. He wrote a novel, *The Jewish State*, in which he described his dream of a state that was a sort of socialist utopia. To bring this vision to reality, he organized the First Zionist Congress in 1897, in Basle, Switzerland, which launched the World Zionist Organization, which in turn began the systematic work of developing a Jewish settlement in Palestine. In 1903, the British offered to give land in Uganda for a Jewish homeland, and Herzl, who was from a highly assimilated background, accepted. The proposal, however, was voted down by the World Zionist Congress, and Herzl thereafter gradually lost his power and influence as more traditionalist Russian Jews took over. **Works:** *The Jewish State* (originally published in 1896; New York, 1988); *Old New Land (Altneuland)*, trans. Lotta Levensohn (originally published in 1902; Princeton, NJ, 1997). **Suggested Readings:** Alex Bein, *Theodore Herzl: A Biography* (Philadelphia, 1940); Desmond Stewart, *Theodor Herzl* (Garden City, NY, 1974); Jacques Kornberg, *Theodor Herzl: From Assimilation to Zionism* (Bloomington, IN, 1993).

Hess, Moses (1812–1875)

German Jewish Socialist thinker who is often regarded as the founder of Socialist Zionism. He argued that the only way to revitalize Jewish life was to change the social and economic situation of the Jewish masses. This was possible only through the establishment of a Jewish political restoration that would allow Jews to have control over their own education and socioeconomic structures. He was attacked by Marx and Engels for seeing socialism in educational and moral terms while ignoring the role of class. He is best known for his work, *Rome and Jerusalem*, which is now considered a classic in Zionist literature. **Work:** *Rome and Jerusalem: A Study in Jewish Nationalism*, translated from the German with introduction and notes by Meyer Waxman (New York, 1918, 1943). **Suggested Readings:** Sir Isaiah Berlin, *The Life and Opinions of Moses Hess* (Cambridge, 1959); Shlomo Avineri, *Moses Hess: Prophet of Communism and Zionism* (New York, 1985); Ken Koltun-Fromm, *Moses Hess and Modern Jewish Identity* (Bloomington, IN, 2001).

Hillel and Shammai (early first century C.E.)

Semilegendary leaders of two rival schools of thought from the earliest stratum of protorabbinic Judaism. They or their schools of thought are cited frequently in the Mishnah and Talmud. Hillel is remembered as a man of mild manners and concern for the common people. In the numerous debates with students from the school of Shammai cited in the Talmud, Hillel prevails in all but a handful of cases. It is from his school that the bulk of the Mishnaic laws come. He is credited with giving early rabbinic literature its concern for individual rights and tolerance of differences. **Suggested Readings:** Nahum Glatzer, *Hillel The Elder: The Emergence of Classical Judaism* (New York, 1956); Yitzhak Buxbaum, *The Life and*

Teachings of Hillel (Northvale, NJ, 1994); Jacob Neusner, *The Rabbinic Traditions about the Pharisees before 70* (Atlanta, GA, 1999).

Hirsch, Samson Raphael (1808–1888)

The intellectual founder of modern Orthodox Judaism. Born in Hamburg, Hirsch was engaged in a lifelong struggle to find a middle way between the Reform Jews of Central Europe who wanted to transform Judaism into an Enlightenment religion, and the traditional Orthodox Jews of Eastern Europe who viewed any deviation from medieval Jewish practice as heresy. In response to this cleavage in the Jewish community, Hirsch developed the notion of "Torah with world manners," meaning one could combine traditional Judaic piety and practice with modern dress and manners. In addition to a commentary on the Bible that shows how traditional Jewish values can be compatible with the Enlightenment, he is known for his fictive collection of letters in which a traditional Jew shows a perplexed young Jewish intellectual how traditional Judaism can answer his concerns. **Works:** I. Grunfeld, trans., *Horeb: A Philosophy of Jewish Laws and Observations* (London, 1962); Bernard Drachman, trans., *The Nineteen Letters on Judaism* (Jerusalem and New York, 1969); Isaac Levy, trans., *The Pentateuch* (London, 1956). **Suggested Readings:** Noah Rosenbloom, *Tradition in An Age of Reform: The Religious Philosophy of Samson Raphael Hirsch* (Philadelphia, 1976); Robert Liberles, *Religious Conflict in Social Context: The Resurgence of Orthodox Judaism in Frankfurt am Main, 1838–1877* (Westport, CT, 1985).

Hisda (third century C.E.)

One of the most frequently quoted Babylonian legal scholars in the Talmud. According to Talmudic tradition, Hisda was from a priestly family but grew up in poverty and always remembered his roots. Humble and modest in his own life, he is often quoted on matters of health and hygiene, which he felt were important topics for religious discussion, a stance for which he was at times criticized.

Hoffman, Abbie (1936–1989)

One of the best-known personalities of the youth counterculture of the 1960s. Hoffman's major contribution was to convince members of the counterculture to turn to political activism. He engaged in a variety of civil rights demonstrations and gained notoriety by nearly starting a riot at the New York Stock Exchange by throwing dollar bills onto the floor and leading nearly 50,000 people to Washington in an attempt to levitate the Pentagon and so exorcize its demons. Along with Jerry Rubin and other activists, he formed the Youth International Party (Yippie!) and became an icon of the age. He committed suicide in 1989. **Works:** *The Autobiography of Abbie Hoffman, Introduced by Norman Mailer* (New York and London, 2000); *Steal This Book* (New York, 1996; 2000). **Suggested Readings:** Jonah Raskin, *For the Hell of It: The Life and Times of Abbie Hoffman* (Berkeley, CA, 1996); Larry Sloman, *Steal This Dream: Abbie Hoffman and the Countercultural Revolution in America* (New York, 1998).

Isaac ben Sheshet Perfet (1326–1408)

A Spanish rabbi and halachic authority. Perfet was born in Barcelona, but anti-Jewish riots in 1391 forced him to flee to North Africa. He eventually returned to Spain and served as rabbi in Saragossa and finally in Valencia. He was a prolific writer of Jewish legal rescripts (*responsa*) and was one of the major authorities drawn on by the decisive medieval code of Jewish law, the *Shulkhan Arukh*. Among other things, he was active in codifying and establishing traditions concerning marriage and other family status matters that were particular to the Algerian Jewish community. **Work:** *She'elot u-teshuvot ha-Ribash ha-hadashot* (Mukachevo, 1901). **Suggested Readings:** Isaac Morali, *Tsofnat Pa'neah Yegaleh Shirim Kadmonim peri Ruah Rabane Aljir Ha-rishonim* (Berlin, 1895); Avraham Hershman, *Rabbi Yitshak bar Sheshet (ha-Ribash): Derekh Hayav u-Tekufato* (Jerusalem, 1956).

Ishmael ben Elisha (first half of the second century C.E.)

An early framer of rabbinic Judaism. Ishmael ben Elisha was a member of the priestly elite, a student of Eliezer ben Hyrcanus and a colleague of Akiba. He differed in his method of biblical exegesis from Akiba, who regarded every letter as having some sort of esoteric significance. Ishmael, on the other hand, regarded the sacred literature to be in human language and so was much more literal in his interpretations. He is also remembered as a very humane scholar who believed that the rulings of the sages should help the common people, not place undue burdens on them.

Suggested Reading: Gary G. Porton, *The Legal Traditions of Rabbi Ishmael: A Form-Critical and Literary-Critical Approach* (Brill, 1976).

Israel ben Haim of Brunn (or Bruna) (ca. 1400–1480)

Rabbi and communal leader in his hometown of Bruenn, Germany. He eventually became a recognized leader in Regensburg where he ran a yeshiva. He wrote numerous rabbinic legal rescripts in response to questions from all over the German speaking lands. His writings are an important source for understanding the lives of Jews in Central Europe in the fifteenth century. **Work:** *Responsa of Israel ben Hayyim of Bruna* (Salonika, 1788).

Jabotinsky, Zeev (Vladimir) (1880–1940)

An assimilated Jewish intellectual and writer who founded the right-wing faction of the Zionist movement. Born in Russia, Jabotinsky worked for several years as a European correspondent for two Odessa newspapers. After the anti-Jewish riot in Kishniev in 1903, he became a convinced Zionist activist and founded the first Zionist military organization, the Jewish Legion, in World War I and also a youth group, Betar, designed to train Jewish youth to engage in self-defense. Because of his militarism, he eventually came into conflict with the leaders of the Zionist movement who were committed to peaceful negotiation with the British and other world powers for the right to have a Jewish homeland. In response, Jabotinsky founded his own movement, the Revisionists, which supported illegal immigration and even terrorist acts against the British forces in Palestine. His position—that the Jews had to fight for their own freedom and could not rely on others for their welfare—seemed vindicated by the Holocaust. Although he died in 1940, his party continued the struggle in British mandatory Palestine and later became a political party in the new state. **Works:** *Judge and Fool* (New York, 1930); *The Story of the Jewish Legion* (New York, 1945); *Ba-derekh la-medinah* (Jerusalem, 1953). **Suggested Readings:** Joseph Schechtman, *Rebel and Statesman: The Vladimir Jabotinsky Story* (New York, 1956); Lenni Brenner, *The Iron Wall: Zionist Revisionism from Jabotinsky to Shamir* (London, Totowa, NJ, 1984); Michael Stanislawski, *Zionism and the Fin de Siècle: Cosmopolitanism and Nationalism from Nordau to Jabotinsky* (Berkeley, CA, 2001).

Jacob ben Asher (ca. 1270 to 1340)

Author of one of the more influential medieval codes of Jewish law. Jacob divided his code into four parts and called it the *Arba'ah Turim* (the four columns), referring to the columns of precious stones on the biblical priest's breastplate. The fourth section, *Hoshen Mishpat*, is largely concerned with personal matters and civil law. This code remained one of the standard reference works of halachah until the publication of the *Shulkhan Arukh* in the sixteenth century. Such was the influence of the *Arba'ah Turim* that the editor of the *Shulkhan Arukh* maintained its four-part structure. On his death he left an ethical will to his children reflecting his high level of spirituality and culture.

Joseph ibn Migash (1077–1141)

Spanish Talmudic scholar. Joseph ibn Migash studied under al-Fasi for many years and eventually succeeded him as head of the yeshiva (rabbinical college) in Lucena. Joseph became a widely renowned scholar and had much to do with the establishment of Talmudic studies in Spain and southern France. He was the author of many legal rescripts, and although little of his own work survives, he is cited by many later authorities. **Work:** *Teshuvot* (Warsaw, 1870).

Josephus, Flavius (died ca. 100 C.E.)

Roman Jewish historian. A member of one of Jerusalem's priestly families, Josephus was given command of the northern defenses during the rebellion against Rome in 66–70 C.E. He arranged for the peaceful surrender of his troops and was taken by the Roman army to Rome, where he spent the rest of his life writing in defense of his people. Josephus is best known for four books: (1) *The Antiquities of the Jews*, a history of the Judean people from Adam down to his time; (2) *The Jewish War*, a detailed description of the events leading up to, and the conduct of, the rebellion; (3) *Life*, his autobiography; and (4) *Against Apion*, a spirited defense of Judaism written in response to a now lost work of the anti-Jewish writer Apion. In all his works Josephus tried to show that the Judean people were peace loving and willing to get along with the Romans and that all the tension and violence that led to the outbreak of the rebellion was the work of a small group of fanatics. His histories, which go into great detail, are our primary source of information about Jews and Judaism in the century before and after the turn of the first millennium. **Works:** *Jewish Antiquities*, English trans. H.St.J. Thackeray (Cambridge, MA, 1930–   ); *The Great Roman-Jewish War, A.D. 66–70 (De bello Judaico): The William Whiston Translation as Revised by D. S. Margoliouth* (New York, 1960); *Josephus, The Essential Writings: A Condensation of Jewish Antiquities and The Jewish War*, trans. and ed. Paul L. Maier (Grand Rapids, MI, 1988). **Suggested Readings:** Seth Schwartz, *Josephus and Judaean Politics* (Leiden and New York, 1990); Mireille Hadas-Lebel, *Flavius Josephus: Eyewitness to Rome's First-Century Conquest of Judea*, trans. Richard Miller (New York and Toronto, 1993); Fausto Parente and Joseph Sievers, eds., *Josephus and the History of the Greco-Roman Period: Essays in Memory of Morton Smith* (New York, 1994); Louis H. Feldman, *Studies in Josephus' Rewritten Bible* (New York, 1998); Gottfried Mader, *Josephus and the Politics of Historiography: Apologetic and Impression Management in the Bellum Judaicum* (Leiden, 2000).

Joshua ben Hananiah (late first century to early second century C.E.)

A pupil of Yohanan ben Zakkai and therefore a founder of early rabbinic Judaism. According to tradition, he earned a living as a blacksmith and thus brought to his scholarship a certain measure of worldly knowledge. According to tradition, he was so renowned as a scholar that he accompanied the patriarch on several missions to Rome. He vigorously defended Judaism against Christian polemics, but at the same time tried to quell the anger of Judeans against the Roman occupation.

Judah ben Eliezer of Minz (1408–1508)

Important medieval Italian rabbi. Although probably of German origin (his name possibly indicating his birth in Mainz), Judah spent most of his career as rabbi of the Jewish community in Padua, Italy. Despite his stay in Italy, he relied heavily on the Jewish traditions of his native Germany and admired in particular Meir of Rothenburg, whom he frequently cited in his *responsa*. His correspondence is an important source of information on Jewish life and values in Germany during this time. **Work:** *She'elot u-teshuvot* (Jerusalem, 1962).

Kalischer, Zvi Hirsch (1795–1874)

With Yehudah Alkalai, one of the earliest rabbis to promote Zionist thinking. Although he studied with some of the most eminent Polish rabbis of his day, Kalischer refused to serve as rabbi in Thorn, where he lived most of his life. Instead, he spent his time and energy promoting the notion that the long-awaited redemption of the Jews would not come through some sudden divine intervention, but had to be effected by the Jews themselves. Like Alkalai, he was strongly influenced by the rise of nationalistic movements in Europe and was roundly criticized by his rabbinic colleagues. He traveled widely throughout Europe to recruit followers who would not just support Zionism materially but who would actually move to the Holy Land. **Suggested Reading:** Biographical notes and excerpts of his writings can be found in Arthur Hertzberg, *The Zionist Idea* (Garden City, NY, 1959; reprint New York, 1972).

Kallen, Horace (1882–1974)

A philosopher who developed the theory of multiculturalism. Although born in Germany, Kallen spent most of his life in the United States, which he saw as the paradigmatic multicultural society. Kallen's argument was that any number of religious, ethnic, and cultural groups could live within a single state and share a single sense of nationality. Along these lines, he argued that each ethnic, religious, or cultural group in the United States should be granted a degree of cultural autonomy, while itself recognizing the importance of the overarching national culture. In this way, he argued, there could be cultural diversity in which each group could contribute to the culture of the greater whole. His thinking provided the intellectual basis for many Jews to argue that they could support Zionism as a cultural or ethnic movement and still be loyal Americans. **Works:** *Individualism: An American Way of Life* (New York, 1933); *Patterns of Progress* (New York, 1950); *A Study of Liberty* (Yellow Springs, OH, 1959); *Creativity, Imagination, Logic: Meditations for the Eleventh Hour* (New York, 1973). **Suggested Readings:** Milton R. Konvitz, ed., *The Legacy of Horace M. Kallen* (Rutherford, NJ, 1987); Sarah Schmidt, *Horace M. Kallen, Prophet of American Zionism* (Brooklyn, NY, 1995).

Katzenellenbogen, Yechezkel (Ezekiel) (1670–1749)

A renowned German rabbi and legal authority. Katzenellenbogen came from a distinguished family of rabbis and his descendants for the next four generations held various rabbinic posts in Poland. He, like other rabbis of his time, wrote numerous *responsa* dealing with communal, legal, and moral issues of the time. **Works:** *Keneset Yechezkel* (Altona, 1632); *Tefillot le-Yartzait* (Altona, 1727); *Tzawwa'at R. Yechezkel* (Amsterdam, 1750).

Maimonides, Moses (1135–1204)

Also known as Moses ben Maimon and by his rabbinic acronym RAMBAM, Maimonides was a rabbi and one of the foremost neo-Aristotelian thinkers of the Middle Ages. He was born in Cordoba, Spain, but traveled considerably in his younger years, eventually settling in Fustat (now Cairo), Egypt. In Egypt he served as rabbi of the local community as well as court physician to the Muslim ruler. He wrote extensively on rabbinic topics, writing numerous *responsa*. He is also renowned for his careful and insightful commentary on the Mishnah (ca. 1168) and for his compilation of the first systematized code of Jewish law, the *Mishneh Torah* (ca. 1180). Maimonides was also a highly respected philosopher and wrote one of the masterpieces of medieval neo-Aristotelianism, *The Guide of the Perplexed* (ca. 1190). **Works:** *The Code of Maimonides* (New Haven, CT, 1949–); *The Guide of the Perplexed*, trans. Shlomo Pines (Chicago, 1963); *The Eight Chapters of Maimonides on Ethics (Shemonah Perakim): A Psychological and Ethical Treatise*, ed. and trans. Joseph I. Gorfinkle (New York, 1912, reprint 1922, 1966). **Suggested Readings:** David Yellin and Israel Abrahams, *Maimonides: His Life and Works* (New York, 1972); Lenn E. Goodman, *RAMBAM: Readings in the Philosophy of Moses Maimonides* (New York, 1976); Abraham Joshua Heschel, *Maimonides: A Biography*; trans. Joachim Neugroschel (New York, 1982).

Meir of Rothenburg (ca. 1215–1293)

One of the key organizers of Jewish communal life in the German-speaking lands in the thirteenth century. Some scholars have claimed that Meir may have even been chief rabbi of Germany, but there is no evidence that such a position existed at that time, much less that Meir occupied it. Born in Worms, Meir studied in both Germany and France. He returned to Germany and had many students who went on to become leading Ashkenazic scholars. He was a poet and the author of numerous *responsa*. Much of his legal writing has to do with business and other economic matters or with issues of civil law. Through these writings, he helped establish the basic relationship between the individual and the community in European Jewry. He was imprisoned by the local bishop while on a journey through Alsace in 1286 and died there. The reason for his imprisonment remains unclear. **Work:** Moshe Aryeh Blokh, ed., *Sefer Sha'are Teshuvot Maharam b.R. Barukh* (Berlin, 1891). **Suggested Reading:** Irving A. Agus, *Rabbi Meir of Rothenburg: His Life and His Works as Sources for the Religious, Legal, and Social History of the Jews of Germany in the Thirteenth Century* (Philadelphia, 1947).

Mendelssohn, Moses (1729–1786)

The most important Jewish philosopher of the early German Enlightenment and a leader in the struggle of German Jewry to achieve civic and legal emancipation. He was friends with some of the greatest Enlightenment thinkers of the time, especially Gotthold E. Lessing (and he was, in fact, the likely inspiration for Lessing's play *Nathan the Wise*). Mendelssohn was also elected to the Prussian Royal Academy of Sciences, something unheard of for a Jew at the time, although in the end his election was never ratified by King Frederick II. Among his numerous writings was the first Jewish translation of the Bible into contemporary German. The intent was to encourage his fellow Jews to learn the Bible and to become familiar with the vernacular German of their home country. At the same time he encouraged Christian Wilhelm von Dohm to write a pamphlet urging the political authorities to enact new laws emancipating the Jewish community from its medieval restrictions. He is understood to be the inspiration for the unique German–Jewish symbiosis that lasted until the Holocaust. **Works:** Alfred Jospe, ed. and trans., *Jerusalem, and Other Jewish Writings* (New York, 1969); Eva Jospe, ed. and trans., *Moses Mendelssohn: Selections from His Writings* (New York, 1975); Alexander Altmann, *Gesammelte Schriften. Jubilaeumsausgabe* (Stuttgart-Bad Cannstatt, 1971). **Suggested Readings:** Allan Arkush, *Moses Mendelssohn and the Enlightenment* (Albany, NY, 1994); David Sorkin, *Moses Mendelssohn and the Religious Enlightenment* (Berkeley, CA, 1996).

Nissim ben Reuben Gerondi (1310–ca. 1375)

Spanish rabbi known for his work on jurisprudence. Although probably born in Gerona (hence the designation, Gerondi), Nissim spent most of his adult life as a highly esteemed Talmudist in Barcelona, Spain. He had a major influnce on Spanish Jewish law and received requests for legal rescripts (*responsa*) from all across the Jewish world, including the Land of Israel. He drew heavily on the precedents and methods of Moses ben Nahman (Nahmanides) and Isaac bar Jacob al-Fasi. **Works:** *She'elot uTeshuvot* (Rome, 1546; Constantinople, 1548; Cremona, 1557); commentaries on several Talmudic tractates, including *Shabbat* (Warsaw, 1862); *Rosh ha-Shanah* (Jerusalem, 1871); *Baba Metzi'a* (Dyhernfurth, 1822).

Novak, David (1941–   )

Professor of Jewish law and ethics. Currently at the University of Toronto, Novak has published extensively on Jewish law, especially as it relates to questions of politics and governance. Born in Chicago, Novak received his A.B. degree from the University of Chicago in 1961 and a Master of Hebrew Literature in 1964. He was ordained as a Conservative rabbi at the Jewish Theological Seminary of America in 1966 and earned a Ph.D. in philosophy from Georgetown University in 1971. At the University of Toronto he currently holds the J. Richard and Dorothy Shiff Chair of Jewish Studies, serves as Director of the Jewish Studies Program, and is a member of the Joint Centre for Bioethics. **Works:** *The Image of the Non-Jew in Judaism: An Historical and Constructive Study of the Noahide Laws* (New York, 1983); *Jewish Social Ethics* (New York, 1992); *Natural Law in Judaism* (Cambridge and New York, 1998); *Covenantal Rights, A Study in Jewish Political Theory* (Princeton, NJ, 2000).

Philo Judaeus (early first century C.E.)

The most important Hellenistic Jewish philosopher. Philo was a member of one of the most prominent Jewish families of Alexandria, Egypt. His brother was an official in the Roman court, one of his nephews was married into the Judean royal family, and another nephew (Tiberius, who apparently broke his ties with the Jewish community) served as procurator of Judea from 46–48 C.E. and as prefect of Egypt from 66–70 C.E., according to Josephus. Late in life, Philo himself was chosen to head an Alexandrian Jewish delegation to the Roman emperor Caius Caligula. Philo was an extraordinarily prolific writer, who wrote on numerous topics of Jewish interest, especially on Bible and on Jewish law. He was the first thinker to try to reconcile the biblical text with Greco-Roman philosophy. To this end, he developed an allegorical method that had great influence on later, especially Christian, theologians. **Work:** F. H. Colson and G. H. Whitaker, trans., *Philo, in Ten Volumes*, Loeb Classics Series (Cambridge, 1929–1942). **Suggested Readings:** Erwin R. Goodenough, *Introduction to Philo Judaeus* (New Haven, CT, 1963); Samuel Sandmel, *Philo of Alexandria: An Introduction* (New York, 1979); Peder Borgen, *Philo of Alexandria, An Exegete for His Time* (Leiden and New York, 1997); Naomi G. Cohen, *Philo Judaeus, His Universe of Discourse* (Frankfurt am Main, 1995).

Pinhas ben Yair (late second century C.E.)

A Tannaitic authority who was close to mystic circles and was known as a miracle worker. Although he is known as a halachic authority, very few of his decisions are recorded in the literature. He is cited in the Mishnah (Sotah 9:15) as saying, "Watchfulness leads to cleanliness; cleanliness leads to purity; purity leads to distinction; distinction to holiness; holiness leads to humility; humility to the fear of sin; The fear of sin to righteousness."

Quintilian, Marcus Fabius (35–ca. 95 C.E.)

One of the outstanding Roman rhetoricians of the first century, publishing some twelve books on oratory. Although born in Spain, he was educated and spent most of his career in Rome. Like many Romans of the upper classes, he held the Jews and their religion in disdain. He refers to Moses, for example, as the founder "of the Jewish superstition," which has been a corrupting influence on other peoples. **Works:**. Lewis A. Sussman, *The Major Declamations Ascribed to Quintilian: A Translation* (Frankfurt am Main and New York, 1987); Donald Russell, ed. and trans., *The Orator's Education* (Cambridge, 2001). **Suggested Readings:** Aubrey Gwynn, *Roman Education from Cicero to Quintilian* (Oxford, 1926; New York, 1966); George Kennedy, *Quintilian* (New York, 1969).

Rackman, Emmanuel (1910–   )

American Orthodox leader, trained in both law and rabbinics and now serving as chancellor of the Orthodox-oriented Bar Ilan University in Israel. Beginning with his position as rabbi of the Fifth Avenue Synagogue in New York and continuing through his leadership of the Bar Ilan University, Rackman has been an outspoken champion of women's rights within the traditionalist community. **Works:** *Jewish Values for Modern Man* (New York, 1962); *Modern Halakhah for Our Time* (Hoboken, NJ, 1995); *One Man's Judaism, Renewing the Old and Sanctifying the New* (Jerusalem and New York, 2000).

Resh Lakish (third century C.E.)

Also known as Shimon ben Lakish, he is one of the most cited Palestinian legal authorities in the Talmud. He seems to have been active in communal affairs, especially in Tiberias, which may have been his hometown. He placed special emphasis in his preaching on the study of Torah as a primary value.

Rothschild

A widely renowned and powerful Jewish banking family that had its roots in Frankfurt, Germany. The family banking business became important under Mayer Amschel (1744–1812). Mayer had five sons, each of whom developed a branch of the bank. Amschel (1773–1855) maintained the branch in Frankfurt, Nathan (1777–1836) established a branch in London, Jakob (1791–1868) developed a branch in Paris, Saloman (1774–1855) operated the bank in Vienna, and Kalman ran the Italian branch in Naples. The London and Paris branches continued to function into the twentieth century. The family retained its Jewish identity and was active in a variety of Jewish causes. Baron Edmond James de Rothschild (1845–1934) of the Paris branch, in particular, was a major philanthropic supporter of the early Zionist movement, providing financial backing for such early settlements in the Land of Israel as Rishon LeZion, Zikhron Ya'akov (named after Edmond's father James [Jakob, Yaacov in Hebrew]), Rosh Pinah and Petach Tikvah. Edmond's son, James, who was a British subject, served on the staff of General Allenby, who took Jerusalem from the Turks during World War I. **Work:**

Edmund de Rothschild: A Gilt-edged Life, A Memoir (London, 1998). **Suggested Readings:** Simon Schama, *Two Rothschilds and the Land of Israel* (New York, 1978); Derek Wilson, *Rothschild: A Story of Wealth and Power* (London, 1988); Niall Ferguson, *The House of Rothschild* (New York, 1998); Ran Aaronsohn, *Rothschild and Early Jewish Colonization in Palestine* (Jerusalem, 2000).

Rubin, Jerry (1938–1994)

Along with Abbie Hoffman, one of the founders of the Youth International Party (Yippie!) that tried to merge politics and the radical youth culture of the 1960s and 1970s. He is remembered most for the 1969 trial of the Chicago Seven, in which he saluted Judge Julius Hoffman with the Nazi salute while crying out, "Heil, Hitler!" Rubin later became a businessman and worked on Wall Street. He died in an automobile accident in 1994. **Works:** *We Are Everywhere* (New York, 1971); *Growing (Up) at Thirty-Seven* (New York, 1976). **Suggested Readings:** Ron Chepesiuk, *Sixties Radicals Then and Now: Candid Conversations with Those Who Shaped the Era* (Jefferson, NC, 1995); Joan Morrison and Robert Morrison, *From Camelot to Kent State: The Sixties Experience in the Words of Those Who Lived It* (Oxford and New York, 2001).

Saadia Gaon (882–942 C.E.)

Babylonian sage and one of the last internationally recognized leaders of the Babylonian Talmudic academies. Saadia was well acquainted with Islamic philosophy and even wrote a philosophical treatise in Arabic. He also wrote one of the first Hebrew grammars. He is probably best remembered for his confrontation with the Jewish Karaite sect, which claimed that only the Bible was authoritative for Jews and not the Talmud or other rabbinic writings. Saadia's spirited defense of rabbinism led to rabbinic Judaism's ultimate triumph over Karaism. **Works:** Samuel Rosenblatt, trans., *The Book of Beliefs and Opinions* (New Haven, London, 1976); Michael Linetsky, ed. and trans., *Rabbi Saadiah Gaon's Commentary on the Book of Creation* (Northvale, NJ, 2002). **Suggested Readings:** Henry Malter, *Saadia Gaon: His Life and Works* (Philadelphia, 1921); Boaz Cohen, *Saadia Anniversary Volume* (New York, 1943); Solomon Skoss, *Saadia Gaon, the Earliest Hebrew Grammarian* (Philadelphia, 1955); Erwin I. J. Rosenthal, *Saadya Studies* (New York, 1980).

Salanter, Israel Lipkin (1810–1883)

Founder of the Musar movement to increase moral sensitivity among rabbinic students. A prodigy in Talmudic learning in Lithuania, Salanter shared the concern of many of the yeshiva heads with the advances made by secularism, Reform, Hasidism, and other non-Orthodox movements. In response, he dedicated himself to improving the educational quality of the yeshivas, in particular by introducing the study of values and ethics. To this end he developed a psychology of education and a method of moral training called Musar. Not content to confine himself to advanced Talmudic students, Salanter attempted to make the reading and discussion of traditional Jewish moralistic literature part of daily Jewish life among the masses. **Works:** *Igeret ha-Musar* (Koenigsberg, 1858); *Sefer Or Yisra'el* (Vilna, 1900). **Suggested Readings:** Menahem Glen, *Israel Salanter, Religious-ethical Thinker: The Story of a Religious-ethical Current in Nineteenth Century Judaism* (New York, 1953); Hillel Goldberg, *Israel Salanter: Text, Structure, Idea, The Ethics and Theology of An Early Psychologist of the Unconscious* (New York, 1982); Immanuel Etkes, *Rabbi Israel Salanter and the Mussar Movement: Seeking the Torah of Truth* (Philadelphia, 1993).

Samuel ben Nahman (late third to early fourth century C.E.)

A Palestinian teacher who was best known for his moral lessons rather than his legal scholarship. He also had poetic abilities. He had two sons who grew to be authorities in their own right.

Schwadron, Shalom Mordechai (1835–1911)

A Polish halachic authority. Although he never held a major rabbinic post, he was nonetheless widely recognized as a halachic authority and was consulted by many of the leading rabbis of his day. His *responsa* are noteworthy because of their clear style and simple structure, obtuse and complex writing being the norm by the ninetheenth century. He generally tried to find reason for lenient rulings when he could, thus trying to moderate the increasing orthopraxis of Polish traditional Judaism. **Works:** *Sheelot Uteshuvot Maharsham*, Part I (New York, 1962; reprint of Warsaw, 1902); Part II (New York, 1962; reprint of St. Petersburg, 1905); Part III (New York, 1962; reprint of Satmar, 1910); Part IV (New York,

1962; reprint of Lemberg, 1913); Part V (New York, 1962; reprint of Satmar, 1926); Part VI (Jerusalem, 1968); Part VII (Jerusalem, 1967).

Seneca, Lucius Annaeus (The Younger) (ca. 4 B.C.E.–65 C.E.)

Along with Cicero and Quintilian, one of the great Roman intellectuals of the first century C.E. Seneca wrote a number of philosophical and dramatic works and even served as an adviser to the Emperor Nero. He alludes to the Jews occasionally in his writings, and like his peers, he regarded Judaism as a degenerate and dangerous religion. He held, for example, that the requirement to rest on the Sabbath only encouraged indolence. His disdain for Judaism was common for the Roman aristocracy of the time, possibly because of the popularity of Judaism among the masses. **Works:** Thomas H. Corcoran, trans., *Seneca. With an English Translation* (London, Cambridge, MA, 1971); Frederick Ahl, trans., *Three Tragedies* (Ithaca, NY, 1986); John G. Fitch, ed. and trans., *Hercules, Trojan Women, Phoenician Women, Media, Phaedra* (Cambridge, MA, 2002). **Suggested Readings:** Anna Motto, *Guide to the Thought of Lucius Annaeus Seneca in the Extant Prose Works, Epistulae Morales, the Dialogi, De Beneficiis, De Clementia, and Quaestiones Naturales* (Amsterdam, 1970); Miriam T. Griffin, *Seneca: A Philosopher in Politics* (Oxford and New York, 1976, 1992); Paul Veyne, *Seneca: The Life of a Stoic* (New York, 2003).

Simeon ben Menasia (late second century to early third century C.E.)

A rabbinic scholar who lived at the time that the Mishnah was compiled. He is rarely cited in the Mishnah but does appear in later sources and is mostly known for his homilies. Unlike other rabbis who thought one should spend time studying only holy books, he supported training in the professions so that the religious scholar could also provide a decent life for himself and his family. He is quoted as saying it is permitted in some cases to profane one Sabbath so that one may fulfill many Sabbaths. He thus seems to have been much more worldly and concerned for the common person than was the norm among his rabbinic peers.

Sofer, Moshe (1762–1839)

Also called the Hatam Sofer after his famous book of *responsa*, Sofer was a leading figure in the traditionalist Jewish community. Born in Frankfurt, a.M., Sofer was a child prodigy and was already an advanced Talmudic scholar at the age of seven. He studied with some of the greatest Talmudic sages of his time. He was fiercely opposed to the Enlightenment and stringently fought against any attempt to alter Jewish tradition in any way. He argued that the *Shulkhan Arukh*, the sixteenth-century code of Jewish law, was fully binding and authoritative, a stance that still marks ultra-Orthodox Judaism today. He is famous for proclaiming that "all what is new is forbidden." Over much opposition from the more liberal elements of the community, he was appointed in 1801 as rabbi in Pressburg, one of the most important centers of Jewish life in Hungary. While in Pressburg, he established a major yeshiva for training traditionalist rabbis, part of a long-term strategy to fortify Judaism against corrosive forces from the outside. **Works:** Avraham Yaakov Finkel, trans., *Pressburg Under Siege: An Autobiographical Account* (New York, 1991); *Hidushe Hatam Sofer Ha-shalem* (Jerusalem, 1976–2000); *Teshuvot Hatam Sofer* (Jerusalem, 2000). **Suggested Readings:** Selig Schachnowitz, *The Light from the West: The Story of the Life and Times of the Chassam Sofer* (Jerusalem and New York, 1958); Shubert Spero, *The Story of the Chasam Sofer* (Cleveland, OH, 1976).

Spinoza, Baruch (1632–1677)

One of the founders of the rationalist movement in modern philosophy, generally associated with figures like René Descartes and Gottfried Leibniz. Born in Amsterdam, Spinoza's antireligious polemics eventually provoked the Amsterdam Jewish authorities to excommunicate him for his "abominable heresies." He argued, among other things, that the Bible was not divinely revealed and that revealed religions, such as Judaism, were mere superstitions, truth being fully available only through reason. His most famous philosophical work was the *Tractatus Theologico-Politicus*, published in 1670. So great was his reputation after the publication of the *Tractatus* that he was offered a chair of philosophy at the University of Heidelberg. Spinoza refused, saying he prefered a quiet life of research and philosophical inquiry. In the mid-1670s he completed a second major book, *Ethics*, but found that opposition from theologians was so fierce that nobody would publish the book. It appeared in print only after his death. He lived out his life as a secular scholar, unaffiliated with any religion. **Works:** R.H.M. Elerd, trans., *The Chief Works of Benedict de Spinoza* (New York, 1951); Edwin Curley, ed. and trans., *The Collected Works of Spinoza*

(Princeton, NJ, 1985); Edwin Curley, ed. and trans., *A Spinoza Reader: the Ethics and Other Works* (Princeton, NJ, 1994). **Suggested Readings:** Henry E. Allison, *Benedict de Spinoza: An Introduction* (New Haven, 1987); Don Garrett, *The Cambridge Companion to Spinoza* (Cambridge and New York, 1996); Harry Austryn Wolfson, *The Philosophy of Spinoza: Unfolding the Latent Processes of His Reasoning* (New York, 1934; reprint 1969).

Tacitus, Cornelius (57–117 C.E.)

A Roman aristocrat who served as a senator, consul, and eventually provincial governor of the Roman province of Asia (the western part of modern Turkey) from 112–113 C.E. He was a Stoic and a strong supporter of traditional Roman patrician values. In his *Annals* and especially his *Histories*, he talks about Jews and Judaism at the time of the great uprising of 68–73 C.E., during which time Jerusalem and its Temple were destroyed. His account of the Jews and their history is a strange amalgam of fact, fable, and myth. He regarded Jewish practice as designed to separate Jews from others and to keep them aloof. In this, his attitudes were similar to other Roman patricians like Cicero and Seneca. **Works:** Alfred John Church and William Jackson Brodribb, trans., *The Complete Works of Tacitus: The Annals. The History. The Life of Cnaeus Julius Agricola. Germany and Its Tribes. A Dialogue on Oratory* (New York, 1942); Alfred John Church and William Jackson Brodribb, trans., *The Annals and the Histories* (Chicago, 1952, 1955). **Suggested Readings:** Clarence Mendell, *Tacitus: The Man and His Work* (New Haven, CT, 1957); Elizabeth Henry, *The Annals of Tacitus: A Study in the Writing of History* (Manchester, 1968; New York, 1981); Ronald H. Martin, *Tacitus* (Berkeley, CA, 1981).

Tarfon (first century C.E.)

One of the prominent members of the first generation of protorabbinic thinkers who reshaped Judaism after the destruction of the Jerusalem Temple in 70 C.E. Tarfon was of priestly background and was likely a pupil of Yohanan ben Zakkai and a colleague, and possibly teacher, of Akiba, with whom he often entered into debate. He is remembered in tradition as a great humanitarian, reportedly at one point marrying 300 women during a drought so that they would have shelter and food (if they were married to a priest they would have access to food designated for the priesthood). When forced to choose between study or observance and the doing of good deeds, he always chose concrete acts. He argued that it was important to do good deeds and work for the redemption of the world, even if one could never finish the work. **Suggested Reading:** Joel Gereboff, *Rabbi Tarfon: The Tradition, The Man, and Early Rabbinic Judaism* (Missoula, MT, 1979).

Yohanan ben Zakkai (first century C.E.)

Reportedly the youngest student of Hillel and the leading figure in the reorganization of Judaism after the destruction of the Temple in 70 C.E. According to legend he opposed the war against Rome and was able to have himself smuggled out of the besieged city of Jerusalem in order to appear before the Roman general Vespasian and beg for leniency. In the end, he was able to receive permission to build a schoolhouse for the training of scholars after the war. When the Temple fell and the priesthood was decimated, Yohanan ben Zakkai's academy in the town of Yavne became the center of intellectual life in Roman Palestine, and it was his students, and his students' students, who constituted the intellectual class known as *Tannaim*. These were the scholars who ultimately compiled the Mishnah and thus set the foundation for the development of rabbinic Judaism. He believed that the destruction of Jerusalem and its Temple was due to poor leadership of the people and dedicated himself to creating a new and better leadership elite, one based on learning, piety, and good deeds. **Suggested Readings:** Jacob Neusner, *A Life of Rabban Yohanan ben Zakkai* (Leiden, 1962); Jacob Neusner, *Development of a Legend: Studies on the Traditions Concerning Yohanan ben Zakkai* (Leiden, 1970); Jacob Neusner, *First-Century Judaism in Crisis: Yohanan ben Zakkai and the Renaissance of Torah* (Nashville, TN, 1975).

Yom Tov ben Abraham Ishbili (Ritba) (1250–1330)

A Spanish Talmudist who, while a community leader and judge in Saragossa, was regarded as the spiritual leader of much of Spain at the time. He defended Moses Maimonides from critics who claimed that Maimonides placed logic and human reasoning over revelation as a source for learning Truth. He is best known for his Talmudic commentaries, which have been republished many times over the last few centuries. **Works:** Joseph Kafah, ed., *She'elot u-teshuvot* (Jerusalem, 1959); Benjamin Z.

Kahana, ed., *Sefer Ha-zikaron* (Jerusalem, 1982); *Hidushe ha-Ritba le-Rabenu Yom Tov ben Avraham Ashbili* (Jerusalem, 1993).

Zola, Emile (1840–1902)

French intellectual, essayist, and novelist who spoke out against French anti-Semitism during the Dreyfus Affair. Zola was a fine example of Enlightenment and scientific thinking in late-nineteenth-century France, arguing that scientific observations of nature could explain human behavior. He is most known in Jewish history for his spirited defense of Captain Alfred Dreyfus, who was falsely accused in 1894 of spying for the Germans. Although Dreyfus was convicted, it soon became clear that the trial had been rigged and that the government, and the French army in particular, was aware of Dreyfus's innocence and had been involved in a massive cover-up. In response, Zola wrote an open letter (*"J'accuse"*, I accuse) to the president of France in which he laid out the basis of his accusation that Dreyfus had been falsely indicted and wrongly convicted with the government's full knowledge and complicity, simply because he was a Jew. Zola's letter raised the case to the level of public scandal. After a series of new trials and scandals, the government fell and Dreyfus himself was eventually found innocent and pardoned. **Works:** Mark Jensen, *Emile Zola's J'accuse! A New Translation with a Critical Introduction* (Soquel, CA, 1992); Alain Pages, ed., *The Dreyfus Affair: J'accuse and Other Writings by Emile Zola* (New Haven, CT, 1996). **Suggested Readings:** Norman Finkelstein, *Captain of Innocence: France and the Dreyfus Affair* (New York, 1991); Michael Burns, *France and the Dreyfus Affair: A Documentary History* (Boston, 1999); Leslie Derfler, *The Dreyfus Affair* (Westport, CT, 2002).

NOTES

Chapter 1. The Biblical Legacy: Biblical Israel Confronts the Other

1. There is considerable debate in the field of biblical studies today whether or not the Hebrew Bible has any materials, or important information, about the preexilic period. The so-called minimalists claim that the Hebrew Bible is a product of postexilic Judea and so can tell us nothing of Israel before the sixth century. Most scholars, conceding the point as to the lateness of the Bible's late redaction, nonetheless hold that the earlier history is essentially reliable in its broad framework if not in all its detail.

2. See, for example, Alice Bach's discussion of this in her *Women, Seduction, and Betrayal in Biblical Narrative* (Cambridge: Cambridge University Press, 1997), 8.

3. Gen. 18:25. This and all other translations (unless otherwise noted) are from the *Tanach: The New JPS Translation According to the Traditional Hebrew Text* (Philadelphia, PA: Jewish Publication Society of America, 1988).

4. Interestingly, the details of the levirate relation as related in the story of Ruth do not match up closely with the details of the law of levirate marriage as spelled out in the Book of Leviticus. This is a good example of why the Biblical materials, whether law or story, have to be read with a certain scepticism as to whether the text is descriptive, telling us how things were, or proscriptive, telling us how things ought to be.

5. Phyllis Bird, "The Place of Women in the Israelite Cultus," in Alice Bach, ed., *Women in the Hebrew Bible* (New York: Routledge, 1999), 3.

6. Ibid., 9 f.

7. See for example the work of Carol Meyers, "Women and the Domestic Economy of Early Israel," in Bach, *Women in the Hebrew Bible*, 33–43.

8. See Carol Meyers, *Discovering Eve: Ancient Israelite Women in Context* (New York: Oxford University Press, 1988).

9. These same arguments have been made in connection with the levirate marriage mentioned above as well. A series of essays on the law of the *sotah* and its various interpretations, defenses, and readings can be found in Bach, *Women in the Hebrew Bible*, 461 ff.

10. David Novak, "Is There a Concept of Individual Rights in Jewish Law?" in *Jewish Law Association Studies* 7 (1994): 56.

11. Novak, op. cit., 129–152; esp. 137.

Chapter 3. "Judaism" and Human Rights in the Greco-Roman World

1. The name itself comes from the biblical Kingdom of Judah, which had its capital in the city of Jerusalem. The Persian province of Yahud included only Jerusalem and its immediately surrounding area. Over the course of the next several centuries, the boundaries of what constituted Judea shifted regularly so that the term has more of a general geographical meaning than a precise political one.

2. An excellent discussion of these issues and the multiplicity of ways different groups tried to work out the social, religious, ethnic, and cultural boundaries involved is found in Shaye J. D. Cohen, *The Beginnings of Jewishness: Boundaries, Varieties, Uncertainties* (Berkeley and Los Angeles: University of California Press, 1999).

3. For example, Ciceros' comment is found in *De Officiis* 1:7 and Aristotle's is found in *Politics* 1:5. See Lenn E. Goodman, *Judaism, Human Rights and Human Values* (New York: Oxford University Press, 1998), 52.

4. Cf. Erwin Goodenough, *Jewish Symbols in the Greco-Roman World*, Vols. 1–13 (New York: Pantheon Books, 1953–1968).

5. From Menachem Stern, ed., *Greek and Latin Authors on Jews and Judaism* (Jerusalem: Israel Academy of Science and Humanities, 1976), 382–386.

6. Ibid., 513.

7. Ibid., 358.

8. Ibid., 431.

9. Tacitus, *Hist.* 5:11–13; quoted in Leon Poliakov, *History of Anti-Semitism* (New York: Vanguard Press, 1985), 1:9–10.

10. Josephus, *Against Apion*, Book II, Chapter 1:11. http://www.studylight.org/his/bc/wfj/. Retrived September 15, 2004.

11. Ibid., 1:11.

12. Ibid., 1:29–30.

Chapter 4. Human Rights in the Talmud

1. The entire passage reads, "11. Surely, this Instruction which I enjoin upon you this day is not too baffling for you, nor is it beyond reach. 12. It is not in the heavens, that you should say, 'Who among us can go up to the heavens and get it for us and impart it to us, that we may observe it.'"

2. This entire passage and a discussion of its meaning for Jewish law can be found in, among other places, Menachem Elon Bernard Anerbach, Daniel D. Chazin, and Melvin J.

Sykes, eds., *Jewish Law (Mishpat Ivri): Cases and Materials* (New York and San Francisco: Matthew Bender, 1999), 17–22.

3. See the discussion of Jacob Neusner in *There We Sat Down: Talmudic Judaism in the Making* (New York: KTAV, 1972 and 1978). A more detailed discussion can also be found in Neusner, *School, Court, Public Administration: Judaism and Its Institutions in Talmudic Bablyonia* (Atlanta, GA: Scholars Press, 1987).

4. Much nineteenth- and early twentieth-century scholarship on Jewish ethics did try nonetheless to fit Jewish thought into these Western Christian theological categories. A number of scholars who deal with Jewish ethics have addressed themselves to the problem of translating from one rhetoric to another. A good discussion of the pitfalls of this approach is found in Jack Lightstone, "Problems and New Perspectives in the Study of Early Rabbinic Ethics," in *Journal of Religious Ethics* 9:2 (fall 1981): 199–209. See also Louis Newman, "Woodchoppers and Respirators: The Problem of Interpretation in Contemporary Jewish Ethics," in *Modern Judaism* 10:1 (February, 1990): 17–42; and Marvin Fox, "The Philosophical Foundations of Jewish Ethics: Some Reflections," presented at the Second Annual Rabbi Louis Feinberg Memorial Lecture in Judaic Studies at the University of Cincinnati, March 27, 1979. David Novak discusses this in terms of the ontological priority in Judaism of the concrete over the abstract. See Novak, *Covenantal Rights: A Study in Jewish Political Theory* (Princeton, NJ: Princeton University Press, 2000), 77 ff.

5. Cf. Novak, op. cit., 65–66.

6. Cf. Novak, op. cit., 190–191.

7. Novak, op. cit., 84.

8. This is also regarded as one of the greatest commandments in the Gospels. Cf. The Gospel According to Mark 12:30.

9. Haim H. Cohen, *Human Rights in the Bible and Talmud* (Tel Aviv: MOD Books, 1989), 27–28.

10. There are, in fact, several such trump cards built into the halachah. These include *darchei shalom* (for the sake of peace), *she'at hedechak* (in times of emergency), and *tikkun olam* (for the repair of the world). See Justice Menachem Elon's opening discussion in Etta Bick, ed., *Judaic Sources of Jewish Rights* (Ramat Aviv: Proceedings of the Israel-Diaspora Institute, Nov. 23–25, 1987), 11, but also his qualifications on pages 28–29. Several of the other participants address themselves to these principles as well in the Proceedings.

11. Emphasis added. A discussion of this concept appears in Louis Newman, "Ethics as Law, Law as Religion: Reflections on the Problem of Law and Ethics in Judaism," in *Shofar* 9:1 (fall 1990): 13–31.

12. See Haim Cohen's discussion in *Human Rights in the Bible*, 11.

13. Haim H. Cohen, *Human Rights in Jewish Law* (New York: KTAV, 1984), 211.

14. Cohen, *Human Rights in Jewish Law*, 213.

15. The language in Hebrew is *"rov tzibur yakholim la'amod bo"*; Cf. Avodah Zara 36a.

16. See, for example, the Babylonian Talmud Kiddushin 39b and Hullin 142a.

17. See Cohen, *Human Rights in Jewish Law*, 126.

18. See Cohen, *Human Rights in Jewish Law*, 31.

19. Cohen, *Human Rights in Jewish Law*, 32. Cf. the Jerusalem Talmud Yoma 8:7 and Shevuot 1:7.

20. This expression is repeated throughout the Talmud in these kinds of situations. See Yoma 82b, Pesahim 25b, and Sanhedrin 74a, for example.

21. See, for example, Berachot 58a and 62b , Sanhedrin72b, et al.

22. The exact meaning of the verse is unclear, but the interpretation given here is the generally recognized rabbinic one.

23. The twelfth- through fourteenth-century commentary to the Talmud, Tosofot, for example, says explicitly at Pesahim 25b that you are not to give water to the other because who, after all, can say that his blood is redder than yours?

24. From Novak, op. cit., 182.

25. See the discussion in Menachem Elon et al., op. cit., 444–445.

26. Cohen, *Human Rights in Jewish Law*, 64.

27. Cohen, *Human Rights in Jewish Law*, 70.

28. See the discussion on this passage in Lenn E. Goodman, *Judaism, Human Rights and Human Values* (New York: Oxford University Press, 1998), pp. 58–59.

29. Although the slavery laws of the Bible are known to, and discussed by, the Talmudic rabbis, it appears that the institution of slavery had itself fallen out of use. The rabbinic discussions of biblical slavery are aimed at explaining the biblical text, not at establishing actual law.

30. Cohen, *Human Rights in Jewish Law*, 99-100.

31. Cohen, *Human Rights in Jewish Law*, 103 f.

32. Cohen, *Human Rights in Jewish Law*, 49.

33. Cohen, *Human Rights in Jewish Law*, 50.

34. Cohen, *Human Rights in Jewish Law*, 51 f.

35. Cohen, *Human Rights in Jewish Law*, 52.

36. Judith Romney Wegner, *Chattel or Person: The Status of Women in the Mishnah* (New York: Oxford University Press, 1988), 40 ff. See also Cohen, op. cit., 170 f.

37. For further discussion on the *mamzer*, see Cohen, *Human Rights in Jewish Law*, 178.

38. Cohen, *Human Rights in Jewish Law*, 169.

39. Such property was to be returned to the woman at the same value at which it was brought into the marriage. If the property increased in value, the husband kept the increase. If the property went down in value, however, the husband had to bear the loss. Thus, for *tzon bazel* property, the benefit and risk were the husband's. This is opposed to *melog* property, in which the property was returned to the woman "as is" at the time of divorce, meaning she enjoyed the benefit of increased value but also bore the risk of any decrease in value.

40. Cohen, *Human Rights in Jewish Law*, 169.

41. The classic work in this connection is Bernadette Brooten, *Women Leaders in the Ancient Synagogue* (Chico, CA: Scholars Press, 1982).

42. In fact Saul was reprimanded by Samuel for not wiping out all of the Amalekites, but keeping some of their sheep and sparing the life of their "king," Agag (1 Sam. 15:7 ff). According to some later traditions, this command was finally fulfilled by King Hezekiah (based on a reference in 1 Chron. 4:41–43). An alternate tradition is found in the Book of Esther, which describes the wicked vizier Haman as an "Agagite," but he and his ten

sons are dispatched by the victorious Jews, hence finally fulfilling the command of destroying the remnants of the Amalekites.

43. On this see Goodman, op. cit., 41, who cites several Talmudic passages to this effect.

Chapter 5. Human Rights in the Medieval Halachah

1. See Peter J. Haas, *Responsa: Literary History of a Rabbinic Genre* (Atlanta, GA: Scholars Press, Semeia Series, 1996), 101 f.

2. *Encyclopedia Judaica* 7, s.v. "Gaon."

3. There are many studies of this sort. Among the better known are: S. D. Goitein, *A Mediterranean Society; the Jewish Communities of the Arab World as Portrayed in the Documents of the Cairo Geniza* (Berkeley: University of California Press, 1967); David Ellenson, *Tradition in Transition. Orthodoxy, Halakhah, and the Boundaries of Modern Jewish Identity* (Lanham, MD: University Press of America, 1989); and Irving A. Agus, *Rabbi Meir of Rothenburg, His life and His Works as Sources for the Religious, Legal, and Social History of the Jews of Germany in the Thirteenth Century* (Philadelphia, PA: Dropsie College for Hebrew and Cognate Learning, 1947).

4. From *Mishneh Torah*, Yessodei HaTorah 9:1, cited in Haim Cohen, *Human Rights in Jewish Law* (New York: KTAV, 1984), 2.

5. Cohen, op. cit., 5.

6. Isidore Epstein, *The Responsa of Rabbi Simon b. Zemah Duran as a Source of the History of the Jews in North Africa* (London: Oxford University Press; repr. New York: KTAV, 1930), 60.

7. Jacob R. Marcus, *The Jew in the Medieval World: A Source Book, 315–1791* (New York: Atheneum, 1972), 186.

8. Ibid., 41 f.

9. For the details of the charter, see Marcus, op. cit., 28–33.

10. See Maimonides, *Guide for the Perplexed*, I:72, cited in Cohen, op. cit., 43.

11. It should be noted that the *Shulkhan Arukh* generally follows the halachic rulings of Jewish authorities residing in the Islamic world and that a series of emendations was added by Moses Isserles in the late 1560s, which brought the code into conformity with Ashkenazic, or European, norms and customs.

12. Cited in Solomon Freehof, *A Treasury of Responsa* (Philadelphia, PA: Jewish Publication Society of America, 1963), 43.

13. Eliezer of Minz cited in Freehof, op. cit., 93–96.

14. The Geonim were the heads of the Talmudic academies in the centuries following the completion of the Talmudic text. As such they were the de jure rulers of Babylonian Jewry in its declining years from about the seventh to the twelfth century.

15. From Jacob Bazak, *Jewish Law and Jewish Life*, trans. Stephen Passamaneck (New York: Union of American Hebrew Congregations, 1979), 3–5.

16. See Mark Warshofsky, "Taking Precedent Seriously: On Halakhah as a Rhetoric Practice," in *Re-Examining Progressive Halakhah*, eds. Walter Jacob and Moshe Zemer (New York: Berghahn, 2002), 1–70.

17. Bazak, op. cit., 27.

18. Avraham Yaakov Finkel, ed., *The Responsa Anthology* (Northvale, NJ: Jason Aronson, 1990), 18.

19. Finkel, op. cit., 44.

20. See also Cohen, op. cit., 30.

21. For a longer discussion of Maimonides' view, see Cohen, op. cit., 32 f.

22. Cohen, op. cit., 51.

23. Cohen, op. cit., 65.

24. Cohen, op. cit., 51f.

25. Finkel, op. cit., 24.

26. Bazak, op. cit., 217.

27. Bazak, op. cit., 219.

28. Cohen, op. cit., 120.

29. Cohen, op. cit., 70.

30. Menachem Elon et al., op. cit., 156.

31. Cited from Elon, op. cit., 459.

32. Cited in Elon, op. cit., 339.

33. Finkel, op. cit., 156.

34. Moses Sofer, *Hatam Sofer*; Orah Hayyim no. 206 (Pressburg, 1855–1864).

35. Cohen, op. cit., 104.

36. *Shulkhan Arukh* YD 357:1.

37. From Finkel, op. cit., 36.

38. From Finkel, op. cit., 67.

39. Bazak, op. cit., 234–239.

40. From Finkel, op. cit., 159.

41. See the discussion in BT Ketubot 61b, for example, which lays out the husband's sexual duties based on his occupation. See also David Feldman, *Marital Relations, Birth Control and Abortion in Jewish Law* (New York: Schocken, 1975), 60 ff.

42. From Finkel, op. cit., 111.

Chapter 6. Jews as Europeans and the Adoption of the Enlightenment

1. From Paul Mendes-Flohr and Jehuda Reinharz, eds., *The Jew in the Modern World* 2d ed. (Oxford: Oxford University Press, 1995), 31 f.

2. From Mendes-Flohr, op. cit., 115.

3. A more complete list of questions can be found in Mendes-Flohr, op. cit., 125–126.

4. Heinrich Heine in a letter to Moses Moser. Cf. Max Biod, *Heinrich Heine: The Artist in Rovolt* (New York: New York University Press, 1957), p. 232.

5. The statement does not appear with this meaning in the Talmud; it is probably taken from Talmud Nedarim 60b or Baba Batra 8a which refer to new grain being forbidden during Passover.

6. Moses Hess, *Rome & Jerusalem: A study in Jewish Nationalism*, trans. Meyer Waxman (New York: Block Publishing, 1918, 1949), p.55.

7. François-Marié Arouet (Voltaire) cited in Mendes-Flohr, op. cit., 304–305.

8. It may well be the case that Spinoza was also heavily influenced by earlier Jewish thinkers in the community, such as Uriel da Costa, who had been twice expelled from the community for teaching that all religions were man-made and that the doctrine of the immortality of the soul was false.

9. Spinoza cited in Mendes-Flohr, op. cit., 59. Emphases in the original.

10. In 1753, the British Parliament actually granted Jews the right to be naturalized as citizens, although the law was forced to be revoked a short while later. Emperor Joseph II of Austria issued his "Tolerenz Patent" in 1781, which allowed a measure of Jewish integration without providing for full emancipation. Outside Britain, full emancipation was achieved only in the wakes of the American and French revolutions at the end of the century.

11. Mendelssohn, *Jerusalem, or On Religious Power and Judaism*, cited in Alan Levenson, *Modern Jewish Thinkers: An Introduction* (Northvale, NJ: Jason Aaronson, 2000), 47–48.

12. Moses Mendelssohn, *Jerusalem*, cited in Margaret Jacob, *The Enlightenment: A Brief History with Documents* (Boston and New York: Bedford/St. Martin's Press, 2001), 219.

13. Mendelssohn, *Jerusalem*, cited in Levenson, op. cit., 43.

14. On this point see David Novak's discussion in *Covenantal Rights* (Princeton, NJ: Princeton University Press, 2002), 27 f. Novak claims that there actually is a Hebrew word that catches the sense of the Enlightenment concept of rights, namely tsa'aqah, which translates as crying out or claiming.

15. *Shulamith* (1808) cited in Mendes-Flohr, op. cit., 86–87.

16. Ginzberg's lecture appears in Judah Goldin, ed., *The Jewish Expression* (New Haven: Yale University Press, 1976), 163 ff.

17. The Hebrew title of Hirsch's work was actually *Iggerot Tzafon* (Letters from the North).

18. From Hirsch's sixteenth letter, "Emancipation," in S. K. Hirsch, *The Nineteen Letters on Judaism* (1836), cited in Levenson, op. cit., 61.

19. Israel-Diaspora Institute, Report no. 1 (April 1989), 22.

20. Ibid., 23.

21. Cf. Ibid., 27.

22. Cf. Ibid., 29.

23. Mendes-Flohr, op. cit., 452.

24. Ibid., 453.

Chapter 7. Jews as a Separate People and Rights Based on Nationality

1. Social Darwinism was based on a reading of Darwin that assumed that different groups of people—"nations"—were in effect the same as species in the natural world. Such species, and by extension, such nations, were naturally engaged in a constant life-and-death struggle for resources. The fittest would win out and survive while the weak would be marginalized or even die out. This reading of Darwin into the social world of humans had two implications. One was that all nations were engaged in this kind of "survival of the fittest" struggle against all other competing nations. Two was that as a consequence, each nation had to insure its own internal genetic strength and purity. This

second view in particular led to a whole series of eugenic and other social movements to improve national gene pools. About this, see, for example, George L. Mosse, *Toward the Final Solution: A History of Racism* (New York: Howard Fertig, 1978) and Hannah Arendt, *Origins of Totalitarianism* (New York: Harcourt Brace and Co., 1951).

2. One of the most influential thinkers along these lines was Count A. de Gobineau. See, for example, *The Moral and Intellectual Diversity of the Races* (Philadelphia, PA: Weybright and Talley, 1856).

3. Cited in Deborah Dwork and Robert Jan van Pelt, *Holocaust: A History* (New York: W. W. Norton, 2002), 103 ff. In this chapter of the book Dwork and van Pelt give a brief history of the introduction of travel restrictions and passports at the turn of the twentieth century.

4. Ibid., 103.

5. From "On the Danger to the Well-being and Character of the Germans Presented by the Jews" (1816). Cited in Paul Mendes-Flohr and Jehuda Reinharz, eds., *The Jews in the Modern World*, 2d ed. (Oxford: Oxford University Press, 1995) 310–311.

6. Mendes-Flohr, op. cit., 311, n. 2.

7. See Mendes-Flohr, op. cit., 321 f.

8. From Wilhelm Marr, Antisemiten-Liga, "League of Antisemites," founded in 1879 to create a popular movement to undo Jewish emancipation. See Mendes-Flohr, op.cit., 331–332.

9. Cited in Arthur Hertzberg, ed., *The Zionist Idea* (New York: Atheneum, 1972), 530.

10. Ibid., 105.

11. Ibid., 111.

12. Mendes-Flohr, op. cit., 532.

13. Mendes-Flohr, op. cit., 537.

14. Herzl himself was never fully committed to placing the homeland in Zion. He had, in fact, accepted the British offer of Uganda, but the offer was rejected by the Sixth Zionist Congress in 1903, and the Seventh Zionist Congress of 1905 reaffirmed its commitment to Palestine. This was largely the effect of the more traditionally minded Eastern European Zionists, who felt that the Land of Israel was the only natural place for the Zionist state since it was the ancestral homeland of the Jews.

15. Mendes-Flohr, op. cit., 551.

16. From L. Lavita and D. Ben-Nahur, eds, *Kitvei Borochov* (Tel Aviv: Sifriat Ha Poalim, 1955) I: 383–387. Cited in Mendes-Flohr, op. cit., 554.

17. This statement concludes a long discussion that makes up chapter 5 of Book 3 of *Altneuland*.

18. Epstein cited in Mendes-Flohr, op. cit., 558–562.

19. Brondeis cited in Mendes-Flohr, op. cit., 496.

20. Jabotinsky cited in Mendes-Flohr, op. cit., 594–597.

21. Ben Gurion cited in Mendes-Flohr, op. cit., 605.

22. Hashomer Hazair Worker's Party Memorandum cited in Mendes-Flohr, op. cit., 622–625.

23. Ben Gurion cited in Mendes-Flohr, op. cit., 629–630.

Chapter 8. Human Rights in Practice: The Liberal Jewish Tradition in North America

1. Lee Levinger, A History of the Jews in the United States (New York: Union of American Hebrew Congregations, 1961), 120–121.

2. See for example Stephen Birmingham's wonderful book, The Grandees: America's Sephardic Elite (New York: Harper and Row, 1971).

3. A good general description of the Jewish community in the United States on the eve of the Civil War can be found in Bertram Korn, American Jewry in the Civil War (Philadelphia, PA: Jewish Publication Society of America, 1957), 14.

4. Annual Report of the American and Foreign Anti-Slavery Society, 114–115. Cited in Korn, op. cit., 15.

5. Cited in Korn, op. cit., 17; emphasis in the original.

6. Ibid., 19.

7. Cf. Korn, op. cit., 15. A controversial book published in 1991 by the Historical Research Department of Nation of Islam, The Secret Relationship Between Blacks and Jews, Volume 1, argued that Jews played a significant role, maybe even a leading role in the slave trade. The book is regarded among scholars, both African American and white, to have overstated its case, especially in light of the relatively small number of Jews in the Americas at the time and the exceedingly small number of Jewish farmers, and the even smaller number of plantation owners.

8. Encyclopedia Judaica (New York: Macmillian, 1971–1972), vol. 15 s.v. "United States of America."

9. See, for example, Stephen Whitfield, Voices of Jacob, Hands of Esau: Jews in American Life and Thought (Hamden, CT: Archon Books, 1984), 77 f.

10. Cited in Abba Eban, Heritage: Civilization and the Jews (New York: Summit, 1984), 276.

11. Upton Sinclair's The Jungle, about the meat packing industry in Chicago, is one well-known example of the abuse of workers in the United States at the turn of the twentieth century.

12. Riis cited in Eban, op. cit., 277.

13. From "Women Wage Workers," in Paul Mendes-Flohr and Jehuda Reinhavz, The Jew in The Modern World: A Documentary History, 2nd ed. (New York: Oxford University Press, 1995), 479.

14. Mendes-Flohr, op. cit., 469.

15. Mendes-Flohr, op. cit., 484.

16. Mendes-Flohr, op. cit., 485.

17. See Larry George, "The Domestic Role of Jewish Women in the Modern Social Context: The Kosher Meat Boycott of 1902," in Recovering the Role of Women, ed. Peter J. Haas (Atlanta, GA: Scholars Press, 1992), 113–130.

18. Eban, op. cit., 277.

19. Brandeis cited in Mendes-Flohr, op. cit., 496.

20. See Whitfield, op. cit., 83 f.

21. See Whitfield, op. cit., 85.

22. See Whitfield, op. cit., 86–87.

23. See Whitfield, op. cit., 87.

24. Milton Konvitz, ed., *Judaism and Human Rights* (2nd expanded edition, New Brunswick, NJ: Transaction Publishers, 2001).

25. Ibid., 139.

26. Ibid., 8.

27. A significant number of young American Jews did take this route and adopted an Eastern European version of Jewish Orthodoxy. This led to the *Baale Teshuvah*, or returnees movement.

28. David Novak, *Covenantal Rights* (Princeton, NJ: Princeton University Press, 2000), 31.

29. Ibid., ix.

30. Ibid., 32–35.

31. Ibid., 40f.; see also "God's Commands as Human Rights," 65ff.

32. Ibid., 218.

33. Ibid., 152.

34. See Elliot Dorff and Louis Newman, eds., *Contemporary Jewish Ethics and Morality* (Oxford: Oxford University Press, 1995), 14. It should be pointed out that not everyone agrees with Kellner's point of view. Even in this collection there are opposing views. See, for example, Elliot Dorff's essay, "The Covenant: The Transcendent Thrust in Jewish Law."

35. In Dorff and Newman, op. cit., 99.

36. Ibid., 101.

37. Dorff and Newman, Ibid., 106–117.

38. Lenn E. Goodman, Judaism, *Human Rights, and Human Values* (New York: Oxford University Press, 1998), xiii–xiv.

39. Ibid., 98.

40. Ibid., 135–136.

41. Rackman cited in Konvitz, op. cit., 54.

Chapter 9. Human Rights in Practice in Israel

1. A good discussion of at least some of these issues is found in Menachem Elon, "The Values of a Jewish and Democratic State: The Task of Reaching a Synthesis," in *Judaism and Human Rights*, ed. Milton Konvitz (2nd expanded ed., New Brunswick, NJ: Transaction Publishers, 2001), 353–418.

2. See Haim H. Cohen, "Religious Freedom and Religious Coercion in the State of Israel," in Konvitz, Ibid., 291.

3. Menachem Elon, Bernard Auerbach, Daniel D. Chazin, and Melvin J. Sykes, eds., *Jewish Law (Mishpat Ivri): Cases and Materials* (New York and San Francisco: Matthew Bender, 1999), 441–443.

4. Translation of the Basic Law: Human Dignity and Liberty are found in Konvitz, op. cit., 5–6.

5. See Menachem Elon et al., *Jewish Law*, 473.

6. See Menachem Elon et al., *Jewish Law*, 449–453.

7. On the general trend in this direction in Supreme Court decisions, see Elon, *Jewish Law*, 491–492.

8. The numbers come from the Israeli peace group Peace Now. Today, these settlements contain approximately 10 percent of the entire population of the West Bank.

9. See for example, the various reports of B'tselem, the Israeli human rights organization, at http://www.btselem.org.

10. See RHR's Web site at http://www.rhr.israel.net/overview.shtml.

11. This information is from the *Guardian's* Web site at http://www.guardian.co.uk/israel/comment/0,10551,801564,00.html.

ANNOTATED BIBLIOGRAPHY |

General Background and References

Amsel, Nachum. *The Jewish Encyclopedia of Moral and Ethical Issues.* Northvale, NJ: Jason Aronson, 1994. A collection of essays in which Amsel describes what the Jewish tradition has to say on a number of topics, including charity, family, friendship, and honesty.

Bick, Etta. *Judaic Sources of Human Rights.* Ramat Aviv, Israel: Israel-Diaspora Institute, 1989. The edited proceedings of a colloquium held in Jerusalem in November 1987 under the auspices of the Israel-Diaspora Institute. This volume provides a general discussion of the issues involved in establishing a policy of human rights based on traditional Judaic sources.

Breslauer, Daniel S. *Judaism and Human Rights in Contemporary Thought: A Bibliographic Survey.* Westport, CT: Greenwood Press, 1993. A remarkably complete survey of the literature on Judaism and human rights up to 1993. Including books and chapters and articles, this survey guides the reader through several major themes that comprise this subject. The survey is divided into five parts: General Works and Anthologies; Human Rights in the Bible and Talmud; Jewish Theories of Human Rights; Judaism and Specific Human Rights; and Human Rights and Contemporary Judaism. The survey is introduced by an essay (pp. 3–21) that places these topics in their historical and intellectual contexts.

Cohen, Haim. *Human Rights in Jewish Law*. New York: KTAV, 1984. A former justice of the Israeli supreme court who has written extensively on Israeli law and its background in Jewish religious law (halachah). This volume indudes a number of his essays that deal with topics such as liberty, justice, the right to life, and the like. While providing a good deal of historical material, the collection also addresses modern applications, especially in Israel.

Fishbane, Michael. "The Image of the Human and the Rights of the Individual in Jewish Tradition." In *Human Rights and World's Religions*, edited by Leroy Rouner. South Bend, IN: University of Notre Dame Press, 1988. An essay looking at the Jewish concept of what it means to be human and investigates how this concept impacts Jewish legal decisions, especially for non-Jews and in nonritual contexts.

Konvitz, Milton, ed. *Judaism and Human Rights*. 2nd expanded ed. New Brunswick, NJ: Transaction Publishers, 2001. A contemporary American book that deals with the general topic of human rights in Judaism. The essays in this volume are from contemporary scholars as well as classical writers such as Lord Acton and Henri Frankfort and cover such topics as the rule of law, democracy, and freedom of conscience. The second edition has added a section that includes three essays on "Human Rights in an Israeli Context."

Wyschogrod, Michael. "Religion and International Human Rights: A Jewish Perspective." In *Formation of Social Policy in the Catholic and Jewish Traditions*, edited by Eugene Fisher and Daniel Polish, 123–141. Notre Dame, IN: Notre Dame University Press, 1980. This chapter offers a cursory look at the major issues in human rights as covered in Judaism. This volume is a good place to turn for a brief overview of the field in the years before Breslauer's bibliography.

Biblical Tradition

Brichto, Chanan. "The Bible on Human Rights." In *Essays on Human Rights: Contemporary Issues and Jewish Perspectives*, edited by David Sidkorsky. Philadelphia: Jewish Publication Society of America, 1979. In this chapter, Brichto takes issue with those who claim that human rights in the modern Western sense do not exist in the biblical literature.

Daube, David. *Studies in Biblical Law*. New York: KTAV, 1969. An examination of laws found in the Bible and how they reflect, or helped construct, religious values. In addition to a general methodological introduction on how one might study the values behind biblical laws, there are chapters investigating particular issues, such as individual versus communal responsibilities.

Harrelson, Walter. *The Ten Commandments and Human Rights*. Philadelphia: Fortress Press, 1980. This work is an attempt by a liberal Protestant biblical theologian to ground contemporary liberal politics in the biblical text.

Nahmani, Hayim Simha. *Human Rights in the Old Testament*. Tel Aviv: Chachik, 1964. Nahmani argues that the concept of individual human rights can already be found in the biblical literature, but that these rights are intimately linked to other rights such as those of the land and of animals, for example. He believes that ultimately all these rights rest on the biblical concept of God.

Weinfeld, Moshe. *Social Justice in Ancient Israel and in the Ancient Near East*. Jerusalem: Magnes; Minneapolis: Fortress Press, 1995. Both rulers and commoners have an obligation given by the God of Israel to relieve their subjects and neighbors from the burdens of oppression and anguish.

Halachic (Jewish Legal) Sources

The Mishnah

Blackman, Philip. *Mishnayoth. Pointed Hebrew Text, Introductions, Translation Notes, Supplements*. London: Mishna Press, 1951–1956. A good text and decent translation of the Mishnah, the first legal document of rabbinic Judaism appearing in the early third century C.E. Because of its short comments on each passage and extensive notes, Blackman's edition is especially good for those who are not familiar with the Mishnah.

Danby, Herbert. *The Mishnah*. London: Oxford University Press, 1933. The standard English translation of the Mishnah. The translation is in British English and has no explanatory interpolations or notes. While basically accurate, it is dated and not very helpful for those unfamiliar with the Mishnah.

Neusner, Jacob. *The Mishnah: A New Translation*. New Haven, CT: Yale University Press, 1988. A modern American translation with no notes but considerable interpolated language to help the reader understand the text. This translation, in turn, is based on an earlier translation with extensive line-by-line commentaries put together by Neusner and some of his students. The earlier translations and commentaries were published by E. J. Brill in Leiden between 1974 and 1981 under the titles *History of the Mishnaic Law of Purities* (1974–1977), *History of the Mishnaic Law of Holy Things* (1978–1979), *History of the Mishnaic Law of Women* (1979–1980), *History of the Mishnaic Law of Appointed Times* (1981), and *History of the Mishnaic Law of Damages* (1982). The translation of the order "Seeds" is drawn from the dissertations of Neusner's students, and are published as separate volumes by Scholars Press. These include Zahavy, Tzvee. *The Mishnaic Law of Blessings and Prayers: Tractate Berakhot*. Atlanta, GA: Scholars Press, 1987; Avery-Peck, Alan J. *Mishnah's Division of Agriculture: A History and Theology of Seder Zeraim*. Chico, CA: Scholars Press, 1985; Jaffee, Martin S. *Mishnah's Theology of Tithing: A Study of Tractate Maaserot*. Chico, CA: Scholars Press, 1981; Haas, Peter J. *A History of the Mishnaic Law of Agriculture: Tractate Maaser Sheni*. Chico, CA: Scholars Press, 1980; Brooks, Roger. *Support for the Poor in the Mishnaic Law of Agriculture: Tractate Peah*. Chico, CA: Scholars Press, 1983; Newman, Louis E. *The Sanctity of the Seventh Year: A Study of Mishnah Tractate Shebiit*. Chico, CA: Scholars Press, 1983.

————. *The Tosefta*. New York: KTAV, 1977–1986; and Atlanta, GA: Scholars Press, 1999. The Tosefta is a six-volume set of another early rabbinic text much like the Mishnah but deemed to be less authoritative. As is the case for Neusner's Mishnah translation, this is in modern American English with interpolated language to make the text more understandable to the American reader who is not otherwise familiar with the Tosefta.

The Talmud

Epstein, Isidore, ed. *The Babylonian Talmud Translated into English with Notes, Glossary, and Indices*. 34 vols. London: Soncino Press, 1935–1952. This is the standard translation of the Talmud into English. The translation does not preserve the form of the original but rather formats the text into modern sentences and paragraphs. This edition includes extensive notes to help the reader understand the elliptical and technical nature of Talmudic discourse, but these notes are of uneven quality, depending on the translator and commentator of each particular volume.

Neusner, Jacob. *The Talmud of Babylonia: An American Translation.* Chico, CA: Scholars Press, c. 1984–1993. This volume, like Neusner's translation of Mishnah, tries to replicate as much as possible the formal structure of the Talmud by avoiding sentences and paragraphs and instead breaking the discussion into short lemmas and pericopes that mimic the original. Although there are no notes, Neusner adds considerable language in brackets to make the text comprehensible. The accuracy of the translation and the clarity of the notes varies considerably.

Steinsaltz, Adin. *The Talmud.* New York: Random House, c. 1989– . An English translation of a project originally begun in modern Hebrew in the late 1960s. This edition includes not only a running translation of the text, but adds extensive interpolated language, notes, sidebars, and other explanatory materials. While several volumes of this work have been translated into English, it is not clear that the entire Babylonian Talmud will be available in the English-language version. Overall, this is the best source for those not fully conversant with the Talmudic style of discourse.

Medieval Jewish Law

Agus, Irving. *Rabbi Meir of Rothenburg: His Life and His Works as Sources for the Religious, Legal and Social History of the Jews of Germany in the Thirteenth Century.* Philadelphia: Dropsie College for Hebrew and Cognate Learning, 1947; reprint New York: KTAV, 1970. A look at the legal decisions in a variety of areas by one of the great legal minds of early medieval Central European Judaism. Although Agus does not translate entire *responsa* from Rabbi Meir, he does give a good sense of how Meir thought and of the kinds of rulings he gave.

———. *Urban Civilization in Pre-Crusade Europe: A Study of Organized Town-Life in Northwestern Europe during the Tenth and Eleventh Centuries Based on the Responsa Literature.* 2 vols. Leiden: E. J. Brill, 1965. This study, as the title indicates, reconstructs daily life in pre-Crusade Europe using *responsa*, that is, rabbinic legal decisions. While covering a wide variety of areas, issues of communcal governance and human rights do come up.

Bazak, Jacob, ed. *Jewish Law and Jewish Life: Selected Rabbincial Responsa*. Translated by Stephen Passamaneck. New York: Union of American Hebrew Congregations, 1997. Topically arranged *responsa* on a number of issues that have relevance to human rights, including the judiciary, but also commercial relations, real property, and tenant/landlord relations, creditor/debtor relations, communal tax and regulation enforcement, and criminal matters.

Ben Maimon, Moses (Maimonides). *The Mishneh Torah*. The Yale Judaica series has published a multivolume translation of *The Code of Maimonides*. New Haven, CT: Yale University Press, 1949– . The first comprehensive code of classical Jewish law, appearing in 1178. Although not regarded as fully authoritative today, the code gives good insight into the state of Jewish law in North Africa and the Islamic world in the twelfth century. The section dealing with Jewish self-governance is entitled, "The Law of Kings." Although in content it is little more than biblical kingship as interpreted through Talmud, this section of the *Mishneh Torah* is important because it is the earliest and most systematic collection of Jewish law on politics and political theory.

Carmilly-Weinberger, Moshe. *Book and Sword: Freedom of Expression and Thought Among the Jewish People*. New York Shulsinger Bros., 1966. An expansive historical look at human rights issues, especially freedom of speech and expression in medieval and modern rabbinic sources.

———. *Censorship and Freedom of Expression in Jewish History*. New York: Sepher-Hermon, 1977. A historical survey from the Talmud through the modern period on censorship and freedom of speech. The book touches not only on attempts to censor religious texts like the Talmud, the Kabbalah, or the writings of the Shabbatains, but also types of literature such as pornography.

Cohen, Haim. *Human Rights in the Bible and Talmud*. Translated by Shmuel Himelstein. Jerusalem: Ministry of Security 1988. A Hebrew monograph that offers a general approach to the theme of human rights in early Jewish tradition with an eye to how these might be relevant to the formation of modern Israeli law.

Cohen, J. Simcha. *Timely Jewish Questions, Timeless Rabbinic Answers.* Northvale NJ: Jason Aronson, ca. 1991 and *How Does Jewish Law Work?* Northvale, NJ: Jason Aronson, ca. 1993. These two volumes examine a number of modern *responsa* in order to adduce how Jewish law works.

Epstein, Isidore. *The "Responsa" of Rabbi Solomon ben Adreth of Barcelona as a Source of the History of Spain.* New York: KTAV, 1925 and *The Responsa of Rabbi Simon B. Zemah Duran as a Source of the History of the Jews in North Africa.* New York: KTAV, 1930. Reprint (2 vols. in 1) New York: KTAV, 1968. The *responsa* of two great medieval Jewish legal scholars, Solomon ben Adreth (Spain, thirteenth century) and Simon Duran (North Africa, fourteenth–fifteenth centuries). While dealing with a range of issues, some aspects of human rights are also discussed by these rabbinic authorities.

Finkel, Avraham Yaakov. *The Responsa Anthology.* Northvale, NJ: Jason Aronson, 1990. A collection of contemporary Orthodox *responsa.* These cover a range of materials, including a few relating directly to human rights.

Freehof, Solomon. *The Responsa Literature.* Philadelphia, PA: Jewish Publication Society of America, 1955. A good general introduction to the literary genre of the *responsa.* These rabbinic rescripts, dating from the eighth century to the present, deal with all aspects of applied Jewish law. In this volume, Freehof gives a general characterization of the literature and how it operates.

———. *A Treasury of Responsa.* Philadelphia, PA: Jewish Publication Society of America, 1963. This is a collection of a few dozen diverse *responsa*, in English translation, designed to give the reader examples of the breadth and depth of the issues dealt with through rabbinic rescripts.

Ginzberg, Louis. *Geonica.* New York: Jewish Theological Seminary of America, 1909. A two volume set that contains a large number of early responsa from the Geonim, that is, the heads of the classical Talmudic academies in Babylonia that thrived in the latter part of the first millenium c.e. The *responsa* are generally quite short, sometimes only a sentence or two, but one can still get a sense of the Geonic view of Jewish law as it related to a variety of topics.

Goitein, S. D. A *Mediterranean Society; the Jewish Communities of the Arab World as Portrayed in the Documents of the Cairo Geniza*. Berkeley: University of California Press, 1967– . This study uses *responsa*, letters, and other documents to reconstruct Jewish communal life in the Middle East and North Africa in the late first millennium C.E. Much of the material collected and discussed here deals with social, political, and economic matters that touch on individual and communal rights.

Goldin, Hyman. *Code of Jewish Law*. New York: Hebrew Publishing Co., 1963. The only translation available of the most comprehensive and authoritative medieval code of Jewish law, the *Shulkhan Arukh* of 1565. Unfortunately, the translation is of a highly abridged version of the medieval code (*kitsur Shulkhan Arukh*), but it nonetheless gives some insight into normative Jewish practices of the late Middle Ages.

Goodman, Lenn E. "The Individual and the Community in the Normative Traditions of Judaism." In *Religious Diversity and Human Rights*, edited by Irene Bloom, J. Paul Martin, and Wayne L. Proudfoot. New York: Columbia University Press, 1996. This is part of a series of chapters by individual authors dealing with a variety of religious traditions. Goodman gives a succinct account of individual versus communal rights in traditional Jewish law and society.

Jung, Leo. *Between Man and Man*. New York: Jewish Education Press, 1976. A basic introduction and overview of human relations according to Jewish law from an Orthodox perspective. Published originally in 1967 under the title *Human Relations in Jewish Law*. Includes a useful bibliography.

Lew, Myer S. *The Humanity of Jewish Law*. New York: Soncino Press, 1985. An examination of the religious and moral values that have shaped classical Jewish law in an attempt to show that the halachah is ultimately concerned with the advancement of the human condition.

Sears, David, ed. *Compassion for Humanity in the Jewish Tradition*. Northvale, NJ: Jason Aronson, 1998. In this collection of quotations and citations, Sears tries to show that even though Judaism is a particularistic community it teaches compassion and concern for all peoples, and it therefore can serve as a model for others. Materials are drawn from the Bible and rabbinic literature.

Touger, Eliyahu. *Mishneh Torah: A New Translation with Commentaries, Notes, Tables, Charts and Index.* New York: Maznaim Pub. Corp., 1986– . This is a more recent and fully annotated translation of Maimonides' code of early medival Jewish law.

Theological Views

Borowitz, Eugene. "Social Justice, the Liberal Jewish Case." In *Exploring Jewish Ethics: Papers on Covenant Responsibility.* Detroit, MI: Wayne State University Press, 1990, pp. 295–307. A contemporary voice from the liberal Reform movement on the importance of social concern and activism. In this chapter, Borowitz argues for the continued need for universal values of human dignity and human rights, and that any future Jewish ethic must take this need into account.

Falk, Zeev. *Law and Religion: The Jewish Experience.* Jerusalem: Mesharim, 1981. This is the published version of a series of lectures given at New York University in 1979–1980. Falk's chapter on human rights offers a view of the theological foundation of a Jewish concept of human rights. He argues that although Judaism is basically theocratic in tendency and often casual about granting rights to non-Jews, nonetheless, notions of democratic ideals and values are embedded in the tradition.

Heschel, Abraham Joshua. *The Insecurity of Freedom: Essays on Human Existence.* New York: Schocken, 1972. Although traditional in his own life, Heschel was active in the civil rights movement in the United States. In this book, as in other works, he argues for human rights and equality on the basis of the sacred nature of the human soul.

Kaplan, Mordecai. *Judaism without Supernaturalism: The Only Alternative to Orthodoxy and Secularism.* New York: Reconstructionist, 1967. An attempt to find an American Judaism that is neither traditional in the old European sense nor secularized as was much of American Judaism. In this volume, Kaplan argues for the need to regard human life and rights as foundational, even if one dispenses with the classical notion of God.

Kurzweil, Zvi. *The Modern Impulse of Traditional Judaism.* Hoboken, NJ: KTAV, 1985. Kurzweil attempts to link modern concepts of democracy and religious freedom to traditional Jewish sources.

Rackman, Emanuel. *One Man's Judaism*. New York: Philosophical Library, 1971. Rackman approaches human rights and dignity from an Orthodox perspective.

Sherwin, Byron. *In Partnership with God: Contemporary Jewish Law and Ethics*. Syracuse, NY: Syracuse University Press, 1990. Sherwin speaks out of a traditional, although not Orthodox, perspective. Although a rather eclectic collection of essays, Sherwin touches on several important elements of human rights ethics, including medical ethics, charity, family relationships, and the need to sanctify life in an age of violence.

Walzer, Michael. *Spheres of Justice: A Defense of Pluralism and Equality*. New York: Basic Books, 1983. The author offers a secular and academic view of pluralism and equality, albeit one that draws on Jewish sources.

Political Theory

Bamberger, Bernard. "Individual Rights and the Demands of the State: The Position of the Classical Judaism." In *Yearbook of the Central Conference of American Rabbis* 54 (1955), 197–212. An example of the argument that human rights in Judaism are not based on natural law but on the fact that humans are created in the image of God. Thus, individuals have certain rights that even the needs of the community can not override.

Belkin, Samuel. *In His Image: The Jewish Philosophy of Man as Expressed in Rabbinic Tradition*. Westport, CT: Greenwood Press, 1979. An apologetic exposition of traditional Jewish anthropology drawn from a variety of traditional rabbinic sources.

Frank, Daniel, ed. *Commandment and Community: New Essays in Jewish Legal and Political Philosophy*. Albany: State University of New York, 1995. This looks at how one might derive a Jewish political philosophy out of the classical religious texts. In particular, are discussions of such classical Jewish philosophers as Moses Maimonides, Judah Abravanel, and Baruch Spinoza.

———. *On Liberty*. New York: St. Martin's Press, 1999. Similar in format and design to his *Commandment and Community*, this book focuses more on the issues surrounding the creation of a contemporary Jewish theory of political governance.

Goodman, Lenn E. *Judaism, Human Rights and Human Values*. New York: Oxford University Press, 1998. A professor of Philosophy at Vanderbilt University, Goodman has struggled to create a basis for a just and democratic social and political order that is philosophically sound. In this endeavor he draws heavily on traditional Jewish philosophical writers, but rarely on halachic or legal writings. In this book, argues that the Jewish tradition from the Bible on has an important contribution to make to the general discourse on ethical issues. He discusses thinkers such as Saadia Gaon and Moses Maimonides and applies their insights to contemporary issues. Other books by Goodman include: *Covenantal Rights: A Study in Jewish Political Theory*. Princeton, NJ: Princeton University Press, 2000; *Jewish Social Ethics*. New York: Oxford University Press, 1992; and *Natural Law in Judaism*. Cambridge: Cambridge University Press, 1998. *Law and Theology in Judaism*. New York: KTAV 1974; *On Justice*. New Haven: Yale University Press, 1991.

Quint, Emanuel. *A Restatement of Rabbinic Civil Law*. Northvale, NJ: Jason Aaronson, 1990–1996. A multivolume study of Jewish law that draws on *responsa* (rabbinic legal rescripts), among other sources, but gives almost no actual citations of the *responsa* texts themselves. Nonetheless, this is a good introduction to the field of Jewish jurisprudence. This volume focuses on civil law, and therefore on a variety of topics that are relevant to human rights.

Quint, Emanuel, and Neil Hecht. *Jewish Jurisprudence: Its Sources and Modern Applications*. New York and London: Harwood Academic Publishers, 1980. A basic presentation of the foundational ideals and values of Jewish legal reasoning from both classical and modern sources. Notions of individual rights, especially as these are to be exercised within a community, are addressed.

Roth, Sol. *Halakhah and Politics: The Jewish Idea of the State*. New York: KTAV, 1988. Vol. 14 of *Library of Jewish Law and Ethics*. The author approaches the subject of Jewish political theory from a decidedly Orthodox point of view.

Shohet, David Menahem. *The Jewish Court in the Middle Ages: Studies in Jewish Jurisprudence According to the Talmud, Geonic, and Medieval German*

Responsa. New York: Commanday-Roth, 1931. Detailed exposition of how Jewish self-government developed from late antiquity into the early Middle Ages. The discussion also examines the rights individuals can claim in response to communal or governmental demands.

Sicker, Martin. *The Judaic State: A Study in Rabbinic Political Theory.* New York: Praeger, 1988. This book is a modern academic discussion of classical Jewish political theory as understood from a variety of traditional sources. It is an attempt to adduce a modern political theory for Judaism.

————. *The Political Culture of Judaism.* Westport, CT: Praeger, 2001. This volume looks specifically at the problem of individual rights in the context of the needs of national security. Sicker argues that while Judaic culture seems to support a theocratic form of government, this is not really so. He tries to show in his book that the ideals of a Judaic polity grow more out of the communal experience of Jewish communities than out of revelation.

Silver, Daniel Jeremy, ed. *Judaism and Ethics.* New York: KTAV, 1970. A collection of essays by some of the great scholars of the day on the relationship between Jewish ethics and Greco-Roman, Christian, and modern philosophical moral thought.

American Judaism and Liberalism

Agus, Jacob. *The Vision and the Way: An Interpretation of Jewish Ethics.* New York: Frederick Ungar, 1966. An attempt to link modern liberal American views on human rights to the Jewish tradtion.

Central Conference of American Rabbis. This organization, which represents rabbis of the Reform movement in North America has been publishing *responsa* for the Reform movement for about a century. An online index to these and other North American Reform *responsa* can be found at http://www.ccarnet.org/resp/tindex.html. Although family and personal issues such as marriage, birth, abortion, and so forth make up most of the material, there are occasional responses to human rights issues.

Dorff, Elliot. *To Do the Right and the Good: A Jewish Approach to Modern Social Ethics.* Philadelphia: Jewish Publication Society of America,

2002. Looks at how Judaism addresses the major social issues of our time such as war and poverty and interreligious relationships.

————. *Love Your Neighbor and Yourself: A Jewish Approach to Modern Personal Ethics*. Philadelphia: Jewish Publication Society of America, 2003. How Judaism's particular understanding of the individual should shape how we conduct ourselves as persons and as members of a community in the modern, technological society.

Elazar, Daniel. *Constitutionalism: The Israeli and American Experiences*. Lanham, MD: University Press of America, 1990. The author tries to show that the Jewish tradition underpinning Israeli law has the same liberal tendencies as American law, but that the different histories of the two states have resulted in different forms of legal developments.

Freehof, Solomon. Collections containing modern American *responsa* written from the liberal perspective of Reform Judaism, among which are: *Reform Responsa*. Cincinatti, OH: Hebrew Union College Press, 1960. *Recent Reform Responsa*. Cincinatti, OH: Hebrew Union College Press, 1963. Reprinted as a single volume including *Reform Responsa*. Cincinatti, OH: Hebrew Union College Press, 1973. *Current Reform Responsa*. Cincinatti, OH: Hebrew Union College Press, 1969. *Modern Reform Responsa*. Cincinatti, OH: Hebrew Union College Press, 1971. *Contemporary Reform Responsa*. Cincinatti, OH: Hebrew Union College Press, 1974. *Reform Responsa for Our Time*. Cincinatti, OH: Hebrew Union College Press, 1977. *New Reform Responsa*. Cincinatti, OH: Hebrew Union College Press, 1980. These various volumes cover a wide range of topics, many dealing with life cycle issues, but some political and human rights topics are touched on.

Jacob, Walter. *American Reform Responsa: Jewish Questions, Rabbinic Answers*. New York: Central Conference of American Rabbis, 1983. A continuation of Freehof's work in writing North American Reform *responsa* by his successor. This has been followed by two further volumes, *Contemporary American Reform Responsa*. New York: Central Conference of American Rabbis, 1987; and *Questions and Reform Jewish Answers: New American Reform Responsa*. New York: Central Conference of American Rabbis, 1992. Like Freehof's work, the material collected here deals mostly with internal Jewish communal issues such as marriage, birth, abortion, the status of children of intermarried couples, burial, funerary rites and so forth, there are occasional responses that touch on issues of human rights issues.

Jacob, Walter, and Moshe Zemer, eds. *Studies in Progressive Halakhah.* Oxford and New York: Berghahn, 1999. This series, edited by the cofounders of the Institute for Liberal Halachah, includes a number of volumes relating to issues of human rights, including *Conversion to Judaism in Jewish Law.* Vol. 3, 1994. *Death and Euthanasia in Jewish Law.* Vol. 4, 1995. *The Fetus and Fertility in Jewish Law.* Vol. 5, 1995. *Aging and the Aged in Jewish Law: Essays and Responsa.* Vol. 7, 1998. *Marriage and Its Obstacles in Jewish Law: Essays and Responsa.* Vol. 8, 1999. *Crime and Punishment in Jewish Law: Essays and Responsa.* Vol. 9, 1999. *Gender Issues in Jewish Law: Essays and Responsa.* Vol. 10, 2000.

Kallen, Horace. *Judaism at Bay: Essays Toward the Adjustment of Judaism to Modernity.* New York: Bloch Publishing Co., 1932, reprint New York: Arno, 1972. *Cultural Pluralism and the American Idea: An Essay in Social Philosophy.* Philadelphia: University of Pennsylvania Press, 1956. In these books, Kallen attempts to show that Judaism is fully compatible with the American liberal tradition. He is often credited with establishing the philosophical basis for "cultural pluralism" as opposed to the "melting pot" theory.

Kliksberg, Bernardo. *Social Justice: A Jewish Perspective.* Jerusalem and New York: Gefen Publishing House; World Jewish Congress, 2003. Published originally in Argentina in 2001, this book explains how Judaism addresses such problems as global poverty, political oppression, and social inequality. The author has been an adviser for social development for a number of United Nations agencies.

Lelyveld, Arthur. *The Steadfast Stream: An Introduction to Jewish Social Values.* Cleveland, OH: Pilgrim Press, 1995. A look, by a leading liberal rabbi, at the attitudes and actions demanded by Judaism to achieve social justice.

Library of Jewish Law and Ethics. New York: KTAV, 1977– . A project begun in the mid-1970s, the series now comprises over twenty volumes that cover business ethics, equity, family law, medical ethics, politics, and women from a traditional perspective.

Plaut, W. Gunther, and Mark Washofsky, eds. *Teshuvot of the Nineties: Reform Judaism's Answers to Today's Questions.* New York: Central

Conference of American Rabbis, 1997. This is one of the most recent collections of North American *responsa* from the Reform movement.

Sherwin, Byron L. *Jewish Ethics for the Twenty-First Century: Living in the Image of God.* Syracuse, NY: Syracuse University Press, 2000. The author argues that Jewish ethics in the twenty-first century are based on the notion that all people should be treated as being in the image of God, and that this should structure how we approach interhuman relations from family through biomedical dilemmas.

Sidorsky, David, ed. *Essays on Human Rights: Contemporary Issues and Jewish Perspectives.* Philadelphia: Jewish Publication Society of America, 1974. This book looks at a number of recent political and social issues and argues that more human rights attention should be paid to the needs of Jews, especially as regards the state of Israel.

Human Rights in Israel

Elon, Menachem, Bernard Auerbach, Daniel D. Chazin, and Melvin, J. Sykes, eds. *Jewish Law (Mishpat Ivri): Cases and Materials.* New York: Matthew Bender, 1999. Compiled by a retired deputy president of the Israeli Supreme Court, this volume is meant to serve as a casebook for introducing students to Israeli common law. It thus includes numerous examples of human rights issues that have come before the Israeli Supreme Court.

Gavison, Ruth, ed. *Civil Rights in Israel.* Jerusalem: The Association of Civil Rights in Israel, 1982. A festschrift in honor of Haim Cohen that offers essays on both theoretical issues and concrete applications.

Hofnung, Menachem. *Democracy, Law, and National Security in Israel.* Brookfield, VT: Dartmouth, 1996. A look at civil rights in Israel in light of the security situation. It includes material on the relationship between civilian civil rights organizations both in Israel proper and in the West Bank.

Israel Yearbook on Human Rights. Tel Aviv: Tel Aviv University Faculty of Law, 1989–. Volumes in this series come out approximately once a year. The volumes contain studies by scholars in Israel and elsewhere on human rights, especially in the context of the political situation in Israel. These volumes can serve also as sources for judicial rulings, legislation, military proclamations, and other primary materials not otherwise available in English.

Kretzmer, David. *The Occupation of Justice: The Supreme Court of Israel and the Occupied Territories.* Albany: State University of New York Press, 2002. Kretzmer examines a number of Israeli Supreme Court cases dealing with human rights issues growing out of the Israeli military occupation of the West Bank and Gaza Strip.

Radi, F. *Women's Rights.* Jerusalem: The Association for Civil Rights in Israel, 1989. This book looks at the particular problem of women in Israeli society and law. It argues that the original declaration of the state guarantees equality regardless of gender and shows that such equality still needs to be worked out in Israeli law.

Rakover, Nahum, ed. *Jerusalem, City of Law and Justice.* Jerusalem: Library of Jewish Law, 1998. A collection of essays growing out of an international seminar held in Jerusalem in June 1996. Contents include discussions of Israel as a Jewish and democratic state, human rights and the individual, penal law, and law and medicine.

Sharfman, Daphna. *Living without a Constitution: Civil Rights in Israel.* Armonk, NY: M. E. Sharpe, 1993. A study of how the notion of civil rights has developed in Israel from early statehood to the early 1990s. Includes a discussion of the proposed basic law on human rights.

Shoham, Shlomo, ed. *Of Law and Man: Essays in Honor of Haim Cohen.* New York: Sabra, 1971. Brings together a number of articles dealing with aspects of liberal legal values as these bear on Jewish, and especially Israeli, law.

Swersky, Ann, ed. *Human Rights in Israel: Articles in Memory of Judge Haman Selah.* Tel Aviv: Edanim and Yediot Ahronot, 1988. A collection of essays that address systematically issues of freedom of expression and the right to dissent in the Israeli context.

Zamir, Itzhak, and Allen Zysblat, eds., *Rabbinic Law in Israel.* New York: Oxford University Press, 1996. A collection of various Israeli Supreme Court decisions and ruling that address a range of human rights issues.

Zemer, Moshe. *Evolving Halakhah: A Progressive Approach to Traditional Jewish Law.* Woodstock, VT: Jewish Lights Pub., 1999. In this book,

Zemer, a liberal Rabbi in Israel argues for a more liberal understanding of the halachic tradition. By example, he shows how a variety of issues could be decided in a humane and liberal way while maintaining fidelity to traditional Jewish legal concepts.

INDEX

About the Author

PETER J. HAAS is Abba Hillel Silver Professor Jewish Studies at Case Western Reserve University. He received ordination as a Reform rabbi from Hebrew Union College in 1974. He then served as an active U.S. Army chaplain. He is the author of *Responsa: Literary History of a Rabbinic Genre* (1996), *Morality after Auschwitz: The Radical Challenge of the Nazi Ethic* (1988) and other titles.